Bibliography on major aspects
of the humanisation of work
and the quality of working life

Bibliography on major aspects of the humanisation of work and the quality of working life

Second edition 1978

International Labour Office Geneva

ISBN 92-2-101948-9

First published 1977
Second edition 1978

The designations employed in ILO publications, which are in conformity with United Nations practice, and the presentation of material therein do not imply the expression of any opinion whatsoever on the part of the International Labour Office concerning the legal status of any country or territory or of its authorities, or concerning the delimitation of its frontiers.
The responsibility for opinions expressed in signed articles, studies and other contributions rests solely with their authors, and publication does not constitute an endorsement by the International Labour Office of the opinions expressed in them.

ILO publications can be obtained through major booksellers or ILO local offices in many countries, or direct from ILO Publications, International Labour Office, CH-1211 Geneva 22, Switzerland. A catalogue or list of new publications will be sent free of charge from the above address.

Printed by the International Labour Office, Geneva, Switzerland

CONTENTS

INTRODUCTION

The 1976-77 Programme and Budget of the International Labour Organisation proposes a new orientation to the ILO's activities concerning conditions of work and environment. In addition to the conditions in which men and women work, the content and organisation of work are emphasized, with a view to humanising both working conditions and work itself.

Within the Conditions of Work and Life Programme, these new concerns were translated into work items on job satisfaction, new forms of work organisation and the economic costs and benefits of measures for the humanisation of work. These items were given added impetus by the discussion, at the 1975 International Labour Conference, of the Director-General's report Making Work More Human and the subsequent adoption of a Resolution calling for an international programme in this field, now called the International Programme for the Improvement of Working Conditions and Environment (PIACT, from the French initials).

In order to increase the information available for this work, the International Labour Office has commissioned the International Institute for Labour Studies to undertake a critical review of research and other literature. These reviews include substantive contributions to the work items mentioned above in addition to the present bibliography, which the ILO is pleased to be making available to a wider audience.

Most of the approximately 2,000 titles presented in the bibliography were identified through a comprehensive survey undertaken in Summer 1976 by the IILS among labour ministries, employers' organisations, unions, universities, relevant research institutes and a number of specialised individual researchers in twenty-six of the more industrialised countries.[1] Nearly 150 replies were received in this process.

The main focusses of the bibliography are the areas of the relationship between working conditions and job satisfaction (together with other literature on job satisfaction), new forms of work organisation, and economic cost and benefits of these new organisational arrangements. The wealth of information obtained through the survey allowed the inclusion also of various other, smaller sections on additional aspects of the humanisation of work, and the quality of working life, as is shown in the table of contents.

---

[1] These are: Australia, Austria, Belgium, Bulgaria, Canada, Czechoslovakia, Denmark, Federal Republic of Germany, Finland, France, German Democratic Republic, Hungary, India, Italy, Japan, the Netherlands, Norway, Poland, Rumania, Spain, Sweden, Switzerland, USSR, UK, USA, and Yugoslavia.

The titles are indicatd in the original language together with their English translation. For languages not using the Latin alphabet usually only the English translation is given. The annotations are all in English. Annotations were made where the volumes in question were available in Geneva or where contributors had furnished abstracts. Materials recommended for basic reading on the subjects are marked with an asterisk. As a matter of principle, priority has been attached to literature of recent origin (last 10 years or so). Given its broad coverage, the bibliography provides a fairly comprehensive selection of titles reflecting major trends in both the conceptual and practical aspects of the areas under review.

To take advantage of the second printing of this volume, the Conditions of Work and Life Branch of the ILO has updated the previous edition by adding some of the most important work published in the last two years. These new entries refer to the five major headings in the Table of Contents. However, for the section on "Other aspects of the humanisation of work and the quality of working life" (V), additional references were found only for the subsections on shopfloor participation, flexible working hours and other time arrangements, general literature on the humanisation of work and the quality of working life and bibliographies relevant to the subjects covered.

ACKNOWLEDGEMENTS

The project was directed by H. Günter, Head, Quality of Life and Social Perspectives Sector of the IILS. The main bibliographic work was undertaken by Rose Marie Greve, Research Associate, IILS, together with Herman van der Laan, IILS, and several short-term assistants, in particular Susan Hagemann, University of Geneva. Maryse Gaudier, Librarian at the IILS, assisted in the proper presentation of the materials.

The IILS benefited from technical advice furnished by George Spyropoulos, Chief, Conditions of Work and Life Branch of the ILO, and Joseph Thurman of the same branch and from its project consultants, Professor Yves Delamotte, Conservatoire des Arts et Métiers, Paris, formerly director of the French National Agency for the Improvement of Labour Conditions (ANACT), and Professor A.T.M. Wilson, London Graduate School of Business Studies, London, and General Secretary of the International Council for the Quality of Working Life. The manuscript was typed by various untiring members of the IILS secretariat: Anne Sanchez, Helen Tulloch, Gunilla Bejne, and Susan Noverraz. The compilation of the bibliography was only possible because of the most valuable support received from the various institutions and persons contributing to it, and to whom the ILO and the IILS express their gratitude.

I. RELATIONS BETWEEN WORKING CONDITIONS AND JOB SATISFACTION

ADAMS, P.G.; SLOCUM, J.W.
"Work groups and employee satisfaction." Personnel administration, 34(2), Mar.-Apr. 1971, pp. 37-43.
The article explores the relationship between job satisfaction, group dynamics and performance records of skilled and unskilled workers in the USA. The authors conclude that while group cohesiveness is positively related to job satisfaction among unskilled workers performing monitoring tasks, no such relationship exists among highly skilled workers.

AKHTAR, S.S.; PESTONJEE, D.M.
"A study of employees' adjustment within and outside work situation." Indian journal of social work, 23, 1963, pp. 327-330.

ALDERFER, Clayton P.
"The organizational syndrome." Administrative science quarterly, 12, 1967, pp. 440-460.
A study in an organization which focuses on the effects of job enlargement on satisfaction. Its major findings were: (1) Satisfaction with respect from superiors decreased as job complexity increased and as seniority increased. (2) Satisfaction with use of skills and abilities increased as job complexity increased. Two explanations for the breakdown in superior-to-subordinate relationships are suggested. The first is that more complex jobs require levels of interpersonal competence not reached in the organization studied. The second explanation is that rapid growth and technological change results in career anxiety which puts strains on the superior-to-subordinate relationship.

ALBEDA, W.
"Inkomensverdeling, arbeidsvreugde en vrije tijd." /Income distribution, job satisfaction and leisure./ Economisch-statistische berichten, (3000), Apr. 1975, pp. 418-420.

ALLENSPACH, H.
Flexible working hours. Geneva, International Labour Office, 1975. v, 64 p.
A report on flexible working hours based on experiments in Switzerland, discussing its advantages and disadvantages, including its effects on job satisfaction and employee and management attitudes.

AMMASSARI, Paolo.
Worker satisfaction and occupational life. A study of the automobile worker in Italy. Roma, Facolta de Scienze Statistiche Demografiche e Attuariali, Università, 1970. 190 p.

ANDERSON, J.W.; DAVIS, Louis.
"Enrichissement des tâches, satisfaction au travail et participation." /Job enrichment, job satisfaction and participation./ UIMM - Documentation étrangère, (279), annexe 1, Oct. 1971, 15 p.

ARMSTRONG, Thomas B.
"Job content and context factors related to satisfaction for different occupational levels." Journal of applied psychology, Fall 1971, pp. 57-65.

ARVEY, Richard D.; DEWHIRST, H. Dudley; BOLING, John C.
"Relationship between goal clarity, participation in goal setting, and personality characteristics on job satisfaction in a scientific organization." Journal of applied psychology. 61, 1976, pp. 103-105.

AUSTRALIA. COMMITTEE TO ADVISE ON POLICIES FOR MANUFACTURING INDUSTRY.
Policies for development of manufacturing industry. V. 1: report to the Prime Minister, October 1975. Canberra, A.G.P.S., 1975.
Report of an advisory committee on policies for the manufacturing industry, the key idea of which relates to the need to adapt to change. Part of the report deals with the organisation of work and other related issues such as the quality of working life and job satisfaction. Stressing the significance of job satisfaction the report categorises it into three groups. These are: (i) Those which address the problems inherent in the bureaucracy or social nature of firms, (e.g. joint consultative committees, works councils, worker representation on board of directors). (ii) Those which attempt to redress the problems of traditional technology and production methods (rigid job design, repetitive and unsatisfactory jobs, e.g. job rotation, job enlargement). (iii) Those which assume that workers' desire for involvement and satisfaction are best achieved by tackling both the social and technical constraints inherent in the way work is organised (e.g. semi-autonomous or autonomous work groups within factories).

BAGLEY-MARRETT, Cora; HAGE, Gerald; AIKEN, Michael.
"Communication and satisfaction in organisations." Human relations, 28(7), Sept. 1975, pp. 611-626.
Based on data obtained in health and welfare agencies, the study attempts to develop some measures for establishing the dimensions of organisational communication and for examining the relationship between formality of communication and satisfaction. The findings demonstrate that systems of communication can be empirically specified and their relationship to satisfaction measured though they varied depending on whether satisfaction with the job or with co-workers was the focus. Hypotheses to be tested by further research are proposed.

BAKER, Cherry.
"Job enrichment and job satisfaction - selected overseas studies, Part I: American studies." Personnel practice bulletin, 29(4), Dec. 1973, pp. 277-288.
The first of three articles summarising US, British and Continental European research projects (all mentioned in this bibliography) experiments in job enrichment, job satisfaction and attitudes to work which reflect these countries' approaches towards explaining employee attitudes and behaviour and improving the quality of working life and organisation effectiveness. Five of the six studies discussed here are examples of practical implementations of job redesign which emphasise job enrichment as a means of improving employee morale and motivation. The sixth, a research project designed to examine the determinants of job satisfaction and work performance, recommends, but does not implement experimental changes.

BAKER, Cherry.
"Job enrichment and job satisfaction - selected overseas studies, Part 2: British studies." Personnel practice bulletin, 30(1), Mar. 1974, pp. 38-46.
Presents four British studies in this field, one of which is an experiment in job redesign conducted with a view to evaluating the effects of job enrichment and employee motivation. The other three studies dealt with research projects which were concerned with describing and explaining the industrial attitudes and behaviour of employees but which did not involve experimental changes to jobs or work environment.

BAKER, Cherry.
"Job enrichment and job satisfaction - selected overseas studies, Part 3: European studies." Personnel practice bulletin, 30(2), June 1974, pp. 149-161.
Summaries of studies in job enrichment, job satisfaction and attitudes to work in Norway, Sweden, Germany and Yugoslavia. Their predominant emphasis is on the redesign of jobs to give greater autonomy and responsibility to employees and on the encouragement of other forms of worker participation.

BAKER, Sally H.; HANSEN, Richard A.
"Job design and worker satisfaction: a challenge to assumptions." Journal of occupational psychology, 48, 1975, pp. 79-91. This paper produces data from a sample of semi-skilled American workers, which "do not strongly support the frequently assumed or, less frequently demonstrated, connection between 'the structure of jobs ... job satisfaction ... workers' orientations and the nature of their jobs which influences satisfaction within this range of jobs.' They conclude: With a caution against ... assumptions that slightly more informed employee selection or modest changes in job design ... are likely to change the fundamental problem of worker dissatisfaction." It is important that the comparisons which they made in fact concern jobs; and there is no indication that their findings relate to systematic change in work organisation.

BANERYD, K.
"Analysis of the psychological job content in sawmill work." In: Proceedings of IUFRO Joint Meeting, Div 3 and 5, Ergonomics in Sawmills and Woodworking Industries, Symposium in Sweden, Aug. 26-30, 1974. Stockholm, Arbetarskyddsstyrelsen 1975, pp. 237-248.

BANERYD, K.; KJELLÉN, U.
Safety in the Swedish explosives industry. Alternative approaches to safety at work and some results from an attitude study of explosives workers and supervisors. Stockholm, Försvarets Forskningsanstalt, [n.d.] (FOA Report A 20007-D 1).

BARNOWE, T.J.; MANGIONE, T.W.; QUINN, R.P.
"The relative importance of job facets as indicated by an empirically derived model of job satisfaction." In: QUINN, R.P., et al. Chronicles of an unfinished enterprise. Ann Arbor, Survey Research Center, 1973, pp. 263-320.

BASU, Gopa; PESTONJEE, D.M.
"Executives and the satisfaction cycle." Indian journal of industrial relations, Apr. 1974, pp. 507-517.
This study tries to determine the satisfaction cycle of executives using Herzberg's two factor theory of satisfaction. A questionnaire containing 26 factors, each assessed on a ten-point graphic rating scale, was used. The sample comprises 80 executives from the private sector divided into three age ranges. A U-shaped relationship emerged between age and job satisfaction. An inverted U type of relationship was found between age and dissatisfaction. It was also found that motivators are more potent than hygienes in creating feelings of satisfaction and also dissatisfaction. Herzberg's classifactory categories for individuals do not seem to be universally applicable.

BAUM, John F.; YOUNGBLOOD, Stuart A.
"Impact of an organizational control policy on absenteeism, performance and satisfaction." Journal of applied psychology, 60, 1975, pp. 688-694.

BEER, Michael.
"Organizational size and job satisfaction." Academy of management journal, Mar. 1964.

BELL, C.R.
Men at work. London, Allen and Unwin, 1974. 144 p.
A discussion of the affective quality of the physical environment of the workplace and its consequences for worker behaviour. Some general factors involved in the interaction between man and his working environment are explored, including types of industrial environments, varieties of work, physical limits in adverse environments and other environmental hazards. In addition the author considers the effects of lighting, noise and temperature on work performance and the effects of the organisation of space on social interaction.

BERKEL, P.; VAN BERTING, J.; VAN DIJCK, J.J.J., e.a.
Arbeidsvoldoening en arbeidsbeleid. /Work satisfaction and labour policy./ Onder red. van J. BERTING en L.U. DE SITTER. Utrecht, Het Spectrum, 1968. 221 p.
(Marka boeken, 87.)

BERNOUX, P.; BROSSARD, M.; DURAND, C.; MAURICE, M.
"Conditions de travail; le taylorisme en question." /Conditions of work: taylorism in question/ Sociologie de travail, 16(4), Oct.-Dec. 1974, pp. 337-425.
A compilation of articles relating to the evolution of conditions for work from the point of view of scientific management theory. Includes papers on ergonomics, the organisation of production, job enrichment and the humanisation of professional life.

BHATTACHARYA, K.P.
"Individual difference in susceptibility to industry monotony." Indian journal of psychology, 36, 1961, pp. 69-77.

BIERFELDER, W.H.
"Mitbestimmung und Arbeitszufriedenheit." /Co-determination and job satisfaction./ Industrielle Organisation, 44(1), 1975, pp. 17-20.

BIJ DE VATE, J.
"Ontevredenheid in de werksituatie. /Dissatisfaction with the work situation./ Management facetten, 25, Oct. 1975, pp. 199-202.

BJORN-ANDERSEN, Niels.
The design and impact of an on-line data entry system on work design and job satisfaction. A case study from a Danish savings bank. Copenhagen, 1975. 74 p. (Nyt fra samfundsvidenskaberne, Forskningsrapport 1975-15.) To be published in 1977 as part of an international publication (Pergamon Press).

BLAKE, Jenny.
"Experiments in job satisfaction." Personnel mananagement, 6(1), Jan. 1974, pp. 32-34.
A discussion of a job-enrichment experiment at Philips (UK). Special attention is given to the problem of job satisfaction measurement. Based on the available data the author concludes that the experiment has been successful, and points out the importance of continued monitoring of the experiment.

BLEIJENBERG, P.
"Arbeidsklimaat en arbeidsmotivatie." /Working climate and work motivation./ Bedrijfsvoering, 23, Nov. 1974, pp. 242-248.

BLOOD, Milton R.
Work values and job satisfaction. Berkeley, 1970. (California. University. Institute of Industrial Relations. Reprint No. 344.)

BLUNT, Peter.
"Cultural and situational determinants of job satisfaction amongst management in South Africa; a research note." Journal of management studies, May 1973, pp. 133-140.

BOOKER, Clare.
"Alienation in the quiet factory." Labour gazette, Jan. 1974, pp. 41-44.

BOSE, S.K.
"Employee morale and supervision." Indian journal of psychology, 30, 1955, pp. 117-125.

BRADLEY, G.
Women's interest in promotion in relation to job satisfaction and home and school background. Göteborg, 1972. (University of Göteborg. Institute of Education. Report, no. 21.)

BRIEF, Arthur P.; ALDAG, Ramon J.
"Employee reactions to job characteristics: a constructive replication." Journal of applied psychology, Apr. 1975, pp. 182-186.

BROOKS, Thomas R.
"Job satisfaction: an elusive goal." The American federationist, 79(10), Oct. 1972, pp. 1-7.

BROWN, Julius S.
"How many workers enjoy discretion on the job?" Industrial relations, May 1975, pp. 196-202.
The author attempts to provide some rough quantitative estimates as to the number of workers in the United States who enjoy jobs which permit discretion. In addition, some related questions are investigated, including: Is the proportion of discretion-permitting jobs increasing? How are such jobs distributed by race and sex? Are pay differentials between discretionary and nondiscretionary jobs increasing or decreasing?

BRUYNS, R.A.C.
De invloed van werk en milieu op arbeidsmotivatie. [The influence of work and environment on work motivation.] Assen, van Gorcum, 1972, 247 p.

BUNZ, A.; JANSON, R.; SCHACHT, K.
Qualität des Arbeitslebens: soziale Kennziffern zu Arbeitszufriendenheit und Berufschancen. [Quality of working life; social indicators for job satisfaction and employment opportunities.] Bonn, Bundesministerium für Arbeit und Sozialordnung, 1974. 267 p.
Report of a survey on social indicators of job satisfaction and equal opportunity undertaken in the Federal Republic of Germany. The report covers employee attitudes regarding income, occupational change, occupational safety, hours of work, worker participation, labour relations etc. Workers' reactions (e.g. absenteeism and labour mobility) to working conditions are also considered. The report also contains extensive bibliographical references.

BURKE, Ronald J.
"Managerial satisfaction with various work and non-work life roles." Studies in personnel psychology, Spring 1973, pp. 53-62.

CAMPBELL, D.B.
"Relative influence of job and supervision on shared worker attitudes." Journal of applied psychology, 55, 1971, pp.521-525.

CAMPBELL, David R.; KLEIN, Kenneth L.
"Job satisfaction and vocational interests." Vocational guidance quarterly, 24, Dec. 1975, pp. 125-131.

CANADA. DEPARTMENT OF MANPOWER AND IMMIGRATION.
National sample surveys on job satisfaction and the work ethic in Canada. (In progress)

CANADA. DEPARTMENT OF REGIONAL ECONOMIC EXPANSION. SOCIAL AND HUMAN ANALYSIS BRANCH.
Work organizations, behaviour and attitudes; by Joseph C. Ryant. 2d. ed. Ottawa, Queen's Printer, 1970. 192p. (Bibliography: p. 182-192. "A study by the Industrial Relations Centre, McGill University.")

CARNALL, C.; WILD, Ray.
"Job attitudes and overall job satisfaction: the effect of biographical and employment variables: research note." Journal of management studies, 2, Feb. 1974, pp. 62-67.

CARPENTER, Harrell H.
"Formal organisational structural factors and perceived job satisfaction of classroom teachers." Administrative science quarterly, 16, 1971, pp. 460-465.
The effects of organisational structure on the satisfaction of sociopsychological needs are tested demonstrating that the greater the number of administrative levels in the organisational hierarchy the more the lower level positions are seen as restrictive, regimented and formalised by the incumbents.

CARRELL, M.R.; ELBERT, N.F.
"Some personal and organizational determinants of job satisfaction of postal clerks." Academy of Management journal, 17, 1974, pp. 368-373.

CHADWICK-JONES, J.K.
Automation and behaviour, a social psychological study. London, Wiley, 1969, 168 p.
Study of psychological aspects of the effects of automation on employees' attitude and behaviour in the UK. Particular reference to the work environment in the iron and steel industry. Covered are teamwork, the impact of technological change on the industrial structure, innovation, job satisfaction, promotion, retirement, working conditions, and other relevant subjects.

CHAKRABORTY, Parul.
"Factors contributing to job satisfaction." Productivity, 7(1), Summer 1966, pp. 93-96.

CHAPMAN, William.
"Job satisfaction: the vanishing blues." The American federationist, 81(1), Jan. 1974, 18 p.

CHATTERJEE, Amitava.
"Some variables related to job satisfaction." Indian labour journal, May 1970, pp. 699-712.

CHAUDHURI, Supriyo K.
"Internal and external control: attitudes towards work and job tension." National Labour Institute bulletin (New Delhi), 1(9), Sept.-Oct. 1975, pp. 14-20.

CHERNIK, Doris A.; PHELAN, Joseph G.
"Attitudes of women in management. 1. Job satisfaction: a study of perceived need satisfaction as a function of job level." International journal of social psychiatry, (1-2), 1974, pp. 94-98.

CHERRINGTON, David J.
"Satisfaction in competitive conditions." Organisational behaviour and human performance, 10, Aug. 1973, pp. 47-71.

CHERRINGTON, David J.; CHERRINGTON, J.O.
"Participation, performance and appraisal." Business horizons, 17(6), Dec. 1974, pp. 35-44.
Article on the use of wage incentives, performance recording and workers' participation in budgeting to improve job satisfaction and job performance among workers in the USA. It includes the research results of several experimental studies.

CHERRINGTON, David J. et al.
"Effects of contingent and noncontingent reward on the relationship between satisfaction and task performance." Journal of applied psychology, 55, 1971, pp. 531-536.

CHRISTLICHER GEWERKSCHAFTSBUND DEUTSCHLANDS.
Humanisierung der Arbeitswelt. /Humanisation of work./ Bonn, 1975.
A two-page statement of the CGB on the relationship between working conditions and job satisfaction which suggests that work cannot be considered merely from the point of view of productivity and that the improvement of working conditions must cater to the satisfaction of workers' needs. Tests the main areas on which working conditions should improve.

CLARK, Alfred W.; McCABE, Sue.
"The motivation and satisfaction of Australian managers." Personnel psychology, 25(4), Winter 1972, pp. 625-639.

COATES, K.
Quality of life and workers' control. Nottingham, Russel Peace Foundation, 1972. 15 p. (Spokesman pamphlet No. 27.)
Political pamphlet which argues that workers' participation and self-management could provide the basis for improved working conditions and therefore for the humanisation of work in the UK.

COBB, W. Jr.
The relationship between quality of employment and job satisfaction among black and white workers. N.p., Multilith, 1973.

THE CONFERENCE BOARD.
The altered work week; a symposium held in Ottawa, November 1973: a report from the Conference Board in Canada. Ottawa, /1974/. 73 p. (Canadian studies, no. 34.)
Examines such aspects as how flexible hours and/or a compressed workweek affect productivity, job satisfaction, transportation and recreation, family life, and the supply and demand for labour.

COSTELLO, John M.; LEE, San M.
"Needs fulfilment and job satisfaction of professionals." Public personnel management, 3, Sept.-Oct. 1974, pp. 454-561.

COUILLAULT, S.
L'humanisation du travail dans l'entreprise industrielle. /The humanisation of work in the industrial enterprise./ Paris, Epi Editeurs, 1973. 157 p.
Faulting ergonomics for limiting itself to the rationalisation aspect of work technology and of neglecting biological and psychological needs, the author - an industrial doctor - suggests that a global (i.e. psychological, physiological and sociological) perception of the worker is a necessary precondition to humanisation of work. He considers recent experiments in the humanisation of work in various enterprises, especially those which address themselves to the diminution of absenteeism - a primary indicator of worker dissatisfaction.

COZAN, Lee W.
"Job enlargement and employee satisfaction." Personnel journal, Jul.-Aug. 1959, pp. 95-96.

CROSS, Denys; WARR, Peter.
"Work-group composition as a factor in productivity and satisfaction." Industrial relations journal, 2, 1971, pp. 3-13.

CUMMINGS, L.L.; ELSALMI, A.M.
"The impact of role diversity, job level and organizational size on managerial satisfaction." Administrative science quarterly, Mar. 1970, pp. 1-10.
Role diversity - operationalised by the number of relevant role senders - job level, subunit size, and company size are examined in this paper as determinants of perceived managerial satisfaction. Perceived need satisfaction, need fulfilment deficiency, need importance, and possibility of need fulfilment serve as the dependent variables. Role diversity and job level are found to be more significantly related to need satisfaction and possibility of need fulfilment than subunit or company size. Results are interpreted in the context of role theory and previous research by Porter. Administrative implications are suggested in the areas of reward system design and managerial motivation.

DALE, A.J.
"Job satisfaction and organization among hospital domestic workers." British journal of industrial relations, Jul. 1965, pp. 164-181.

*DAVIS, Louis E.
"Job satisfaction research: the post-industrial view." Industrial relations (Berkeley, Calif.), May 1971, pp. 176-193.
The author contends that research in job satisfaction has been too concerned with examining the worker's environment and working conditions. Research should examine the structure and content of the job itself and changing social values and goals.

DE, Nitish R.
"Employee motivation through work re-design on participative lines in the salary saving scheme of New Delhi Divisional Office of Life Insurance Corporation of India." To be published in National Labour Institute bulletin.
The author, in association with a colleague, V. Nilakant, carried out exploratory discussions with the management and then with the employees of the Divisional Office about the possibility of enriching the quality of work life in the office. After initial discussions, the management and the employees decided to start a pilot project in the Salary Saving Scheme Section which was one of the problem areas in the office. The study discusses the work-flow system in detail and its dysfunctions in relation to the employee expectations. The employees decided to set up a composite task force which, through a series of research conferences worked out an alternative plan which started working from the month of June 1976. Although the Scheme is in operation, there is a continuous review of the progress and continuous improvements are being effected in making the work system more efficient in terms of customers' service and at the same time creating a culture of job satisfaction for educated white-collar employees.

DERMER, Jerry D.
"Interactive effects of uncertainty and self-control on the acceptance of responsibility for and satisfaction with performance." Human relations, Dec. 1974, pp. 911-924.

DESHIRST, H. Dudley.
"How work environment affects job involvement." Research management, July 1973, pp. 33-37.

DIMARCO, Nicholas; NORTON, Steven.
"Life style, organization structure, congruity and job satisfaction." Personnel psychology, Winter 1974, pp. 581-591.

DIRKEN, J.M.
"Industrial shift work: decrease in well-being and specific effects." Ergonomics, 9(2), 1966, pp. 115-124.

DOWNEY, H. Kirk et al.
"Analysis of relationships among leader behaviour, subordinate job performance and satisfaction: a path-goal approach." Academy of Management journal, 18, 1975, pp. 253-262.

DOWNEY, H. Kirk et al.
"Congruence between individual needs, organizational climate, job satisfaction and performance." Academy of Management journal, 18, 1975, pp. 149-155.

DOWNEY, H. Kirk et al.
"Organizational climate and job satisfaction: a comparative analysis." Journal of business research, 2, 1974, pp. 233-248.

DUNNETTE, Marvin D.; CAMPBELL, John P; HAKEL, Milton D.
Factors contributing to job satisfaction and job dissatisfaction in six occupational groups, Minneapolis, 1967. 31 p. (Minnesota University. Industrial Relations Center. Reprint 54.)

EDWARDS, R.A.
"Shift work: performance and satisfaction." Personnel journal, 54, 1975, pp. 578-579, 587.

ELBING, A.O.; GADON, H.; GORDON, J.R.M.
"Flexible working hours: it's about time." Harvard business review, 52(1), Jan.-Feb. 1974, pp. 18-33.
An article on the current trend towards the adoption of flexible working hours in the USA. It also describes the experience of a European enterprise in this field. It includes a discussion of problem areas, the involvement of supervisors and the importance of mutual trust between workers and management and concludes that given appropriate management techniques, the system reduces absenteeism and labour turnover, increases productivity, improves labour relations and fosters job enrichment and job satisfaction.

ELBING, A.O.; GADON, H.; GORDON, J.R.M.
"Time for human time-table." European business, (39), Autumn, 1973, pp. 46-54.
Description of the implementation and results of flexible working hours schemes for European non-manual workers, covering such aspects as job satisfaction and absenteeism and documenting the attitudes of the industrial relations partners.

EMERY, Fred E.; EMERY, Merrelyn.
Participative design, work and community life. Canberra, 1974. 21 p. (Australian National University. Centre for Continuing Education. Occasional papers in continuing education, No.4.)
In Part I Fred Emery lists the factors which have been identified as important determinants of job satisfaction: i.e. adequate 'elbow room', chances for learning on the job, an optimal level of variety, conditions where men can get help and respect from work mates, meaningful work and a desirable future. An alternative organisational module is suggested (semi-autonomous groups).

Part II deals with participative design seminars. These notes are a descriptive selection of issues that may arise in implementing change from bureaucracy to democracy and cover areas such as: selection of persons to be involved in seminars, participation of unions, foremen and managers, the role of facilitator/external resource, the method of analysis and implementation of design.

*EMERY, Fred, E.; PHILLIPS, Chris.
Living at work: Australia 1973. Canberra, A.G.P.S., 1975. 106 p.
Reports on a national study of 2000 urban employees with jobs below supervisory level, carried out for the Minister for Labour and Immigration. Results provide a comprehensive picture of the respondents' objective conditions of work, subjective reactions and overall feelings about their jobs, health problems and other aspects of non-working life including leisure activities.

The effects of bureaucratisation of work on the individual are examined, together with other issues such as the disadvantaged worker and facets of industrial relations behaviour. The theme concept is the quality of work life in terms of the variety, learning, elbow room, mental challenge and desirable job future offered in work. The authors reflect briefly on the implications of the quality of work life for future social trends such as recreation leave and participation in community life.

EVANS, M.G.
"Longitudinal analysis of the impact of flexible working hours." Studies in personnel psychology, 6(2), Spring 1975, pp. 1-10.
Illustrates the impact of flexible working hours on the job satisfaction of British workers by comparing two survey samples of workers on flexible and standard hours respectively.

EWEN, Robert B.
"Pressure for production, task difficulty, and the correlation between job satisfaction and job performance." Journal of applied psychology, 58, 1973, pp. 378-380.

EXTON, W.
The age of systems; the human dilemma. New York, American Management Association, 1972. xxiii, 261 p.
Monograph which examines the business organisational system as an obstacle to the job satisfaction of employees in enterprises and shows how to improve the motivational content of jobs. Both the ergonomic and psychological aspects of the work situation are considered, as are communications, human relations, depersonalisation and alienation, etc.

FALCIONE, R.L.
"The relationship of supervisor credibility to subordinate satisfaction." Personnel journal, 52, 1973, pp. 800-803.

FAZAKERLEY, G.M.
The contribution of group technology to job satisfaction. Paper prepared for a Symposium on the Effects of Group Production Methods on the Humanisation of Work, Turin, July 1975. Turin, International Centre for Advanced Technical and Vocational Training, 1975. 21 p. (Roneod.)
The study examines the impact of group technology on those aspects of workers' needs which are most likely to contribute to job satisfaction. The author claims that "workers want from their employment a challenge they can meet, some immediacy in knowing how well they are doing, interesting work, a congenial

social climate and a degree of security which not only allows them to meet their financial commitments but also enables them to work in what is essentially a co-operative rather than a conflict ridden situation." She suggests that group technology, which allows for present technological knowledge to be applied in ways which bring about both economic benefits and social gains has an advantage over most other forms of work reorganisation in meeting these needs and contributing, thereby, to job satisfaction.

FIELD, Hubert S.; RIDENHOUR, Calvin B.
"Presentation of positive and negative policy changes: what effects on members' satisfaction with their organization?" Personnel psychology, Winter 1975, pp. 525-532.

FLAM, Tamás; MAKKAY, László; SÁNDOR, Jenő.
Az ember a változó munkakörnyezetben. /Man and the changing conditions of work./ Budapest, Közgazdasági és Jogi Kiadó, 1974.

FLANAGAN, R.J.; STRAUSS, G.; ULMAN, L.
"Workers discontent and workplace behaviour." Industrial relations, 13(2), May 1974, pp. 101-123.
An analysis of worker behaviour in relation to working conditions and job satisfaction which covers absenteeism, labour turnover, hours of work, job enrichment, etc.

This excellent paper examines job satisfaction issues and measures of job behaviour from an economic point of view.

The author argues that strikes, high turnover and absenteeism do not necessarily imply an increase in worker dissatisfaction. He concludes that if there has been an increase in worker dissatisfaction, there is no evidence of serious economic consequences arising out of it.

FORM, William H.
"Auto workers and their machines: a study of work, factory, and job satisfaction in four countries - U.S., Italy, Argentina and India." Social forces, Summer 1973, pp. 1-15.

FRENCH, J.R.P.; ISRAEL, I.; AAS, D.
"An experiment on participation in a Norwegian factory." Human relations, 13(1), 1960, pp. 3-19.
This report is an attempt to replicate a previous study on participation (Coch and French, 1948) in another culture.

The hypothesis states that there is "... a positive relationship between participation and ... (i) production; (ii) management-worker relations; (iii) job satisfaction."

"There was no difference between the experimental and control groups in the level of production. With respect to worker-management relations, there was support for the hypothesis that the effects of participation hold only for subjects who experience at least as much participation as they consider legitimate. There was equal support for the hypothesis that the effects of participation increase with decreasing resistance to the participation methods."

FRIEDMANN, G.
Où va le travail humain? /What is the future of human work?/ Paris, Gallimard, 1967. 385 p.
This book on industrial psychology comprises critical speculation on the effects of continuing technological change on job satisfaction and human relations. It analyses work environment factors with particular reference to payment by result in plants in the USA, and covers psychological aspects and sociological aspects of mass production, the importance of leisure and cultural activities.

FÜRSTENBERG, F.
"The relationship between work structure and attitudes to work in the chemical industry." In: GRAVES, D., ed. Management Research: a cross-cultural perspective. Amsterdam, 1973, pp. 115-124.

GANGULY, O.N.; JOSEPH, J.S.
A study of management morale in an iron and steel industry. New Delhi, Ministry of Labour, 1969. 61 p. (Classified report.)
This report is of various facets of job satisfaction and working conditions of officers of a large Iron and Steel Industry in the Public Sector. Out of 1,300 officers, 459 officers at various levels from all the plants were covered. The results were presented in terms of a Morale Index by department, age, salary and experience; a correlational matrix between different variables and percentage of officers expressing favourable, unfavourable and neutral attitudes towards various aspects of job content and motivation and work organisation. The majority of officers expressed a high degree of overall job satisfaction, interest in work, satisfaction towards working conditions and pay. Officers on the whole registered low feeling towards future prospects, authority and responsibility, timely supply of equipment and material, communication and system of promotion. Besides these general findings, the study pin-pointed several specific areas for management action.

GANGULY, O.N.; JOSEPH, J.S.
Quality of working life: work prospects and aspirations of young workers in Air India. Bombay, Central Labour Institute, 1976. (Classified report.)
A study on the quality of working life of young workers in Air India with special reference to life and job satisfaction issues. Findings indicate that, of the various physical and psychological working conditions, pride in organisation, job-earned community respect, reasonable working hours etc. are more positively correlated with job satisfaction than friendship with colleagues, good work location, physical strain, variety of skills and risk of injury or illness. Data also indicate that strong family ties and a rural background are more positively correlated with life and job satisfaction; that the self esteem engendered by having a job (in a country of limited employment opportunities) counteracts the effects of boredom and monotony in certain jobs and that pre-employment values, expectations and aspirations of young workers affect the quality of their working life.

GANNON, Martin J.; REECE, B. Keith.
"Personality characteristics, job satisfaction, and the four-day week." In: INDUSTRIAL RELATIONS RESEARCH ASSOCIATION. Proceedings of the twenty-fourth Annual Winter Meeting, Dec. 27-28, 1971. Madison, Wisc., 1972.

GARDELL, B.
"Alienation and mental health in the modern industrial environment" In: LEVI, L., ed. Society, stress and disease: the psychological environment and psychosomatic diseases. London, Oxford University Press, 1971, pp. 164-166.

GARDELL, B.
"Produktionsteknik och arbetsglädje. En socialpsykologisk studie av industriellt arbete." /Production techniques and job satisfaction./ PA-rådet meddelande, (63) 1971.

GHISELLI, Edwin E.; JONSON, Douglas A.
"Need satisfaction, managerial success and organisational structure." Personnel psychology, 23, 1970, pp. 569-576.
A study of the effects of organisational structure on the perceived job satisfaction of 413 managers from various business and industrial enterprises in the U.S. indicating that structures with few supervisory levels and large areas of control were associated more with the fulfilment of social, esteem, autonomy and self-actualisation needs than organisations having many supervisory levels and small areas of control.

GHOSH, S.N.; SHUKLA, S.N.
"A study of the correlates of job satisfaction of a group of telegraphists." Indian journal of applied psychology, 4, 1967, pp. 43-50.

GLUCK, Adrian; EVANS, Martin G.
"The status and job satisfaction of computer operators." Relations industrielles - Industrial relations, 27(3), Aug. 1972, pp. 423-430. (Abstract in French.)

GOLEMBIEWSKI, Robert T. et al.
"Factor analysis of some flexitime effects: attitudinal and behavioral consequences of a structural intervention." Academy of Management journal, 18, Sept. 1975, pp. 500-509.
"Factor analysis is used to establish the multidimensional impact of a specific programme of flexible work hours on attitudes of employees and supervisor. The factor analytic results support a previously published item analysis of questionnaire responses. Hard data also suggest the breadth of the effects of the flexitime installation." - abstract.

GOODMAN, R.
"Job content and motivation; hypothesis." Industrial engineering, May 1969, p. 40 et seq.

GOWLER, Dan.
"Values, contracts and job satisfaction." Personnel review, 3, Autumn 1974, pp. 4-14.

GRAY. J.L.
A study into the nature and causes of factory employee turnover and absenteeism at Carter Temro Limited. Winnipeg, Manitoba Institute of Management, 1973. 1 v.

GREAT BRITAIN. DEPARTMENT OF EMPLOYMENT.
Improving satisfaction of work by job redesign. London, 1974. (Its: Work Research Unit. Report, 1.)

GREENE, Charles N.
"Causal connections among managers' merit pay, job satisfaction, and performance." Journal of applied psychology, Aug. 1973, pp. 95-100.

GREENE, Charles N., ORGAN, Dennis W.
"An evaluation of causal models linking the received role with job satisfaction." Administrative science quarterly, Mar. 1973, pp. 95-103.

GRUPP, Fred W. Jr.; RICHARDS, Allan R.
"Job satisfaction among state executives in the US." Public personnel management, 4(2), Mar.-Apr. 1975, pp. 104-110.

GUEST, R.H.
The man on the assembly line revisited; a main paper given at the 36th Annual Meeting of the American Academy of Management, Kansas City, August 1976.
A significant paper on two studies of assembly-line work, done in the same plant of the same US company with a gap of 25 years. "The results of both studies can be summed up briefly. In the repeat study ... we found that nothing had substantially changed over 25 years in the way people feel about the intrinsic nature of assembly-line work itself."

"These results were 'somewhat surprising' because in an objective sense there were many changes over the years which, taken as a whole, pointed to substantial improvements in the quality of work life."

The author is convinced that "work alienation is viewed as a very real problem, and furthermore, that labour, management and governments are grappling with it as a matter of high priority."

He particularly notes the way in which "formal experiments" could be unsuccessful because they were "superimposed without any real involvement of the workers or their representatives". He makes a particularly important point: informal modifications in job content have long been going on "in the form of arrangements between workers, work groups and their supervisors, to explore better ways of doing an efficient job while at the same time alleviating the frustrations inherent in such highly rationalised machine-pace environments."

His conclusion puts forward "an important hypothesis. Success in quality of working life experiments breeds more than job satisfaction. There is a 'dynamic' set in motion."

GUPTA, Nina.
The impact of performance contingent rewards on job satisfaction: direct and indirect effects. Ann Arbor, Mich., 1975. 234 p. (Michigan. University. Ph.D. psychology.)

HACKER, N.; RUHLE, R.; SCHNEIDER, N.
"Psychologische Grundlagen von Arbeitsverfahren." /Psychogical basis of work reorganisation./ Sozialistische Arbeitswissenschaft, (Berlin, GDR), 6, 1976, pp. 428-429.
Discusses psychological factors for the improvement of individual and collective work organisation with the aim of both optimising productivity and development of the personality of the workers by using more fully their intellectual potential.

*HACKMAN, J.Richard.; LAWLER, Edward E. III.
"Employee reactions to job characteristics." Journal of applied psychology monograph, 55(3), 1971, pp. 259-286.

HAMMER, W. Clay.
"How to ruin motivation with pay." Compensation review, 7(3), 1975, pp. 17-27.

HARKER, H.J.
"Causes of unhappiness in the public service." Canadian personnel and industrial relations journal, 19, Nov. 1972, pp. 38-40.

HEGEDÜS, András; MÁRKUS, Mária.
Ember, munka, közösség. /Man, work and the community./ Budapest, Közgazdasági és Jogi Kiadó, 1955.
A basic work which considers the theoretical aspects of the humanisation of work and incorporates the results of the first Hungarian surveys on job satisfaction.

HERBERT, T.T.
"The influence of organization and technology on job satisfaction." Akron business and economic review, 5(4), 1974, pp. 28-33.

HERMAN, J.B.; DUNHAM, R.B.; HULIN, C.L.
"Organizational structure, demographic characteristics, and employee responses." Organizational behavior and human performance, (13), 1975, pp. 206-232.
Behavioural sciences report on the correlations between job satisfaction, motivation levels, work environment and demographic characteristics in the USA.

HERZBERG, Frederick; MAUSNER, Bernard; SYNDERMAN, Barbara B.
The motivation to work. New York, John Wiley, 1959. 157 p.
A pioneering work in the theory of job satisfaction which used the "critical incident technique" to define the components of job satisfaction.

HERZBERG, Frederick; ZAUTRA, A.
"Orthodox job enrichment: measuring true quality in job satisfaction." Personnel, 53(5), Sept.-Oct. 1976, pp. 54-68.
The main premise of this article is that trying to enrich jobs without changing their structure is not especially conducive to job satisfaction. The authors suggest that employees respond more readily to more responsible tasks, which involve greater learning and new skills than they do to changes in hygienic factors.

HETHY, Lajos; MAKÓ, Csaba.
Workers, automation and society. Budapest. Sociological Research Institute of the Hungarian Academy of Sciences, 1975.
The study aims at throwing light on the effects of the advance of automation in industry on the contents of industrial production work, on working conditions and workers' attitudes in countries with different political, social and economic systems. The study treats workers' attitudes, working conditions and the contents of work, around which it is centred, as dependent variables and traces these largely from automation as the main variable and the characteristics of the socio-economic system as a background factor, also taking into consideration the role of certain control factors, characteristics of the enterprise, the production unit and the individual worker.

HUNT, J.W.; SAUL, P.N.
"Relationship of age, tenure, and job satisfaction in males and females." Academy of Management journal, 18(4), Dec. 1975, pp. 690-702.
Article based on a survey of the relationship of age and tenure of non-manual workers to job satisfaction among male and female workers in Australia.

IRIS, B.; BARRETT, G.V.
"Some relations between job and life satisfaction and job importance." Journal of applied psychology, 56, 1972, pp.301-304.

IVANCEVICH, John M.
"Effects of the shorter workweek on selected satisfaction and performance measures." Journal of applied psychology, 59, 1974, pp. 717-721.

IVANCEVICH, John M.; BAKER, James C.
"The job satisfaction of American managers overseas." MSU business topics, Summer 1969, pp. 72-78.

IVANCEVICH, John M.; DONNELLY, J.H., Jr.
"Relation of organizational structure on job satisfaction, anxiety-stress, and performance." Administrative science quarterly, 20, 1975, pp. 272-280.
This study of 295 trade salesmen in three organisations reports on the relationship between organisation shape or structure (tall, medium and flat) to job satisfaction, anxiety-stress, and performance. The findings indicate that salesmen in flat organisations (1) perceive more satisfaction with respect to self-actualisation, and autonomy, (2) perceive lower amounts of anxiety-stress, and (3) perform more efficiently than salesmen in medium and tall organisations.

JAWA, Sarla.
"Anxiety and job satisfaction." Indian journal of applied sociology, 8(2), Jul. 1971, pp. 70-71.

JOHANSSON, G.
"Psychopsysiological stress reactions in the sawmill; a pilot study." In: Proceedings of IUFRO Joint Meeting, Div 3 and 5, Ergonomics in Sawmills and Woodworking Industries, Symposium in Sweden, Aug. 26-30, 1974. Stockholm, Arbetarskyddsstyrelsen, 1975, pp. 261-271.

JOHNSTON, Ruth.
"Pay and job satisfaction: a survey of some research findings." International labour review, 111(5), May 1975, pp. 441-449.
Several enterprise-level studies done in the US, the UK and Australia (including three of the author's own studies) are cited to support the view that workers often value factors such as job interest and good working relations above pay and that even dissatisfied workers indicate that pay is not crucial in determining positive or negative attitudes towards work. The author concludes that pay becomes the most important factor in job satisfaction only when it is seen as a compensation for dissatisfying and alienating job situations.

JONES, D.H.; GANGULY, T.; SEQUEIRA, C.E.
Studies of attitude and morale in three units of a large chemical process undertaking. Bombay, Central Labour Institute, 1964.

JOSEPH, J.S.
"Differential perception of factors in job attitudes." Psychology annual, (Mysore University), June-Jul. 1970.

JUROVSKÝ, A.
"Sociálnopsychologické appekty práce a pracovná motivácia." /Socio-psychological aspects of work and work motivation./ Syntéza, 7(1), 1974, pp. 4-13.

JUROVSKÝ, A.
Spokojnosť s prácou a jej činitele. /Job satisfaction and its determinants./ Bratislava, Czechoslovak Research Institute of Labour and Social Affairs, 1971. 200 p.
The book describes and summarises the results of job satisfaction studies carried out by the author. He comprehends job satisfaction as a generalised attitude of men to work which is

composed of a whole series of detailed opinion and points of view to different components of work, of working place and to everything connected with work. He assumes that job satisfaction is one of the main parts of a cyclical process, by which the man adjusts himself to work. The correct solution of the questions of "human psychology at work" concerns the individual living equilibrium as well as prosperity of the whole society.

KALSBEEK, J.W.H.
"Mentale werkbelasting en arbeidssatisfaktie." /Mental work load and work satisfaction./ TNO Project, 2(9), Sept. 1974, pp. 323-327.

KATZELL, Raymond A.; BARRETT, Richard S.; PARKER, Treadway, C.
"Job satisfaction, job performance, and situational characteristics." Journal of applied psychology, Apr. 1961, pp. 65-72.

KATZELL, Raymond A.; YANKELOVICH, Daniel; FEIN, M.; ORNATI, O.A.
Work, productivity, and job satisfaction; an evaluation of policy related research. New York, Psychological corporation, 1975. xii, 432 p.
Interdisciplinary research report on factors affecting motivation, job satisfaction and productivity in the USA. It examines management attitudes and practices, labour relations aspects, employees attitudes, management by objectives, workers participation and job enrichment, wage incentive issues, employment policy implications, etc. Extensive bibliographical references.

KATZELL, Raymond A.: YANKELOVITCH, Daniel, et al.
"Pay vs. work motivation and job satisfaction." Compensation review, 8(1), 1976, pp. 54-66.

KAVANAGH, Michael J.; MACKINNEY, Arthur C.; WOLINS, Leroy.
"Satisfaction and morale of foremen as a function of middle manager's performance." Journal of applied psychology, 54, 1970, pp. 145-156.
Demonstrates a relationship between high rating of department needs on their performance of personnel-related job functions and high group satisfaction of foremen in the areas of pay, on-the-job learning opportunity, authority and control and lack of undue pressure and fatigue.

KELLER, Robert T.
"Role conflict and ambiguity: correlates with job satisfaction and values." Personnel psychology, Spring 1975, pp. 57-64.

KERPOLLA, K.
"Participatory administration and teamwork in labour-management cooperation." American journal of economics and sociology, 33(1), Jan. 1974, pp. 19-32.
Referring to Maslow's hierarchy of human needs, the author contends that modern development leads to more autonomy for the individual, more information and more participation in planning, thus moving away from elitism, mechanical organisation and formal subjection to authority. Searching for ways of increasing motivation (and therefore job satisfaction) it is found that motivation is more likely to be created by the delegation of

decision-making power, participation and teamwork than by improving the "hygiene factors" that cause dissatisfaction initially. This is illustrated by reference to an empirical study of Finnish factory workers.

KILBRIDGE, M.D.
"Turnover, absence and transfer rates as indicators of employee dissatisfaction with repetitive work." Industrial and labour relations review, 15, Oct. 1961, pp. 21-32.

KILLINGWORTH, J.S.M.
"Sources of work satisfaction in Australia." Australian psychologist, 9, 1974, pp. 126-140.

KIM, Jay S.; HAMNER, W. Clay.
"Effect of performance feedback and goal setting on productivity and satisfaction in an organizational setting." Journal of applied psychology, Feb. 1976, pp. 48-57.

KLEIN, Lisl.
"There is satisfaction in blue-collar work." Social policy, Jul.-Aug. 1973, pp. 23-26.

KLEIN, Stuart M.
"Pay factors as predicators to satisfaction: a comparison of reinforcement, equity and expectancy." Academy of Management journal, 16, Dec. 1973, pp. 598-610.

KRISTOL, Irving.
"Job satisfaction: daydream or alienation?" The American federationist, 80(22), Feb. 1973, pp. 11-13.

KUHN, D.G., et al.
"Does job performance affect employee satisfaction?" Personnel journal, 50, 1971, pp. 455-459.

LAFOLLETTE, William R.; SIMS, Henry P. Jr.
"Is satisfaction redundant with organizational climate?" Organizational behavior and human performance, 13, Apr. 1975, pp. 257-278.

LAHIR, Dilip K.; SRIVASTVA, Suresh.
"Determinants of satisfaction in middle-management personnel." Journal of applied psychology, June 1967, pp. 254-265.

LANSBURY, Russel, ed.
Sources of worker dissatisfaction in Australia: a symposium. Victoria, Monash University, 1974. 127 p.
A collection of papers from a symposium on worker dissatisfaction in Australia. The symposium which brought together employers, trade unionists, government officials and academics generated a wide variety of views on the subject of the sources of dissatisfaction and the possible solutions to the problem.

Noting that "a poor social environment and bad working conditions lead to a low quality of working life, which results in a high degree of dissatisfaction" the symposium suggests - among other solutions - improved communications, better training and recreational facilities, flexible working hours, various forms of codetermination, job enrichment and job redesign. Some experiments and innovations (notably those at ICI) are also described.

There is a feeling that "in order to establish the preconditions for an improvement in job satisfaction, there must be a concerted attack on deep-rooted social and economic disadvantages and not just cosmetic changes."

LASLETT, B.
"Mobility and work satisfaction: a discussion of the use and interpretation of mobility models." American journal of sociology, 77, 1971, pp. 19-35.

Two different models for studying the effects of intergenerational occupational mobility on three types of work satisfaction are compared and discussed. The interpretive consequences of using one model rather than another are considered. The analysis shows that mobility, whether studied by the interaction or additive models, is not significantly related to satisfaction with earnings. The additive model can predict a significant relationship between mobility and satisfaction with the kind of work done and overall work satisfaction and is preferable to the interaction model on grounds of simplicity.

LATHAM, G.; YUKL, G.
"Effects of assigned and participative goal setting on performance and job satisfaction." Journal of applied psychology, 61(2), 1976, pp. 166-171.

LAURENCE, Mary W.
"Sources of satisfaction in the lives of working women." Journal of gerontology, Apr. 1961, pp. 163-167.

LAUTERBURG, C. H.
"Motivation durch Aufgabenstrukturierung." /Motivation through task structuring./ Industrielle Organisation, 42(72), 1973, pp. 554-559.

LAWLER, Edward E. III.
Motivation in work organizations. Monterey, Brooks and Cole, 1973.
A review of the current major psychological theories of work motivation, presenting also some empirical data on the subject. Topics covered include theories of motivation, the determinants of satisfaction and the relationship between it and work performance through the use of rewards, the impact of the nature of tasks on job performance, satisfaction, self-esteem and perceived competence and the influence of peers on productivity. Discussing three types of management patterns (paternalistic, scientific and participative) the author concludes that a combination of all three is necessary for an organisation to be truly effective.

LAWLER, Edward E. III; HALL, Douglas T.
"Relationship of job characteristics to job involvement, satisfaction and intrinsic motivation." Journal of applied psychology, 54, 1970, pp. 305-312.
A study demonstrating the relationship between perceived job characteristics and job behaviour and job involvement, higher order need satisfaction and intrinsic motivation.

LOCKE, Edwin A.
"Satisfiers and dissatisfiers among white-collar and blue-collar employees." Journal of applied psychology, 58(1), Aug. 1973, pp. 67-77.

LOCKE, Edwin A.; WHITING, R.J.
"Sources of satisfaction and dissatisfaction among solid waste management employees." Journal of applied psychology, 59, 1974, pp. 145-156.

LOGAN, Nancy; O'REILLY, Charles II; ROBERTS, Karlene.
"Job satisfaction among part-time and full-time employees." Journal of vocational behavior, Jan. 1973, pp. 33-41.

LONDON, Manuel; KLIMOSKI, Richard J.
"Self-esteem and job complexity as moderators of performance and satisfaction." Journal of vocational behavior, 6, June 1975, pp. 293-304.

LYON, Herbert L.; IVANCEVICH, John M.
"An exploratory investigation of organizational climate and job satisfaction in a hospital. Academy of Management journal, 17(4), 1974, pp. 635-648.

LYONS, Thomas F.
"Role clarity, need for clarity, satisfaction, tension and withdrawal." Organisational behaviour and human performance, 6, 1975, pp. 99-110.
A questionnaire-survey of 156 female nurses testing the relationship between perceived role clarity and work satisfaction, withdrawal and tension. Findings indicate that perceived role clarity is positively correlated with satisfaction and negatively correlated with withdrawal and tension.

MANNHEIM, Bilha.
"A comparative study of work centrality, job rewards and satisfaction: occupational groups in Israel." Sociology of work and occupations, 2(1), Feb. 1975, pp. 79-103.

MARRETT, Cora B.; HAGE, Jerald; AIKEN, Michael.
"Communication and satisfaction in organizations." Human relations, 28, Sept. 1975, pp. 611-626.

MATĚJŮ, P.
"Dynamika vzdělání a některé aspekty změn ve sféře pracovní motivace." /Dynamics of education and some aspects of the changes in the sphere of worker motivation./ Syntéza, (3), 1975, pp. 84-90.

MAURICE, M.; MONTEIL, C.
Vie quotidienne et horaires de travail; enquête psychosociologique sur le travail des équipes successives. /Daily life and hours of work - a psychosociological survey of shift work./ Paris, Institut des Sciences Sociales du Travail, 1965. 318 p.
A report of research on the psychological aspects and the sociological aspects of shift work in France. It covers employees attitude towards shift work, job satisfaction, social implications, leisure activities of shiftworkers.

MAYEROVÁ, M.
"Sociální potřeby - činitelé pracovní motivace." /Social needs - factors on work motivation./ Psychologie v ekonomické praxi, (1-2), 1966, pp. 37-48.

MAYES, K.
"Four days shalt thou labour ..." Industrial management, 3(3), Mar. 1973, pp. 37-38.
Article discussing various schemes, such as the condensed work week for the promotion of job satisfaction in the USA.

MEHTA, Prayag.
"Work satisfaction and democratic outlook: the role of worker participation." National Labour Institute bulletin (New Delhi), 2(6), June 1976, pp. 231-234.
Data were collected from 152 worker representatives of joint shop-floor committees in a large public sector undertaking on work satisfaction, socio-political outlook and life satisfaction. Out of this sample, 35 per cent seemed satisfied with the nature of influence and autonomy they enjoyed in the organization; 28 per cent were satisfied with working conditions; 39 per cent with challenge on their jobs; 27 per cent with supervisory behaviour. The paper also explores the nature of intercorrelations between the variables.

MIKALICHKI, A.
"The effects of job design on turnover, absenteeism and health." Relations industrielles - Industrial relations, Aug. 1975, pp. 377-389.

MILES, R.H.; PETTY, M.M.
"Relationships between role clarity, need for clarity, and job tension and satisfaction for supervisory and nonsupervisory roles." Academy of Management journal, 18, 1975, pp. 877-883.

MILES, Raymond E.
"Work, performance and satisfaction: a complementary collection." Industrial relations, (9), 1970, pp. 405-474.

MITCHELL, Terence R.; SMYSER, Charles M.; WEED, Stan E.
"Locus of control: supervision and work satisfaction." Academy of Management journal, Sept. 1975, pp. 623-631.

MONIE, P.M.
"Job satisfaction of female employees in the clothing industry; case study No. 4." Personnel practice bulletin, Sept. 1967, pp. 183-190.

MOORS, S.; VANSINA, I.; VERBORGH, E.
Travail en groupe et satisfaction au travail dans un atelier de confection: une transformation du travail à la chaîne. /Group work and job satisfaction in the workplace; a transformation of the assembly line./ Bruxelles, Office Belge pour l'Accroissement de la Productivité, 1975. 1 v + annexes.

MORIN, F.
"Le non-intéressement des travailleurs à l'entreprise: analyse de quelques causes d'ordre juridique." /Workers' disinterest in the enterprise: an analysis of some legal reasons./ Relations industrielles - Industrial relations, 28(4), 1973, pp. 862-871.

MOUNTAIN, Ann D.
"Job satisfaction of female employees in the clothing industry; case study No.1." Personnel practice bulletin, Dec. 1965, pp. 7-17.

MUMFORD, Enid.
Job satisfaction: a study of computer specialists. London, Longman, 1972. 242 p.
Using a sample of computer specialists from eight organisations, the study examines their work needs, the factors which contribute to job satisfaction and the reconciliation of occupational efficiency needs with individual needs for a satisfactory and stimulating work environment.

MUMFORD, E.
Work design: a method for achieving job satisfaction and efficiency. Manchester, Manchester Business School, 1976.
A collection of articles used in the Computer and Work Design Research Unit in practical design of work systems. It contains twelve articles, including two dealing with technologists and engineers as designers and one dealing with "trade unions - new users of research" by two Scandinavian workers.

NICHOLSON, Edward A.; MILJUS, Robert C.
"Job satisfaction and turnover among Liberal Arts College professors." Personnel journal, Nov. 1972, 6 p.
The purpose of this article is to examine those factors or conditions of employment with which faculty members are the most satisfied or dissatisfied. The focus on this excellent study is not on the propensities of professors to move from arts colleges, but on the organisational conditions which underlie the disposition of the faculty members to move or to remain in their present positions.

NILSSON, C.
"Working conditions in the sawmill industry: a sociopsychological approach based on subjective data." In: Proceedings of IUFRO Joint Meeting, Div 3 and 5, Ergonomics in Sawmills and Woodworking Industries, Symposium in Sweden, Aug. 26-30, 1974. Stockholm, Arbetarskyddsstyrelsen, 1975, pp. 249-260.

NOVARA, F.
"Aspetti psicologici dell'assenteismo e del ricambio del personale." /Psychological aspects of absenteeism and turnover./ Studi organizzativi, (2), 1971.
Absenteeism and turnover are studied as an effect of work organisation.

OBRADOVIČ, J.; FRENCH, John R.P. Jr.; RODGERS, Willard.
"Workers' councils in Yugoslavia: effects on perceived participation and satisfaction of workers." Human relations, 23(5), Oct. 1970, pp. 459-471.
This research studies the effect of the distinctive Yugoslavian Workers' Councils, but views this form of participation within a general theoretical framework including: (1) the relation of the factory to the larger political and economic system of which it is a part; (2) the distribution of power and participation among the various formal positions and levels in the factory hierarchy; (3) the processes of election or selection by which members get into these positions; (4) informal participation and influence.

One interpretation of the data presented in this paper is as follows: membership on a Workers' Council tends to be perceived as providing a greater opportunity to participate in the management of the factory, and perhaps for this reason members tend to be more satisfied with their situation than non-members. However, Workers' Council members from the worker levels do not have nearly as much influence within the Workers' Council as do those from management roles. Hence, there is a discrepancy between the amount of influence that many members of Workers' Councils think they should have and the amount they perceive they actually have; this produces frustration in those with a high aspired level of participation, and this frustration offsets to some extent the greater satisfaction that would otherwise accompany membership on the Workers' Council.

O'REILLY, Charles A. III; ROBERTS, Karlene H.
"Individual differences in personality, position in the organization, and job satisfaction." Organizational behavior and human performance, 14, Aug. 1975, pp. 144-150.

ORGAN, D.W.; GREENE, C.N.
"Role ambiguity, locus of control, and work satisfaction." Journal of applied psychology, 59, 1974, pp. 101-102.

ORGANISATION FOR ECONOMIC CO-OPERATION AND DEVELOPMENT.
Advances in work organisation; international management seminar, Paris, 3rd-6th April 1973: final report. Paris, 1974. 59 p.
Designed to examine, evaluate and elicit lessons from developments in work reorganisation, the report of this seminar describes new practices, analyses reported cases and considers their results and their implications for managers, supervisors and workers. While reports told of improvements in productivity and job satisfaction resulting from changes in work organisation, the conclusions stress the impracticability of assuming the existence of a single solution, given the greater variety of approaches to the management of change.

OSBORN, R.N.; HUNT, J.G.
"Relations between leadership, size and subordinate satisfaction in a voluntary organization." Journal of applied psychology, 60, 1975, pp. 730-735.

PAUL, R.J.
"Role clarity as a correlate of satisfaction, job-related strain and propensity to leave, male vs. female." Journal of management studies, 11, 1974, pp. 233-245.

PENTZLIN, Kurt.
Die organisierte Unzufriedenheit; Eine "Rolle" der Gewerkschaften. /Organised dissatisfaction and the "function" of trade unions./ Stuttgart, Seewald Verlag, 1973. 156 p.
The author examines the problem of the apparent increase in worker dissatisfaction (rather than satisfaction) in the face of improving standards of living and suggests that trade union wage policies may contribute to this phenomenon.

PESTONJEE, D.M.
"Effect of financial incentive on job satisfaction." Indian journal of applied psychology, 8(2), Jul. 1971, pp. 61-63.

PESTONJEE, D.M.
Organisational structure and job attitudes. Calcutta, Minerva, 1973. 152 p.
This book describes an emperical study of job satisfaction and morale under two types of organisational structures: autocratic and democratic. Data indicates that employes under democratic supervision reported more satisfaction with different job areas and management, than employees under autocratic supervision, thereby confirming findings of several earlier studies in India and abroad. Additionally, conditions within the work context and work conditions outside it do not have a reciprocal influence on job satisfaction and social life outside the factory environment appears to counteract employees' feeling of stress, strain and job dissatisfaction.

PESTONJEE, D.M.
A study of employee morale and job satisfaction as related to organisational structure. Aligarh Muslim University, 1976. (Unpubl. Ph.D. thesis.)

PHILIPSEN, H.
"De voorwaardelijkheid van algemene uitspraken toegelicht aan de samenhang tussen werkvoldoening en afwezigheid wegens ziekte." /Restriction on general statements explained from the relationship between work satisfaction and absence due to sickness./ Sociologische gids, 17(4), Jul.-Aug. 1970, pp. 320-332.

PORTER, Lyman W.; LAWLER, Edward E.III.
"The effects of 'tall' versus 'flat' organization structures on managerial job satisfaction." Personnel psychology, (2), 1964, pp. 135-148.

PORTER, Lyman W.; SIEGEL, Jacob.
"Relationship of tall and flat organization structures to the satisfactions of foreign managers." Personnel psychology, Winter 1965, pp. 379-392.

"Pressure for production, task of difficulty, and the correlation between job satisfaction and job performance." Journal of applied psychology, 58, 1973, pp. 378-380.

PRITCHARD, Robert D.
"Effects of varying performance-pay instrumentalities on the relationship between performance and satisfaction: a test of the Lawler and Porter Model." Journal of applied psychology, 58, 1973, pp. 122-125.

PRITCHARD, Robert D.; DUNNETTE, Marvin D.; JORGENSON, Dale O.
"Effects of perceptions of equity and inequity on worker performance and satisfaction." Journal of applied psychology, 57, 1972, pp. 75-94.

PRITCHARD, Robert D.; KARRASICK, B.W.
"The effects of organizational climate on managerial job performance and job satisfaction." Organizational behavior and human performance, 9, 1973, pp. 126-146.

PRITCHARD, Robert D.; PETERS, Lawrence H.
"Job duties and job interests as predictors of intrinsic and extrinsic satisfaction." Organizational behavior and human performance, 10, 1974, pp. 315-330.

PRUDEN, H.O.; REESE, R.M.
"Interorganization role-set relations and the performance and satisfaction of industrial salesmen." Administrative science quarterly, 17, 1972, pp. 601-609.

PRYBIL, Lawrence D.
"Job satisfaction in relation to job performance and occupational level." Personnel journal, 52(2), Feb. 1973, pp. 94-101.

RAO, G.V.S.
"Job content and context factors in job satisfaction of female electrical employees." Indian journal of social work, 32(1), Apr. 1971, pp. 45-51.

REGINI, M.; REYNERI, E.
Lotte operaie e organizzazione del lavoro. /Labour grievances and the organisation of work./ Padova, Marsilio, 1972.
The authors study the 1968-1972 labour grievances in relationship to the discontents about work organisation. Implicit or explicit workers demands for change are also examined.

REHN, Gösta.
"For greater flexibility of working life." OECD observer, (62), Feb. 1973, pp. 3-7.
Discusses proposals for flexible hours of work and other methods of promoting job satisfaction, including greater personal control over time allocation for work, leisure, education, etc., over the life span.

Abridgement of the author's report to the OECD International Conference on New Patterns for Working Time, Paris, 1972.

"The relationship between education and satisfaction with job content." Academy of Management journal, 18, 1975, pp. 888-892.

RITTI, Richard R.
"Underemployment of engineers." Industrial relations, 9(4), 1970, pp. 437-452.
Uses the results of research to support the argument that lack of opportunity to perform meaningful work is at the root of the frustration and dissatisfaction among engineers. Cites the fact that "field" engineers, who have more autonomy and responsibility are more satisfied than "laboratory" engineers, who feel that they are underemployed or misemployed, as evidence supporting the theory that greater performance leads to greater satisfaction.

ROBINSON, John P.; ATHANASION Robert; HEAD, Kendra B.
"Measures of occupational attitudes and occupational characteristics." In: Measures of political attitudes. Ann Arbor, Mich., University of Michigan, Survey Research Centre, 1969, appendix A.

RONAN, W.W.
"Individual and situational variables relating to job satisfaction." Journal of applied psychology monograph, 54(1), 1970, Part 2, pp. 1-31.

RYDER, Leonie A.
"Job satisfaction of female employees in the clothing industry; case study no.5." Personnel practice bulletin, 25(4), Dec. 1969, pp. 309-320.

SARAPATA, Adam.
Socjologiczne problemy przedsiebiorstwa przemyslowego. /Sociological problems of industrial enterprises./ Warsaw, Panstwowe Wydawnictwo Ekonomiczne, 1965.

SCANLAN, Burt K.
"Determinants of job satisfaction and productivity." Personnel journal, 55, 1976, pp. 12-14.

SCHNEIDER, Benjamin; SNYDER, Robert A.
"Some relationships between job satisfaction and organizational climate." Journal of applied psychology, June 1975, pp. 318-328.

SCHULER, Randall S.
"Role perceptions, satisfaction, and performance: a partial reconciliation." Journal of applied psychology, 60, 1975, pp. 683-687.

SCHWAB, Donald P.
"Conflicting impacts of pay on employee motivation and satisfaction." Personnel journal, 53, Mar. 1974, pp. 196-200.

SCHWAB, Donald P.; CUMMINGS, Larry L.
"Theories of performance and satisfaction: a review." *Industrial relations*, 9(4), Oct. 1970, pp. 408-430.
Traces the development of concepts and theories of performance and satisfaction commencing with the view expressed by the Human Relations School in the 30's and 40's that satisfaction led to better performance and ending with the most recent theories which hold that satisfaction is caused by performance rather than being the cause of it. The Porter and Lawler model is described in detail as an example of the latter view.

SCHWAB, Donald P.; HENEMAN, H.G.III.
"Aggregate and individual predictability of the two-factor theory of job satisfaction." *Personnel psychology*, 23, 1970, pp. 55-66.

SCHWAB, Donald P.; HENEMAN, H.G.III.
"Pay: a road to motivation and satisfaction?" *Personnel administrator*, 19, 1974, pp. 19-21.

SCHWAB, Donald P.; WALLACE, Marc J.
"Correlates of employee satisfaction with pay." *Industrial relations*, Fall 1974, pp. 78-89.
This study examines six personal and organisational correlates of pay satisfaction of both male and female nonexempt employees in a large firm manufacturing durable consumer goods. In general, the results indicate that although satisfaction with pay is related to several of the observed variables, the vast majority of the variance in pay satisfaction is not explained with the variables used in this study. Based on these results, additional variables worth investigating are suggested for future research.

SCOTT, R.D.
"Job enlargement: the key to increasing job satisfaction?" *Personnel journal*, 52, 1973, pp. 313-317.

SEASHORE, Stanley E., BARNOWE, J. Thad.
"Behind the averages: a closer look at America's lower-middle-income workers." *In*: INDUSTRIAL RELATIONS RESEARCH ASSOCIATION. *Proceedings of the 24th Annual Winter Meeting, Dec. 27-28, 1971*. Madison, Wisc., 1972, pp. 358-365.
The authors constructed an index of blue-collar blues to test the proposition that dissatisfaction is associated with certain demographic and socio-economic characteristics of the worker. They conclude that specific features of the job and work setting are responsible for dissatisfaction which is common to workers of disparate personal backgrounds, occupations and incomes.

SHARMA, V.K.
"Fringe benefits and employee satisfaction." *Indian management*, 10(10), Oct. 1971, pp. 33-37.

SHEPARD, Jon M.
Automation and alienation: a study of office and factory workers. Cambridge, Mass., M.I.T. Press, 1971. 163 p.
The author compares the impact of mechanisation and automation on worker alienation of office workers and blue-collar workers and finds that office employees are less alienated than semi-skilled factory workers.

SHEPARD, Jon M.
"Functional specialization, alienation and job satisfaction." Industrial and labor relations review, Jan. 1970, pp. 207-219. A review of previous research on the relationship between job satisfaction, functional specialisation and alienation from middle-class work norms.

SHEPARD, Jon M.
"Specialization, autonomy and job satisfaction." Industrial relations, 12(3), Oct. 1973, pp. 274-281.
A comparative study of three groups of workers, with different degrees of functional specialisation, which demonstrates that job satisfaction is more closely related to the "objective" factor of specialisation than to the "subjective" factor of perceived lack of autonomy.

SHEPPARD, Harold Lloyd; HERRICK, Neal W.
Where have all the robots gone? Worker dissatisfaction in the seventies. New York, Free Press, 1972. 222 p.
The authors use data from interviews with white, male blue-collar union members and from the national survey of employed workers conducted by the University of Michigan to analyse worker dissatisfaction and its linkages with social and political behaviour. Unhappiness about the lack of variety, autonomy and responsibility in the job are more important than the wage level and the degree of job security.

SHERIDAN, John E.; SLOCUM, John W.
"The direction of the causal relationship between job satisfaction and work performance." Organizational behavior and human performance, 14, Oct. 1975, pp. 159-172.

SIMS, Henry P. Jr.; SZILAGYI, Andrew D.
"Leader reward behavior and subordinate satisfaction and performance." Organizational behavior and human performance, 14, Dec. 1975, pp. 426-438.

SIMS, Henry P. Jr.; SZILAGYI, Andrew D.
"Leader structure and subordinate satisfaction for two hospital administrative levels: a path analysis approach." Journal of applied psychology, Apr. 1975, pp. 194-197.

SINGH, A.P.; PESTONJEE, D.M.
"Supervisory behaviour and job satisfaction." Indian journal of industrial relations, Jan. 1974, pp. 407-416.
An attempt to determine the differential effect of supervisory behaviour on the job satisfaction of blue-collar workers. The results indicate that overall job satisfaction scores, social relations area scores, and management area scores are higher under employee-oriented supervision. The scores on job and personal adjustment areas are not influenced by supervisory orientation. The results are analysed in terms of mean, S.D., critical ratio, and analysis of variance.

SINGH, A.P.; SRIVASTAVA, A.K.
"Occupational level and job satisfaction." Journal of psychological researchers, 19(2), May 1975, pp. 56-59.

SINGH, R.P.; NANDKEOLYAR, S.
"Personnel characteristics and job satisfaction." Khadi gram, 20(8), May 1974, pp. 408-411.

SINGHAL, Sushila.
"Psychology of men at work. II: Communication and job perception." Indian journal of industrial relations, 8(3), Jan. 1973, pp. 415-424.

SINHA, Duganand.
"Job satisfaction in office and manual workers." Indian journal of social work, 19, 1958, pp. 39-46.

SINHA, D: AGARWALA, U.N.
"Job satisfaction and general adjustment of Indian white-collar workers." Indian journal of industrial relations, 6(4), apr. 1971, pp. 357-367.
This paper tries to find out job satisfaction among white-collar workers with the help of a comprehensive job satisfaction questionnaire and Saxena's Adjustment Inventory along with a brief personal data form on 60 white-collar workers. The product-moment correlation of the two (r=.52) indicated that workers who were satisfied tended to have better score on adjustment and those less satisfied were generally poorer in their adjustment. Inter-correlation of job satisfaction score with different areas of adjustment, viz., home, social, and emotional, revealed all the coefficients to be positive and statistically reliable. Significant relationship of job satisfaction with age, education, income, and length of service was observed. Lastly, those who evaluated their job in positive terms tended to score higher on the job satisfaction questionnaire. The relationship with marital status and number of dependants was negligible. The author then discusses the inter-relationship of adjustment with job satisfaction and concludes that general adjustment of individual is an important determinant of the satisfaction that he experiences on the job and from the conditions surrounding it.

SINHA, D.; GUPTA, N.
"Need-satisfaction and absenteeism." Indian journal of industrial relations, 10(1), Jul. 1974, pp. 3-14.
Article on the relationship between job satisfaction and absenteeism, based on a survey of 188 unskilled workers in an Indian enterprise.

SMITH, P.I.S.
Job involvement and communications. London, Business Books, 1973, x, 126 p.
A study of various means (job enrichment, workers' participation, intrafirm communications, etc.) used by firms in the UK, the USA and elsewhere to raise the level of job satisfaction and improve the quality of work. It covers theoretical issues, trade union attitudes, and emphasises management initiative in communication through joint consultation, mass communication and briefing groups.

SNEIDER, B.; SNYDER, R.A.
Some relationships among and between measures of employee perceptions and other indices of organizational effectiveness. College Park, Md., University of Maryland, 1974. 41 p.
Report on the relationships between job satisfaction, work environment, productivity and labour turnover.

STARCEVICH, M.M.
"Job factor importance for job satisfaction and dissatisfaction across occupational levels." Journal of applied psychology, 56, 1972, pp. 467-471.

STEEL, M.H.
"The supervisor: dissatisfier or satisfier?" Supervision, 34, May 1972, pp. 30-31.

STEERS, Richard M.
"Factors affecting job attitudes in a goal-setting environment." Academy of Management journal, Mar. 1976, pp. 6-16.

STONE, Eugene F.; PORTER, Lyman W.
"Job characteristics and job attitudes: a multivariate study." Journal of applied psychology, Fall 1975, pp. 57-64.

***STRAUSS, George.**
"Worker dissatisfaction: a look at the causes." Monthly labour review, 97, Feb. 1974, pp. 57-58.
This paper examines the causes of worker dissatisfaction. According to the author dissatisfaction is reported on jobs with short job cycles or relatively little challenge. But dissatisfaction can also be caused by low incomes, job insecurity, inadequate fringe benefits or tyrannical supervision. A lack of challenge is much less oppressive than a lack of income, because people are willing to accept boredom, if they are paid enough. This however is no reason to ignore the problem of work with little or no challenge, since this is also an important source of dissatisfaction.

SUSMAN, Gerald I.
"Process design, automation, and worker alienation." Industrial relations, 11, 1972, pp. 34-45.
Study on worker alienation in automated plants in continuous process industries which considers the possibility that (i) the degree of alienation observed in continuous process industries is due to characteristics of work process other than automation and (ii) that alienation decreases as plants become more automated. The result of the study question the generally-accepted idea that automation reduces alienation.

SUSMAN, Gerald I.
"Job enlargement: effects of culture on worker responses." Industrial relations, 12(1), Feb. 1973, pp. 1-15.
Tests previous research findings indicating that community attitudes play a large part in determining employee reactions to job enlargement schemes. Uses data from 26 plants with continuous process technologies to challenge the assumption that rural workers respond more favourably to such schemes than urban workers. Indicates that, while all workers respond positively to job enlargement programmes, rural workers show more pride in job accomplishment and urban workers show greater intrinsic job interest. Notes, however, that the characteristics of continuous process industries create initially favourable job attitudes and suggests that these might colour worker response to job enlargement.

SWART, J. Carroll; BALDWIN, R.A.
"EDP clerical employees, and work satisfaction." Academy of Management journal, 15, 1972, p. 240.

SYMPOSIUM ERGONOMIJA, Niška Banja, 1976.
Collection of papers. T. 1-4. N.p., 1969-1974.
4 v. (Papers on application of technical, biological and humanistic sciences for the optimisation of working conditions, effects and products. Also contains a collection of regulations of safety at work with commentary and technical regulations.)

SZTUMSKI, J.
"Le travail et la satisfaction." /Work and satisfaction./ Humanisation du travail, (2), 1974.

TELLIER, R.D.
Cross-sectional study of the impact of the transition to the four-day work week on employee job satisfaction. Ann Arbor, Mich., University of Michigan, 1975. viii, 261 l.
Thesis on the impact of changes in hours of work and weekly rest on job satisfaction in several enterprises in the USA. It presents survey data on employees attitudes to the transition to a 4-day work week, and includes the degree of workers' participation in planning the transition. Includes bibliographical references.

TERKEL, Louis.
Working; people talk about what they do all day and how they feel about what they're doing. New York, Pantheon Books, 1974. 589 p.

THIERRY, H.
"Arbeidsinstelling en personeelsbeleid." /Work attitude and personnel policy./ Personeelsbeleid, 4(10), Oct. 1968, pp. 290-297.

TRUELSEN, Hans Tage; SØE, Mogens.
Helbred, trivsel, jobforhold. /Health, job satisfaction, job conditions./ Copenhagen, 1975. 87 p.

TURCOTTE, William E.
Control systems, performance, and satisfaction in two state agencies." Administrative science quarterly, 19, Mar. 1974, pp. 60-73.

TURNER, Arthur N.; LAWRENCE, Paul R.
Industrial jobs and the worker. Boston, Mass., Harvard University, Graduate School of Business Administration, 1965, 177 p.
Forty-seven different jobs in eleven industries were studied and measured in terms of such attributes as variety, autonomy, responsibility, knowedge and skill to determine which characteristics of the intrinsic job influence workers' response. A positive relationship was found between job level and job satisfaction for rural workers; a negative relationship appeared for urban workers.

UNITED STATES. CONGRESS. SENATE. COMMITTEE ON LABOUR AND PUBLIC WELFARE.
Changing patterns of work in America. Washington, GPO, 1976. v, 497 p.
Record of hearings on alternative hours of work and work arrangements in the USA - covering part-time employment, flexible hours of work, job sharing, etc. The paper considers their implications for job satisfaction.

VAID, K.N.
"Work behavior and work attitude: a study of absentees." Indian journal of industrial relations, 2(3), Jan. 1967, pp. 378-392.

VAN BEEK, H.G.
"Der Einfluss der Organisation eines Fliessbandes auf die Produktion und die Einstellung zur Arbeit." /The influence of assembly line organisation on production and attitude towards work./ Mitteilungen. Institut für Angewandte Arbeitswissenschaft (Köln), (41), Sept. 1973, pp. 15-32.

VAN BEEK, H.G.
"The influence of assembly line organisation on output quality and morale." Occupational psychology, 38, 1964. pp.161-172.

VAN BEINUM, H.J.J.
The morale of the Dublin busmen. Dublin, Mount Salus Press, 1966. 94 p.
A study directed towards determining the attitudes of busmen towards their work situation through the analysis of three major components of the work environment: the job, the management system and the trade union role. The reasons for the busmen's attitudes were also analysed in this attempt to consider the relationship between the three components and low morale. Findings indicate that socio-technical factors and problems of structured design; certain employment conditions and company policy and values are determinants of low morale. The author indicates areas and directions of change and the role of management and unions regarding change.

WALKER, Charles R.; GUEST, Robert H.
The man on the assembly line. Cambridge, Mass., Harvard University Press, 1952. 180 p.
One of the first studies of the automobile assembly plant. The workers expressed dissatisfaction with the repetitiveness, mechanical pacing and drudgery of the assembly line. (A 1976 repitition of the study by Robert Guest indicates that this situation has not changed substantially in the intervening years.)

WALSH, Edward Joseph.
Dirty work, race, and self-esteem. Ann Arbor, Institute of Labor and Industrial Relations, University of Michigan-Wayne State University, 1975. 95 p. (Policy papers in human resources and industrial relations, 23.)

WANOUS, John P.
"A casual-correlational analysis of the job satisfaction and performance relationship." Journal of applied psychology, Apr. 1974, pp. 139-144.

WATERS, L.K.; ROACH, Darrell.
"Relationship between job attitudes and two forms of withdrawal from the work situation." Journal of applied psychology, Fall 1971, pp. 92-94.

WATERS, L.K.; ROACH, Darrell.
"The two-factor theories of job satisfaction: empirical tests of four samples of insurance company employees." Personnel psychology, 24, Winter 1971, pp. 697-705.

WATERS, L.K.; WATERS, Carrie Wherry.
"Correlates of job satisfaction and job dissatisfaction among female clerical workers." Journal of applied psychology, Oct. 1969, pp. 388-391.

WEAVER, C.N.
"Correlates of job satisfaction: some evidence from the national surveys." Academy of Management journal, 17, 1974, pp. 373-375.

WEDDERBURN, D.; CROMPTON, R.
Workers' attitudes and technology. Cambridge, University Press, 1972. 176 p.
A study of the relationship between worker attitudes, in particular the greater or lesser degree of satisfaction derived from occupational activity, and the technology used at the workplace, based on a survey conducted in northern England by means of interviews. The study shows that the use of similar technologies does not necessarily result in identical working conditions or similarity in worker attitudes, and that, if such attitudes are to be evaluated, account should be taken of many other variables relating to the economic situation and the environment of the undertaking, the style of management and the size of the production unit, not to mention the workers' background, experience, skills and personal aspirations. The authors nevertheless reach the conclusion that the technologies adopted can serve as a useful point of departure for the study of behaviour patterns in an undertaking; the same role can be

fulfilled by management-designed systems for the planning, performance and supervision of tasks. The authors provide instructive comments on the factors making for positive reactions of wage earners (particularly the degree of independence they enjoy in their work) and on many other aspects of working life.

WEITZEL, W. et al.
"The impact of the organization on the structure of job satisfaction: some factor analytic findings." Personnel psychology, 26, 1973, pp. 545-557.

WERNIMONT, P.F. et al.
"Comparison of sources of personal satisfaction and of work motivation." Journal of applied psychology, 54, 1970, pp.95-102.

WHITE, G.C.
Job design and work organisation: diagnosis and measurement. London, n.d. (Great Britain. Department of Fmployment. Work Research Unit. Paper, No. 2.)
Outlines framework in which organisational development must take place and the need for methods to establish objective measures of organisational behaviour related to job satisfaction. Includes sample employee questionnaires for use in the diagnosis of technical, social and other internal problems.

WILD, R.
"Job needs, job satisfaction and job behaviour of women manual workers." Journal of applied psychology, 54, 1970, pp. 157-162.

WILD, R.; DAWSON, A.
"The relationship of specific job attitudes with overall job satisfaction and the influence of biographical variables." Journal of Management studies, 9, 1972, pp. 150-158.

WILD, Ray; HILL, A.B.
Women in the factory: a study of job satisfaction and labour turnover. London, Institute of Personnel Management, 1970.

WILSON, N.A.B.
On the quality of working life. London, H.M.S.O., 1973. v, 52 p. (Great Britain. Department of Employment. Manpower papers, No. 7.)
The quality of working life depends on both the output and the satisfaction of workers, the present report describes the effects that some of the characteristics of modern industrial systems have, first on the work experience of employees and then on their feelings of responsibility and their enthusiasm for their work. Noting that one must take into consideration the fact that conditions of the future will be very different from those of today, the report makes several recommendations for future government in this area.

WINTHER, Erik.
EDB og trivsel. Delrapport til projektet. /ADP and job satisfaction. Partial report for the projekt./ Copenhagen, 1974. 85 p. + annexes. (Nyt fra samfundsvidenskaberne, Forskningsrapport 1974-4.)

WOOD, D.A.
"Background charateristics and work values distinguishing satisfaction levels among engineers." Journal of applied psychology, 55, 1971, pp. 537-542.

"Worker participation and job satisfaction." Labour and employment gazette, Nov. 1975, pp. 4-5.
Increasing interest is being focussed on worker participation as a means of creating greater job satisfaction. A survey conducted by the Department of Labour, New Zealand in the manufacturing sector in 1972 showed that one in every eight firms employing more than 20 people reported that they were utilising some form of participation. Studies of the schemes introduced into some of these firms have shown that increased job satisfaction is an important objective of participation.

ZWERDING, Daniel.
"Beyond boredom: a look at what's new on the assembly line." Washington monthly, Jul.-Aug. 1973, pp. 80-91.

II. OTHER LITERATURE ON JOB SATISFACTION

"Absenteeism in industry: can it be checked altogether?" Tamil Nadu labour journal, 16(12), Dec. 1974, pp. 1-2.

ALBERS, H.J.
"Pädagogische Aspekte der Arbeitszufriedenheit." /Educational aspects of job satisfaction./ Deutsche Berfus- und Fachschule, 71(7), Jul. 1975, pp. 438-489.
This article discusses relationships between satisfaction, motivation, performance record and attitudes.

ALLEN, George.
"Sources of job satisfaction, a concluding report." Banking, Dec. 1967, pp. 64, 66, 68, 70.

ALTIMUS, C.A.; TERSINE, R.J.
"Chronological age and job satisfaction: the young blue collar worker." Academy of Management journal, 16(1), Mar. 1973, pp. 53-66.
Article on the significance of age groups in determining job satisfaction among manual workers in the USA, based on a questionnaire survey of older workers and young workers.

ANAND, K.K.; BAJAJ, Anita.
"Employee morale survey." Indian management, 14(2), Feb. 1975, pp. 52-56.

ARDY, P.
"Qualité de vie dans le travail." /The quality of working life./ Journal des associations patronales, 70(10), Mar. 1975, pp. 175-177.
Article on employees' attitudes towards job satisfaction and the work environment in OECD countries.

ASEEV, V.
"Psikhologicheskie faktory preoddeniia monotonnosti truda." /Psychological factors causing monotony of work./ Sotsialisticheskii trud (Moskva), 18(2), Feb. 1973, pp. 81-89.
Article on psychological aspects of boredom and fatigue in the work environment, and their adverse effects on labour productivity, with particular reference to assembly line work. The article covers motivation, job enrichment, and the participation of workers in the setting of their own standards performance, etc.

ASH, P.
"Job satisfaction differences among women of different ethnic groups." Journal of vocational behavior, 2, 1972, pp. 495-507.

ATCHISON, T.J.; LEFFERTS, E.A.
"The prediction of turnover using Herzberg's job satisfaction technique." Personnel psychology, 25(1), Spring 1972, pp. 53-65.

BACKER, W.
Some aspects of motivation patterns of a group of coloured factory workers. Cape Town, Centre for Intergroup Studies, University of Cape Town, 1975.
The objective of this study was to ascertain the major factors responsible for satisfaction and dissatisfaction of workers on different job levels.

This investigation used the interviewing technique within the framework of Herzberg's Motivation-Hygiene Theory.

It concludes that better motivation can be reached by resolving the "hygiene" problems and by introducing higher level motivators by job enrichment.

BAKER, C.
"Job evaluation and job satisfaction." Personnel practice bulletin, Dec. 1973, Mar. 1974, June 1974.

BARBASH, Jack.
"The tensions of work. Can we reduce the cost of industrialism?" Dissent, 19(1), 1972.

BARBASH, Jack.
Job satisfaction, attitudes surveys. Paris, Organisation for Economic Co-operation and Development, 1976. 36 p.
Report on current trends in the methodology and use of attitude surveys for measuring job satisfaction in OECD countries.

BARTH, Richard T.
"A comparison of weighted and unweighted inter-group climate satisfaction scores." Relations industrielles-Industrial relations, 28(2), 1973, pp. 362-379. (Summary in French.)

BARTOL, K.M.
"Male versus female leaders: the effect of leader need for dominance on follower satisfaction." Academy of Management journal, 17, 1974, pp. 225-233.

BASU, Gopa; PESTONJEE, D.M.
"Executives and the satisfaction cycle." Indian journal of industrial relations, Apr. 1974, pp. 507-517.

BEATON, Allan.
"Worker participation: overseas trends and lessons for Australia." Personnel management, 13(2), July 1975, pp. 18-22.
The author presents his account of overseas experiences in worker participation based on a study tour completed in 1974. He comments on developments in South Australia, and in conjunction with his overseas impressions concludes: "There are tremendous dangers inherent in the whole concept. I don't go as far as some of the people in Europe saying that it represents the greatest danger yet to the free enterprise system ... But I do go as far as to say that we are indeed 'dragging our feet' not as to its implementation, but as to our basic understanding of the nature of the threat and issues which confront us as managers."

BERTING, J.; DE SITTER, L.U.
Arbeidssatisfactie; theorie, methodiek, feiten. In samenwerking met de Stichting Interuniversitair Instituut voor Social-Wetenschappelijk Onderzoek. /Work satisfaction; theory, methodology, facts. In cooperation with the SISWO Foundation (Interuniversity Institute for Socio-Scientific Research)./ Assen, van Gorcum and Prakke, 1971. 228 p. (SISWO-reeks, 1.)

BHALLA, M.M.
"Absenteeism: the current causes." Economic times, 15, Feb. 1970, p. 7.

BIDDLE, D.; HUTTON, G.
"Toward a tolerance theory of worker adaptation." Human relations, 29(9), Sept. 1976, pp. 863-872.
This article "examines the ways in which people can achieve toleration of what is to them, and may appear to others, an unsatisfying or impoverished work situation." It is based on empirical study of six workshop in an engineering company in the south of England and make its analysis in terms of 'living space'. "Adaptive actions ... are exemplified ... links are made with ... play and creativity and the social psychology of the neighborhood."

BIDERMAN, A.D.; DRURY, T.F.
"Quality of employment indicators." American behavioral scientist, 18(3), Jan.-Feb. 1975, pp. 299-432.
Compilation of social research articles on the quality of social indicators relating to employment and the work environment which covers the measurement of job satisfaction, non-money equivalents of fringe benefits, concepts of equity in income distribution and the evaluation of the effect of social policy on occupational structure.

BLAI, Boris, Jr.
"A job satisfaction predictor." Personnel journal, October 1963.

BLAU, Paul.
Die zerstoerte Arbeitsfreude: aktuelle Probleme unserer Zeit. /The joy of work destroyed: problems of our era./ Wien, Verlag d. OeGB, /N.d./

BLAUNER, Robert.
Alienation and freedom: the factory worker and his industry. Chicago, University of Chicago Press, 1964. x, 222 p.
This writer spent four years as an employee, first as an electric assembler, and then as a labourer in an automative factory before becoming a sociological research worker. His study was made in four different production units: a printing works; a textile factory; an automobile assembly line; and a chemical process plant. It has remained a standard work for over 12 years. It gives a balanced picture from contrasting types of manufacturing units.

BLAUNER, Robert.
"Work satisfaction and industrial trends in modern society." In: BENDIX, R.; LIPSET, S.M. Class, states and power. London, Routledge and Kegan Paul, 1967.

BLOOD, M.R.; HULIN, C.L.
"Alienation, environmental characteristics and worker responses." Journal of applied psychology, 51, 1967, pp. 284-290.

BOGAERT, Michael V.D.; DASS, N.C.
"Absenteeism in a public sector industry: the case of Rourkela Steel Plant." Social action, 23(2), Apr.-June 1975, pp. 132-144.

BORDEMANN, G.H. "Arbeitszufriedenheit und Arbeitskonflikt." /Job satisfaction and labour disputes./ Dokumentation der CDU Rheinland, (2), 1973.

BOYER, Ronald K.; SHELL, Richard L.
"The end of the line at Lordstown; workers have always groaned over the drudgery of the assembly line. Now they are beginning to say 'no'." Business and society review, Autumn 1972, pp. 31-35.

BRITTO, A.J.
"Job satisfaction and absenteeism in India." Social action, 16(5-6), May-June 1966, pp. 252-258.

BROAD, Bruce M.
"He is well paid that is well satisfied." Canadian personnel and industrial relations journal, Mar. 1976, pp. 31-34.

BRUGGEMANN, Agnes; GROSKURTH, Peter; ULICH, Eberhard.
"Arbeitszufriedenheit." /Job satisfaction./ Schriften zur Arbeitspsychologie, (17), 1975.

BRUGGEMANN, Agnes.
"Zur Unterscheidung verschiedener Formen von 'Arbeitszufriedenheit'." /Distinguishing between different types of job satisfaction./ Arbeit und Leistung, 28(11), 1974, pp. 281-284.

BUNNAGE, David; ROSDAHL, Andus.
Teknikken og arbejderen II. Arbejderens indstilling til Arbejdet, jobskift og uddannetse. /Technology and the worker II. Attitudes of workers to the work situation, job change and training./ Socialforskningsinstituttet Publikation 75. Copenhagen, 1976.
Study on the workers' experience of and reactions to various aspects of their work situation including job satisfaction. A questionnaire survey of 666 workers in 17 firms in the chemical, graphic and printing and engineering industries disclosed that positive attitudes to work and the work situation are especially frequent where the job involves a relatively high degree of complexity and autonomy. The study also covers data on workers' desires for change of job, for more education and training. On the basis of the findings recommendations are made with regard to the questions of work situation, job content and worker influence and on the issues of provision and support for further education and training. The volume contains an English summary.

BURSTEIN, M.; TIENHAARA, N.; HEWSON, P.; WARRANDER, B.
Canadian work values; findings of a work ethic survey and a job satisfaction survey. Ottawa, Information Canada, 1975. 104 p.
Report on research results of two sample surveys relating to the 'work ethic' motivation and attitude and job satisfaction in Canada. It includes statistical information on attitudes in general and on attitudes of young workers and women workers.

BUTANI, D.H.
"Studies in absenteeism." Productivity, 9(1-2), Apr.-Sept. 1970, pp. 168-177.

BUTLER, W.P.
"Job satisfaction among foremen." Personnel practice bulletin, Mar. 1959, pp. 7-15.

BUTLER, W.P.
"Job satisfaction among foremen; case study No.2." Personnel practice bulletin, Mar. 1961, pp. 5-14.

CAMERON, C.G.
"Job satisfaction of employees in a light engineering firm: a case study." Personnel practice bulletin, Mar. 1970, pp. 34-41.

CAMERON, Sheila.
Job satisfaction: the concept and its measurement. London, Department of Employment, 1973.
Directed towards academics, this paper examines the theory of job satisfaction and its relevance to leading theories of job behaviour. It compares alternative measures of job satisfaction and explores its relationship with worker productivity. It also suggests a distinction between satisfaction and motivation and considers reasons for attempting to increase job satisfaction.

"Can job satisfaction be explained by Herzberg's 'dual-factor' theory?" IRC current news, 2 Feb. 1968, p. 20; 9 Feb. 1968, p.24.

CARPENTIER, J.
"Organisational techniques and the humanisation of work." International labour review, 110(2), Aug. 1974, pp. 93-116. (Also publ. in French and Spanish.)
An article examining factory organisation techniques for improving the humanisation of work. It discusses the impact of mass industrial production and assembly-line work on productivity and the work environment, and describes techniques for increasing job satisfaction (including job enrichment, reassignment, etc.), and reducing alienation.

CARROLL, Bonnie.
"Job satisfaction." Key issues, (3), Feb. 1969.

CARROLL, Bonnie.
Job satisfaction; a review of the literature. Revised and updated by Mary W. Blumen. Ithaca, New York State School of Industrial and Labor Relations, Cornell University, 1973. 57 p. (Key issues series, No. 3.)

CERNEA, M.
"Individual motivation and labour turnover under socialism." Studies in comparative international development, 8(3), Fall 1973, pp. 303-323.
On the basis of several surveys of mobile and potentially mobile workers in Rumania, the author considers the motivational factors behind labour turnover and labour mobility among industrial workers. The influence of job satisfaction on workers attitudes towards leaving is examined.

CHAKRAVARTY, T.K.
"Need-orientation as related to extension job satisfaction: a profile analytic exploration." Indian journal of psychology, 49(Part 3), 1974, pp. 201-212.

CROSS, Denys.
"The worker opinion survey: a measure of shop-floor satisfactions." Occupational psychology, 47, 1973, pp. 193-208.

DAS, S.R. Mohan.
"Why more mandays are lost in India." Labour chronicle, 4(4), Sept. 1971, pp. 5-8.

DAVIS, Keith; ALLEN, George, R.
"Length of time that feelings persist for Herzberg's motivational and maintenance factors." Personnel psychology, Spring 1970.

DE, Nitish R.
"Contents and discontents of work commitment." Lok Udyog, 9(1), Apr. 1975, pp. 23-28.

DE, Nitish R.
"Work commitment and work ethics in public enterprises a framework for consideration." National Labour Institute bulletin, 1(4), Apr. 1975, pp. 13-15.

DENT, Frederick B. "The myth of the dissatisfied worker." Public relations journal, Oct. 1973, pp. 10-11.

DESAI, K.C.
"Absenteeism: a problem solving approach." Tamil Nadu labour journal, 16(7), July 1974, pp. 1-10.

DICKENS, Denise.
Colorless, odorless, invisible: boredom on the job." Job safety and health, Feb. 1976, pp. 22-27.

"Does your job bore you, or does Professor Herzberg?" Economist, 6 June 1970, p. 66.

DONOIAN, Harry A.
"Survey shows AIWers have strong opinions on jobs." Allied industrial worker, June 1973, pp. 6-7.

DORÉ, Russel; MEACHAM, Merle.
"Self-concept and interests related to job satisfaction of managers." Personnel psychology, Spring 1973, pp. 49-59.

"Douze jeune travailleurs parlent de leur entreprise." /Twelve young workers talk about their undertaking."/ Fabrimetal, (8), Oct. 1975, pp. 15-26.
Article reporting an interview of 12 young workers in an industrial enterprise in Belgium with regard to their attitudes concerning working conditions, job satisfaction, the work environment, etc.

DROWKERS, P.L.
Labour management co-operation for productivity and job satistion. Paris, Organisation for Economic Co-operation and Development, /n.d./
The author considers three strategies for changing organisational behaviour: (1) the missionary approach through lectures and courses, (2) the formal approach through structural measures such as wage systems and technology, and (3) the cybernetic approach through co-operative and continuous guidance, adjustment, joint problem solving. He argues that the experimentation needs a margin of free movement and that this margin should not be diminished by formalisation at too early a stage, let alone by freezing participation in a legalistic form. Twelve experiments in work structuring in Phillips plants are described, showing that both the economic and the psychological indicators of success are predominantly positive.

DUBIN, Robert; CHAMPOUX, Joseph E.
"Workers' central life interests and job performance." Sociology of work and occupation, 1, Aug. 1974, pp. 313-326.

DUNCAN, Otis Dudley.
"Does money buy satisfaction?" Social indicators research, (2), Dec. 1975, pp. 267-274.

DUNHAM, Randall B.; HERMAN, Jeanne B.
"Development of a female faces scale for measuring job satisfaction." Journal of applied psychology, 60, 1975, pp. 629-631.

DUPRIEZ, F.
"Le travailleur et le travail; recherche opérationnelle menée en juin-juillet 1975 en vue de mesurer la satisfaction ou l'insatisfaction ressentie par les travailleurs dans leur milieu de travail." /The worker and his work; operational research carried out in June-July 1975 to measure the degree of satisfaction or dissatisfaction of workers at the workplace./ Revue du travail, 77(2), Feb. 1976, pp. 155-185.
Article describing an operational research approach to the measurement of job satisfaction in Belgium. It discusses research methods and research results from a survey of employees attitudes toward the work environment.

DYER, Lee; PARKER, Donald F.
"Classifying outcomes in work motivation research: an examination of the intrinsic-extrinsic dichotomy." Journal of applied psychology, 60, Aug. 1975, pp. 455-458.

DYSON, B.
"Leading to satisfaction." Management today, Apr. 1975, pp. 76-78.

"Enrichissement du potential humain." /The enrichment of human potential./ Personnel, (160), May 1973, pp. 9-51.
Compilation of articles expressing management attitudes with respect to working cnditions and job satisfaction in France. In connection with social change and industrial sociology of the future, and referring particularly to the need for job enrichment and workers' participation in production management.

EVANS, M.G.
"Herzberg's two-factor theory of motivation: some problems and a suggested test." Personnel journal, Jan. 1970.

EVANS, G.
"The moderating effects of internal versus external control on the relationship between various aspects of job satisfaction." Studies in personnel psychology, 5, Spring 1973, pp. 37-46.

EVANS, Martin G.
"Relations among weighted and non-weighted measures of job satisfaction." Studies in personnel psychology, 4, Oct. 1972, pp. 45-54.

EWEN, Robert B.
"Some determinants of job satisfaction." Journal of applied psychology, 48(3), 1964, pp. 161-163.

EWEN, Robert B.
"Weighing components of job satisfaction." Journal of applied psychology, 51(1), 1967, pp. 68-73.

"A factor-analytic study of job satisfaction." Indian journal of industrial relations, Apr. 1970, pp. 429-439.

FEIN, M.
Motivation for work. New York, 1971. 81 p. (American Institute of Industrial Engineers. Monograph, No. 4.)
Essay on the motivation of workers in the USA, appraising various schemes for increasing job satisfaction and covering wage incentives, workers participation, job enrichment, and employment security.

FEIN, M.
"Nachbemerkung zur Darstellung der Herzberg'schen Lehre." /Comment on the presentation of Herzberg's theory./ Fortschrittliche Betriebsführung, 23(1), 1974, 17 p.

FINE, S.A.
Guidelines for the design of new careers, Kalamazoo, W.E. UpJohn Institute for Employment Research, 1967. 23 p.
Guide, based on industrial psychology, to the improvement of job satisfaction through employer commitment to the career concept of employment - covers aspects of occupational choice, job description, promotion, recruitment, job evaluation, etc., and refers in particular to the USA.

FISCHER, L.; LÜCK, H.E.
"Entwicklung einer Skala zur Messung von Arbeitszufriedenheit (SAZ)." /Developing of a rating scale to measure job satisfaction./ Psychologie und praxis, 16(2), 1972, pp. 64-76.

FISHER, Vivian Ezra; HANNA, Joseph V.
The dissatisfied worker. New York, Macmillan, 1931. 260 p.

FLOWERS, Vincent S.; HUGHES, Charles L.
"Why employees stay." Lok Udyog, 7(2), Feb. 1974, pp. 21-31.

FOUNDATION FOR RESEARCH ON HUMAN BEHAVIOR.
The worker in the new industrial environment. Ann Arbor, Braun and Brumfield, 1964. ii, 50 p.
Conference report on a seminar to discuss problems of industrial psychology in the USA - covers job satisfaction factors, employees attitude to technological changes and research methods in respect thereof. Bibliography pp. 37 to 40.

FORD, R.N.; BORGATTA, E.F.
"Satisfaction with the work itself." Journal of applied psychology, 54, 1970, pp. 128-130.

FOSSUM, John A.
"Urban-rural differences in job satisfaction." Industrial and labor relations review, 27, 1974, pp. 405-409.

FRIEDLANDER, F.
"Underlying sources of job satisfaction." Journal of applied psychology, 47(4), 1963, pp. 246-250.

FÜRSTENBERG, F.
"Menschliche Selbstverwirklichung in einer technischen Arbeitswelt." /Human self-realisation in a technological work environment./ BKU, 1974, pp. 43-44.

GADEL, Marguerite S.; KRIEDT, Philip H.
"Relationships of aptitude, interest, performance, and job satisfaction of IBM operators." Personnel psychology, Aut. 1952, pp. 207-212.

GANNON, Martin J.; HENDRICKSON, D.H.
"Career orientation and job satisfaction among working wives." Journal of applied psychology, 57, 1973, pp. 339-340.

GARDELL, Bertil.
"Reactions at work and their influence on non-work activities: an analysis of a sociopolitical problem in affluent societies." Human relations, 29(9), 1976, pp. 885-904.
The author contends that the conflict between the organisation of work and basic human needs has important consequences not only for work and for self-esteem and mental health but also for participation in organised cultural, political and educational activities. He suggests that since the advance of the welfare state has increased peoples expectations as regards both their quality of working life and their non-work activities there is a need for a broader approach to social change than the purely socio-technical one. This change would include such issues as shorter working hours, more flexible career patterns and greater flexibility in the relation between work, family and non-work activities. His overall conclusion is, therefore, that "development in the job world must be subordinated to social policy and to human life goals."

GEARE, A.J.
"The use of two dimensions to achieve a practical measure of factors determining job satisfaction." The journal of industrial relations, 16(4), Dec. 1974, pp. 351-362.
Using a research study of three groups of workers in a medium-sized process firm, the paper demonstrates how a combined measure incorporating measures of both the importance attached to various aspects of work and job satisfaction items could provide the information required by a manager interested in raising job satisfaction. The author contends that such a measure is superior to measures of job satisfaction alone and makes a case for the use of both dimensions to examine factors affecting job satisfaction.

GECHMAN, Arthur S.; WIENER, Yoash.
"Job involvement and satisfaction as related to mental health and personal time devoted to work." Journal of applied psychology, Aug. 1975, pp. 521-523.

GELLERMAN, Saul W.
Motivation and productivity. New York, American Management Association, 1968.

GIBSON, R.O.
"Toward a conceptualization of absence behavior of personnel in organizations." Administrative science quarterly, 2(1), June 1966, pp. 107-133.
An industrial psychological survey of employees attitudes towards their work environment which examines the effect of such factors as age, sex, job satisfaction and personnel management on the duration and frequency of absences.

GIROUX, C. Rodrigue.
"Suervisors' incentives and job satisfaction." Relations industrielles-Industrial relations, Dec. 1954, pp. 15-39.

"GM zeroes in an employee discontent." Business week, May 12, 1973, pp. 140-142, 144.

GOLDRING, Patrick.
Multipurpose man: a new work style for the modern age. New York, Taplinger Pub. Co., 1974.
Among the problems facing the advanced industrial nations in the seventies, none is more difficult and dangerous or more widely neglected than boredom. The author presents a broad discussion of the phenomenon and proposes the introduction of widespread multiple job holding (i.e. having two or three substantially different part-time jobs simultaneously) as a way of reducing work-related boredom and therefore, alienation and job dissatisfaction.

GOLDTHORPE, J.H.; LOCKWOOD, David; BECHHOFER, Frank, et al.
The affluent worker, industrial attitudes and behaviour. Cambridge, The University Press, 1968. vii, 206 p.

GOMBERG, William.
"Job satisfaction: sorting out the nonsense." The American federationist, 80(6), June 1973, pp. 14-20.

GORDON, Michael E., et al.
"An examination of scaling bias in Herzberg's theory of job satisfaction." Organizational behavior and human performance, 11, Feb. 1974, pp. 106-121.

GRAEN, George B., et al.
"Need type and job satisfaction among industrial scientists." Journal of applied psychology, Aug. 1968, pp. 286-289.

GRAHAM, Kenneth.
"Union attitudes to job satisfaction." In: WEIR, Mary, ed. Job satisfaction: Challenge and response in modern Britain. London, Fontana, 1976.
The paper reports the fact that the trade union objectives of the past 30 years are strongly reflected in the findings of the Donovan Commission. The author notes that improvements in job satisfaction have been made largely in response to serious personnel problems and points out that the improvement of hygienic factors should be regarded as the removal of causes of dissatisfaction rather than as the positive promotion of satisfaction. He examines the attitudes of those concerned with organisational change (including the unions) and argues that prior consultation of the workers concerned is necessary. He concludes that these schemes will not mean that workers will be less concerned with pay or less interested in the unions.

GREAT BRITAIN. DEPARTMENT OF EMPLOYMENT. WORK RESEARCH UNIT.
The Job Satisfaction Research Programme. London, /n.d./
(Its: WRU information note, No.5.)
Describes the objectives and planning of research co-ordinated by the Work Research Unit. The research is directed towards the content of jobs, their organisation and the effects on individual satisfaction. Details of ten projects are included covering work in manufacturing, process and service industries, offices, hospitals, construction and mining.

GREENE, Charles N.
"The satisfaction-performance controversy." Business horizons, Oct. 1972, pp. 31-41.

GROSKURTH, P.
"Arbeitszufriedenheit als normatives Problem." /Job satisfaction as a normative problem./ Arbeit und Leistung, 28(11), 1974, pp. 285-288.

GUPTA, J.S.
"Importance of front-line supervisors in promoting productivity and human relations." Industrial relations (Calcutta), 18(2), Mar.-Apr. 1966, pp. 65-69.
A conference paper which considers the possibility of industrial development and of increased labour productivity through the promotion of better human relations. It suggests that the role of the front-line supervisor is to improve the work environment of the industrial employees and to increase their job satisfaction.

HAAVIO-MANNILA, Elina.
Sex differences in satisfaction; a study of satisfaction with family, work, leisure, and life among men and women. Helsinki, University of Helsinki, 1970. (Helsingin Yliopisto. Sosiologian laitoksen tutkimuksia, 153.)

HACKSTEIN, R.
"Informationen und Fragen zu Herzbergs Dualitätstheorie." /Information and questions on Herzberg's duality theory./ Fortschrittliche Betriebsführung, 33(2), pp. 67-77.

HALDANE, B.
Career satisfaction and success; a guide to job freedom. New York, Amacom, 1974. 194 p. Monograph intended as a guide for individual employees in the USA in their search for greater job satisfaction - suggests a programme for self-evaluation, reappraisal of one's skills and occupational qualifications, identification of the sources of motivation, etc., it recommends a strategy for promotion of more satisfying work.

HAMERMESH, Daniel S.
"Economic considerations in job satisfaction trends." Industrial relations, 15, 1976, pp. 111-114.

HANDYSIDE, J.D.; SPEAK, N.
"Job satisfaction: myths and realities" British Journal of industrial relations, 2(1), 1964.

HARRIS, T. C.; LOCKE, E. A.
"Replication of white-collar - blue-collar differences in sources of satisfaction and dissatisfaction." Journal of applied psychology, 59, 1974, pp. 369-370.

"Has recession made job satisfaction a dead issue?" Industrial relations news, what's ahead in personnel? (144), Feb. 1975, 4p.

HENLE, Peter.
"Worker dissatisfaction: a look at the economic effects." Monthly labor review, Feb. 1974, pp. 58-59.

HERRICK, Neal Q.
"Who's unhappy at work and why." Manpower, Jan. 1972, 4, pp. 2-7.
"University of Michigan survey which seeks to identify dissatisfied workers and what makes them that way."

HERZBERG, Frederick
"The motivation-hygiene-theory. In: PUGH, D.S., ed. Organization theory: selected readings. Harmondsworth, Penguin, 1971, pp. 324-344.

HERZBERG, Frederick.
Work and the nature of man. 5. Auf. New York, 1971.

HILTON, Bernard. "An empirical investigation of the Herzberg methodology and Two-Factor Theory." Organizational behavior and human performance, Aug. 1968.

HINES, George H.
"Cross-cultural differences in two-factor motivation theory." Journal of applied psychology, Dec. 1973, pp. 375-377.

HINRICHS, John R.; MISCHKIND, Louis A.
"Empirical and theoretical limitations of the Two-Factor Hypothesis of job satisfaction." Journal of applied psychology, Apr. 1967.

HINRICHS, J. R.
Motivation crisis; winding down and turning off. New York, Amacom, 1974. vii, 164 p.
Considers the psychological aspects of alienation, job satisfaction and worker motivation in the United States of America and discusses job enrichment and the humanisation of work as possible solutions to the problems of boredom etc.

HINRICHS, J. R.
"A replicated study of job satisfaction dimensions." Personnel psychology, Winter 1968, pp. 479-503.

HOLLON, Charles J.; GEMMILL, Gary R.
" A comparison of female and male professors on participation in decision making, job related tension, job involvement, and job satisfaction." Educational administration quarterly, Winter 1976, pp. 80-93.

HOWARD, John H.; RECHNITZER, Peter A; CUNNINGHAM, D. A.
"Coping with job tension: effective and ineffective methods." Public personnel management, 4, Sept.-Oct. 1975, pp. 317-326.

HULIN, Charles L.
"Effects of changes in job-satisfaction levels on employee turnover." Journal of applied psychology, Apr. 1968, pp. 122-126.

HULIN, Charles L.; SMITH, Patricia, C.
"An empirical investigation of two implications of the Two-Factor Theory of job satisfaction" Journal of applied psychology, Oct. 1967.

HULIN, Charles L.; SMITH, Patricia C.
" A linear model of job satisfaction." Journal of applied psychology, 49(3), June 1965, pp. 209-246.
Study of job satisfaction by age group, sex, wages, duration of employment, etc. 13 references.

HUTTON, M. A.; O'Brien, G.E.
A regression test of Herzberg's two-factor theory of job satisfaction. Bedford Park, 1974. 14 l. (The Flinders University of South Australia. Institute of Labour Studies. Working paper series, 6.)

INDANA, Alphons; KHISTY, Cyril H.
"Study of absenteeism." Indian labour journal, 15(7), Jul. 1974, pp. 1183-1190.

JENKINS, G. Douglas Jr.; NADLER, David A., et al.
"Standardized observations: an approach to measuring the nature of jobs." Journal of applied psychology, 60(2), 1975, pp. 171-181.

"Job satisfaction: models, methods, and empirical results." Journal of applied psychology, 50(6), 1966; 51(5), 1967; 52(4, 15), 1968.

"Job satisfaction and productivity." Gallup Opinion index, Apr. 1973, pp. 1-40.
While the latest Gallup Poll indicates that 77% of the people were satisfied with their jobs, there was a 10 point drop in job satisfaction between April 1969 and January 1973. The most dissatisfaction was found among blacks and young persons. Testimony by workers, union officials, management representatives and academic researchers is also presented. Of particular interest is the report of a study team, sponsored by the Ford Foundation, which looked at European experiments in increasing job satisfaction.

JOHNSTON, Ruth; BAVIN, Ronald A.
"Herzberg and job satisfaction." Personnel practice bulletin, June 1973, pp. 136-147.

JOHNSTON, Ruth; GHERARDI, J. C.
"Workers' attitudes to their job; a survey of a small soap factory in Western Australia." Economic activity, 13(4), Oct. 1970, pp. 37-47.
Article on a questionnaire survey of employees attitudes and the degree of job satisfaction in a soap factory in Western Australia - analyses the results according to age group, trade union membership and indicates that there is much less satisfaction among immigrants than among Australian employees.

"Joint study to seek ways to improve job satisfaction." Department of employment gazette, June 1973, pp. 551-552.

JOSHI, V. P.
"Some aspects of job satisfaction." Industrial management, 13(9), Sept. 1974, pp. 30-32.

JUNGBLAT, M.
"Gesucht: das Glück am Arbeitsplatz." /Wanted: happiness at the workplace./ Die Zeit (Hamburg), 6 Mar. 1973.

KALLEBERG, Arne L.
"A causal approach to the measurement of job satisfaction." Social science research, Dec. 1974, pp. 299-322.

KANUGO, Radindra N.; MISRA, Sasi B.; DAYAL, Iswar.
"Relationship of job involvement to perceived importance and satisfaction of employee needs." International review of applied psychology, 24, 1975, pp. 49-59.

KARMARKAR, S.B.
"Positive approach to the problem of absenteeism" Labour gazette, 50(9), May 1971, pp. 1055-1061.

KATZELL, Raymond Abrahm; YANKELOVICH, Daniel.
"Improving imperfections in job satisfaction." Organizational dynamics, 4, Summer 1975, pp. 69-80.

KEENE, D. F.
"Man's inherent rebellion against God and satisfaction." Personnel administrator, 18, 1973, pp. 33-36.

KESSELMAN, Gerald A., et al.
"A factor analytic test of the Porter-Lawler expectancy model of work motivation," Personnel psychology, 27, Winter 1974, pp. 569-579.

KHISTY, Cyril H.
"Problem of absenteeism in industry." Labour gazette, 50(6), Feb. 1971, pp. 648-651.

KLEBER, C. F.
"Job satisfaction: who needs it?" Vital speeches of the day, July 1, 1973, pp. 558-562.

KOCH, James L.
"Job and career needs in the contemporary setting." Human resource management, 13, Winter 1974, pp. 14-24.

KOKKILA, L.M., et al.
"Perceptions of job satisfaction in differing occupations." Business perspectives, 9, 1972, pp. 5-9.

KOSHAL, Rajindar K.; KOSHAL, Manjulika.
"Absenteeism in the manufacturing industries: an econometic approach." Indian journal of industrial relations, 8(4), Apr. 1973, pp. 543-548.

KOTLIAR, A.
"Problems of younger workers in the USSR." International labour review, 109(4), Apr. 1974, pp. 359-371. (Also publ. in French and Spanish.).
Article examining the problems of adjustment to work by young workers in the USSR and the need to provide vocational guidance and vocational training that will provide job satisfaction and stability. It also includes the research results of a survey of young workers in respect of part time education, housing problems and labour turnover.

KOWALEWSKA, Salomea
Psychospoleczne warunki pracy w przedsiebiorstwie przemyslowym. /The social and psychological conditions of work in an industrial enterprise./ Wroclaw, Ossolineum, 1962.

KRAMER, C.
"Absentéisme; pourquoi?" /Why absenteeism?/ Journal des associations patronales. 70(6), Feb. 1975, pp. 95-97.
Article analysing the major causes and variables of the absenteeism phenomenon, with particular reference to psychological aspects.

KRAUT, Allen I.
"Predicting turnover of employees from measured job attitudes." Organizational behavior and human performance. 13 Apr. 1975, pp. 233-243.

KRISHNA, Km. Anshula.
"Job satisfaction and general adjustment of Indian white-collar workers." 33(7), July 1973, Labour bulletin, pp. 1-5.

KRISHNAMURTHY, V.A.
"Absenteeism in coal mines." Indian journal of commerce, 98(104), Part. III, Sept. 1975, pp. 65-70.

KUČERA, J.
Pracovitost', pracovní morálka a iniciativa. /Effort, job morale and initiative./ Praha, Práce, 1972. 175 p.

LABERGE, R.
"Canadians and the work ethics." Labour gazette, 75(5), May 1975, pp. 285-288.
Article outlining research results of an interview survey of job satisfaction and employees attitudes to work in Canada.

LANDY, F.J.
"Motivational type and the satisfaction-performance relationship." Journal of applied psychology, 55, 1971, pp. 406-413.

LAROUCHE, Viateur.
"Inventaire de satisfaction au travail: validation." /Testing the validity of the job satisfaction inventory./ Relations industrielles - Industrial relations, 30(3), Aug. 1975, pp. 343-376.
Article on methodology for measurement of job satisfaction. The author tests the validity of the job satisfaction inventory using survey data for two groups of workers in Canada. (English abstract.)

LAROUCHE, Viateur; DELORME, François.
"Satisfaction au travail: reformulation théorique." /Job satisfaction: a theoretical reformulation./ Relations industrielles - Industrial relations. 27(4), 1972, pp. 567-602.
A review of existing definitions of job satisfaction, demonstrating that the lack of a valid analytical framework is the root of the confusion surrounding this concept. The authors propose a definition which takes account of how the worker regards his role in the production process; they conclude that job satisfaction or dissatisfaction depends on the congruence between the worker's view of his own job and the stimulants actually offered by the task to which he is assigned.

LAROUCHE, Viateur; LEVESQUE, André; DELORME, François.
"Satisfaction au travail? Problèmes associés à la mesure." /Job satisfaction: the problems of measurement./ Relations industrielles - Industrial relations, 28(1), 1973, pp. 76-109.
Article on the problems linked to the measurement of job satisfaction, with particular reference to Canada. Outlines guidelines to follow in measuring job satisfaction, and contains a critical analysis of operational measures, a descriptive review of questionnaires currently used, and estimates of their value. (English abstract.)

LEFKOWITZ, J.
"Job attitudes of police; overall description and demographic correlates." Journal of vocational behavior, 5(2), Oct. 1974, pp. 221-230.
Article on employees' attitudes and job satisfaction among policemen in the USA, based on a survey conducted in a midwest urban area. Data show that there is more dissatisfaction in this group than in comparable occupational groups, and that job attitudes are highly correlated with age group, rank and job assignment.

LEVITAN, Sar A., ed.
Blue-collar workers: a symposium on middle America. New York, N.Y., McGraw-Hill, 1971. 393 p.
Nineteen social scientists, including economists, political scientists, sociologists and public officials, discuss the

problems and complaints of blue-collar workers. The articles range from analysis of the changing economic position of the workers to attitudes and aspirations, political behavior and the impact of governmental programs. Despite some contradictory evidence and conclusions, the majority of the contributors discount widespread alienation among industrial workers.

LEVITAN, Sar A.; JOHNSTON, William B.
Work is here to stay, alas. Salt Lake City, Olympus Pub. Co., /1973/. 184 p.

"Life on the assembly line: why auto workers complain." U.S. news and world report, May 1972, pp. 82-84.

LIST, Wilf.
"Labour report; evidence is not conclusive for 'blue collar blues'." Engineering and contract record, Mar. 1973, p.16.

LIU, Michel.
Putting the job satisfaction debate in perspective. Brussels, European Institute for Advanced Studies in Management, 1972. 185 p.

LIU, Michel.
"Putting the job satisfaction debate in perspective." Management international review, 13 (4-5), 1973, pp. 27-36.

LOFQUIST, Lloyd H.; DOWIS, René V.
"Vocational needs, work, reinforcers and job satisfaction." Vocational guidance quarterly, 24, Dec. 1975, pp. 132-139.

MACARTHUR, D.
"One Canadian's search for job satisfaction." The Canadian personnel and industrial relations journal, 22(3), May 1975, pp. 178-196.

MANGIONE, T. W.
The validity of job satisfaction. Ann Arbor, Mich., University Microfilms, 1973. (Doctoral dissertation.)

MANGIONE, T. W.; QUINN, R.
"Job satisfaction, counter-productive behavior, and drug use at work." Journal of applied psychology, 60, 1975, pp. 114-116. (Also presented at the 82nd annual meeting of the American Psychological Association, New Orleans, September, 1974.)

MARCUSE, Herbert.
"Further reflections on work, alienation..." Canadian journal of political science, 6, June 1973, pp. 295-302.

MASLOW, Abraham H.
Motivation and personality. 2nd ed. New York, Harper and Row, 1970.

MEHR, M.R.
Importance of job satisfaction in raising productivity." Capital, 172(4311), May 1974, pp. 608-609.

MEHTA, Pradeep Kumar.
"Labour absenteeism in cotton textile industries." Survey, 14(3-4), July-Dec. 1974, pp. 27-31.

MIKES, P.S.; HULIN, C.L.
"Use of importance as a weighing component of job satisfaction." Journal of applied psychology, 52(5), 1968, pp. 394-398.
Report on a survey of job satisfaction conducted in Montreal to establish employees' attitudes to job importance and the relationship thereof to labour turnover.

MILES, R.E.; ROBERTS, K.H.; WALTER, G.A.
"Factor analytic study of job satisfaction items designed to measure Maslow need categories. Personnel psychology, 24(2), Summer 1971, pp. 205-220.
An article appraising the methodological usefulness of Maslow's theory of hierarchical needs for the measurement of job satisfaction based on an evaluation of the survey responses of 380 managers.

MITCHELL, T. R.
Expectancy models of job satisfaction, occupational preference and effort; a theoretical, methodological and empirical appraisal. Springfield, National Technical Information Service, 1973. iii, 49 p.
Technical report comprising an evaluation of expectancy models of job satisfaction, occupational choice and effort which includes methodological considerations and theory.

MITCHELL, Vance F.; BABA, Vishwanath; EPPS, Timothy.
"On the relationship between job involvement and central life interest." Relations industrielles - Industrial relations, 30(2), Apr. 1975, pp. 166-177. (Summary in French.)

MORSE, Nancy C.
Satisfaction in the white-collar job. Ann Arbor, Mich., Institute for Social Research, 1953. 235 p.

MUKHERJEE, Bishwa Nath.
"Factor-analytic study of job satisfaction." Indian journal of industrial relations. 5(4), Apr. 1970, pp. 429-439.

MUKHERJEE, Bishwa Nath.
"Interrelationships among measures of job satisfaction and job involvement." Indian journal of psychology, 44, Parts 1-4, 1969, pp. 21-32.

MUMFORD, E.
"Job satisfaction; a method of analysis." Personnel review. 1(3), Summer 1972, pp. 48-57.
Article presenting an analytical model of job satisfaction based on a series of interrelationships between employers' and employees' needs, individual expectations, and individual work experience.

MUMFORD, E.
"Job satisfaction: a new approach derived from an old theory." Sociological review, 18, Mar. 1970, pp. 71-101.

MUSTAFA, H.; SYLVIA, R. D.
"Factor-analysis approach to job satisfaction." Public personnel management, 4, 1975, pp. 165-172.

MUTHAYYA, B. C.; GNANAKANNAN, I.
Development personnel; psychosocial study across three states in India. Hyderabad, National Institute of Community Development, 1973. vi, 185 p.
Paper based on a survey of development personnel and community development administrators. The survey which covered such issues as employee attitudes, social status, educational level and leadership qualities aimed at exploring the job satisfaction of the personnel concerned.

MYERS, M. Scott.
"Who are your motivated workers?" Harvard business review, Jan.-Feb. 1964.

NATARAJ, C. L.; HAFEEZ, A.
"A study of job satisfaction among skilled workers." Indian journal of social work, 26(1), 1965, pp. 9-12.

NATHANSON, Constance A.; BECKER, Marshall H.
"Job satisfaction and job performance: an empirical test of some theoretical propositions." Organizational behavior and human performance, 9, Apr. 1973, pp. 267-279.

NAYAR, P. K.
"Motivation and morale in industry." Management in enterprise and management education in universities, (New Delhi), 1(243), Nov. 1971 - Jan. 1972, pp. 10-18.
The paper is concerned with the role of the supervisor in motivation and morale of the workers on the shopfloor. The author concludes that the factors that lead to positive job attitudes do so because they satisfy the individual's need for self-actualisation in his work. A successful supervisor is instrumental in structuring the work in such a way that his subordinates could realize their ability for creative achievement. In this complex world, few people could fulfil their potentialities entirely by their own effort. Hence they go to organisations. This aspect of the worker's motivation has to be properly realised and provided for in any work supervision.

NEELEY, J. D. Jr.
"A test of the need gratification theory of job satisfaction." Journal of applied psychology, 57, 1973, pp. 86-88.

NEUBERGER, O.
Theorien der Arbeitszufriedenheit. [Theories of job satisfaction.] Stuttgart, 1974.

NEWMAN, John E.
"Understanding the organizational structure: job attitude relationship through perceptions of the work environment." Organizational behavior and human performance, 14, Dec. 1975, pp. 371-397.

OREGON, BUREAU OF LABOR.
Life from 8 to 5: Oregonians talk about their jobs; a report on job satisfaction among employed Oregonians. [N.p.], 1975. 91 p.

O'REILLY, Charles A. III; ROBERTS, Karlene H.
"Job satisfaction among whites and non-whites: a cross-cultural approach." Journal of applied psychology, 57, 1973, pp. 295-299.

ORGANISATION FOR ECONOMIC CO-OPERATION AND DEVELOPMENT. MANPOWER AND SOCIAL AFFAIRS DIRECTORATE.
Emerging attitudes and motivations of workers; report of a management experts' meeting, Paris, 24-26 May 1971. Paris, 1972. vi, 38 p. (Also publ. in French.)
Conference report on changing employees' attitudes and motivations in OECD countries, with particular reference to job satisfaction. The report outlines the need for specific action by top management respecting job enlargement.

ORPEN, C.
"Social desirability as a moderator of the relationship between job satisfaction and personal adjustment." Personnel psychology, 27, 1974, pp. 103-108.

ORR, Carole.
"Assembly line blues: the souring of Henry's dream." Last Post, Dec. 1972, pp. 8-9.

OSIPOV, G.W.; SZCZEPANSKI, Jan, eds.
Spoleczne problemy pracy i produkcji. Polsko-radzieckie badania porownawcze. [Social problems of work and production. The Polish-Soviet comparative studies.] Warsaw, Ksiazka i Wiedza, 1970.

ÖSTERMAN, S.
Lön, arbetstillfredsställelse och avgång; en undersökning av en grupp industriarbetare. /Wages, job satisfaction and retirement: a study of a group of industrial workers./ Stockholm, 1971. 180 p. (Personaladministrativa Rådet. Rapport 71, No. 0039.)
A socio-psychological study of motivation and job satisfaction in Sweden which analyses work environment factors and employees attitudes with regard to organisational systems, situational behaviour communications, human relations, financial compensation, retirement, etc.

O'TOOLE, James.
"Work in America and the great job satisfaction controversy." Journal of occupational medicine, 18(11), 1974, pp. 710-715.

PACE, D.E.
"A job satisfaction approach to a management problem." Management services in government, 30, 1975, pp. 209-213.

PALIWAL, M.B.; PALIWAL, K.M.
"Study of need importance in relation to personal characteristics of industrial employees." Psychological studies, 19(2), July 1974, pp. 118-126.

PALLONE, Nathaniel J.; HURLEY, Robert B.; RIKARD, Fred. S.
"Emphases in job satisfaction research: 1968-1969." Journal of vocational behaviour, 1, Jan. 1971, pp. 11-28.

PALLONE, Nathaniel J.; RIKARD, Fred. S.; HURLEY, Robert B.
"Job satisfaction research of 1966-67." Personnel and guidance journal, Fall 1970, pp. 469-478.

PALOLA, Ernest G.; LARSON, William R.
"Some dimensions of job satisfaction among hospital personnel." Sociology and social research. Jan. 1965, pp. 201-213.

PAREEK, U.
"Conceptual model of work motivation." Indian journal of industrial relations, 10(1), Jul. 1974, pp. 15-31.
The paper presents an integrated model of job satisfaction and work motivation. It covers such issues as the psychological aspects of individual needs, altered needs resulting from commitment to work and individual role satisfaction through work.

PESKIN, D.B.
Doomsday job; the behavioral anatomy of turnover. New York, American Management Association, 1973. ix, 162 p.
A management development textbook on ways in which to increase employee motivation and job satisfaction so as to reduce labour turnover. Among the topics covered are such issues as the importance of the work environment centralisation versus decentralisation of management and job specialisation.

PESTONJEE, D.M.; BASU, G.
"Study of job motivations of Indian executives." Indian journal of industrial relations, 8(1), Jul. 1972, pp. 3-16.
An article on a job satisfaction questionnaire survey of middle management motivation in the private sector and public sector manufacturing industries in India which discusses results of social research supporting Herzberg's two-factor theory of content-context variables.

PETERSEN, Eggert.
Trivsel på arbejdspladsen. Bind 1: Trivsel og trivselmåling. Bind 2: Ledelsevaner og trivselfaktorer. /Job satisfaction. Vol. 1: Job satisfaction and its measurement. Vol. 2: Managerial habits and factors of job satisfaction./ Copenhagen, Danish National Institute for Mental Health Research, 1968. 2 v. (With a summary in English, v.2)

PIERCE, Karlton W.
Increasing the job satisfaction of white-collar workers. Part 1: What white-collar workers want. Ann Arbor, Mich., 1958. 13 p. (University of Michigan. Bureau of Industrial Relations. Bulletin No. 26.)

PINTO, Patrick R.; DAVIS, Thomas C.
"The moderating effect of need type on the prediction of overall job satisfaction." Journal of vocational behaviour, 4, 1974, pp. 339-348.

PORTER, Lyman W.; LAWLER, Edward E. III.
"What job attitudes tell about motivation." Harvard business review, Jan.-Feb. 1968.

PORTER, Lyman W., et al.
"Organizational commitment, job satisfaction, and turnover among psychiatric technicians." Journal of applied psychology, 59, 1974, pp. 603-609.

PORTIGAL, Alan A.
"Current research on the quality of working life in industrial relations." Industrial Relations: quarterly review, 28(4), Oct. 1973, pp. 736-767.
Reviews some viewpoints on QWL and comments on some of the studies purporting to document the apparent dissatisfaction of workers with the prevailing working conditions. Contends that QWL must be viewed not only from the perspective of the workers but also those of government and employers if findings are to be comprehensive and relevant.

Discusses job satisfaction, alienation and experiments in work humanisation and looks ahead at future prospects of QWL and their implications for governments and labour.

Notes that experiments which deal simultaneously with the multiple facets of job satisfaction and worker motivation generally live up to management expectations and considers the varied reactions of European and American unions to such experiments. Suggests that QWL should be an objective of legitimate interest and concern to governments.

PORTIGAL, Alan.
Measuring work satisfaction. Paris, 1976. 51 p. (Organisation for Economic Co-operation and Development. Social indicator development programme. Special Studies, No.1.)
The author proposes a method of devising social indicators involving the extensive use of behavioural surveys, with a view to working out a scale based on multiple criteria. This will make it easier to interpret the results of behavioural surveys and make it possible to determine the origin of work satisfaction and its effects on worker behaviour.

PRASAD, K. Nagaraj.
"Problem of labour absenteeism in Indian industries." Southern economist, 10(2), May 1971, pp. 15-16.

PREWITT, Lena B.
"Discontent in the ranks: is the operative worker really trapped?" Personnel journal, Oct. 1973, pp. 879-884.

PRICE, C.R.
New directions in the world of work; a conference report. Kalamazoo, W.E. Upjohn Institute for Employment Research, 1972. vii, 40 p.
A conference report on strategies for promoting job satisfaction and improving the work environment in response to cultural change as reflected in employees attitudes in the USA.

PRINCETON UNIVERSITY. INDUSTRIAL RELATIONS SECTION.
Blue-collar blues: fact or fiction? Princeton, N.J., 1973. 4 p. (Its: Selected references, No. 168.)

QUINN, Robert P.; MANDILOVITCH, Martha; MANGIONE, Thomas W.
"Job satisfaction: a new survey; no more, no less." American federationist, 81(1), 1974, pp. 22-24.

QUINN, Robert P.; MANGIONE, Thomas W.
"Evaluating weighted models of measuring job satisfaction: a Cinderella story." Organisational behavior and human performance, 10(1), Aug. 1973, pp. 1-24.

RAINVILLE, J.M.
"La satisfaction à l'égard de la tâche et la satisfaction à l'égard de la carrière." /Job satisfaction and career satisfaction./ Relations industrielles-Industrial relations, 29, 1974, pp. 83-97.

RAMSER, Charles D.
"Performance, satisfaction, effort." Personnel administration and public personnel review, Jul.-Aug. 1972, pp. 4-8.

RAMSEY, Douglas.
"Banishing the assembly line blues." European Community, Aug.-Sept. 1973, pp. 14-17.

RAO, G.V. Sarveswara.
"Determinants of job satisfaction of Indian engineers: a test of the two-factor theory." Indian journal of industrial relations, 8(4), Apr. 1973, pp. 605-619.
An empirical investigation of 124 engineers which tests the validity and the generality of the two-factor theory of job satisfaction. Data indicated that the two-factor theory could find only partial support and satisfaction and dissatisfaction were found to be independent feelings.

RAO, G.V. Sarveswara.
"Socio-personal correlates of job satisfaction." Indian journal of applied psychology, 7(2), Jul. 1970, pp. 63-70.

RAO, G.V. Sarveswara.
"Study of weighting components of job satisfaction with importance ratings of industrial employees." Indian journal of industrial relations, 9(4), Apr. 1974, pp. 537-546.
Discusses the choice of methodology for the measurement of job satisfaction, based on a survey conducted in an Indian firm.

RAO, G.V. Sarveswara.
"Theoretical and empirical considerations of the two-factor theory of job satisfaction." Indian journal of industrial relations, 7(3), Jan. 1972, pp. 311-330.
A brief survey of the theoretical foundations of the two-factor theory of job satisfaction and its empirical results. The implications of the theory for management is also discussed.

RAO, G.V. Sarveswara.; RAO, V. Ganapathi.
"A study of factors contributing to satisfaction and importance of industrial personnel; a test of the two-factor theory." Indian journal of industrial relations, 9(2), Oct. 1973, pp. 233-262.
The study attempts to verify Herzberg's two-factor theory of motivation based on a sample of 113 supervisors, 137 clerks and 250 skilled workers. Multivariate analysis revealed that motivators and hygiene factors were not mutually exclusive and their effect was not unidirectional. The factor theory did not receive unequivocal support in this study.

RAO, P.D.P. Prasada.
"Workers and the absenteeism." Andhra Pradesh labour bulletin, 2(1), Apr. 1971, pp. 7-11.

REYNOLDS; SHISTER.
Job horizons. A study of job satisfaction and labor mobility. Downsview, Ont., Labor and Management Center, 1949.

RIDGEWAG, C.C.
"Job dissatisfaction and labour turnover." Personnel and training management, Dec. 1968, pp. 18-20.

RIEKER, Heinrich.
"Rebellion against the assembly-line." Scala, (4), 1975, pp. 36-37.

RITTI, R.R.
The engineer in the industrial corporation. New York, Columbia University Press, 1971. xi, 266 p.
A study of the work role behaviour and job satisfaction of engineers in a large, private enterprise in the USA. Covers such issues as management attitudes, workers' participation in decision-making and underutilisation of workers.

ROBERTS, Karlene H.; SAVAGE, Frederick.
"Twenty questions: utilizing job satisfaction measures." California management review, 15(3), Spring 1973, pp. 82-91.

ROBERTS, Karlene H., et al.
"A factor analytic study of job satisfaction items designed to measure Maslow need categories." Personnel psychology, 24, 1971, pp. 205-220.

ROCHE, William J.; MACKINNON, Neil L.
"Motivating people with meaningful work." Harvard business review, May-June 1970.

RONAN, W.W.; MARKS, E.
"The structure and stability of various job satisfaction measures." Studies in personnel psychology, 6(1), 1973, pp. 2-27.

ROSOW, J.M.
Workers and the job; coping with change. Englewood Cliffs, N.J., Prentice-Hall, 1974. x, 208 p.
A compilation of conference papers on job satisfaction covering such topics as alienation, boredom, attitudes towards jobs and job enrichment and considering the usefulness of the revision of employment policies and the humanisation of work.

ROTHSCHILD, Emma.
"Beating boredom on the job." Saturday review of the society, Apr. 1973, pp. 18, 20.

ROUSSELET, J.
Allergie au travail. [Allergy to work.] Paris, Ed. du Seuil, 1974. 282 p.
A study of the causes of the alienation of youth in relation to the work environment. Elements examined include the role of education, parental attitudes to work, the impact of technological change and other ideological and cultural factors. The author suggests that youth should be encouraged to seek personal success in leisure activities.

ROUSTANG, G.
Les enquêtes sur la satisfaction au travail. [Job satisfaction surveys.] Communication au Congrès 'Etude des effets des méthodes de production en groupes sur l'humanisation du travail', Turin, 30 juin - 5 juillet 1975. Turin, Centre International de Perfectionnement Professionnel et Technique, 1975. 18 p. (Roneogr.)
Paper for the Seminar on Effects of Group Production Methods on the Humanisation of Work, Turin, 30 June - 5 July 1975.

RUDRABASAVARAJ, M. N.
"Case of missing mathbal: problems in absenteeism." Integrated management, Feb. 1970, pp. 15-16.

RUSSELL, Kevin J.
"Variations in orientation to work and job satisfaction." Sociology of work and occupations, (2), 1975, pp. 299-322.

SAIYADAIN, Mirza S.
"Group size and satisfaction: a test of undermanned-overmanned hypothesis." Indian journal of industrial relations, Oct. 1973, pp. 227-231.

SAIYADAIN, Mirza S.
"Personality predisposition and satisfaction with supervisory style." Indian journal of industrial relations, 10(2), Oct. 1974, pp. 153-161.

SALEH, Shoukry Dawood.
Development of the job attitude scale (JAS). Waterloo, University of Waterloo, 1971.

SALEH, Shoukry Dawood.
"Job involvement: concepts and measurements." Academy of Management journal, June 1976, pp. 213-224.

SAND, Herman.
"Questions concerning job satisfaction." Management international review, (4-5), 1973, pp. 55-59.

SANDERSON, George.
"Are blue-collar workers really blue?" Labour gazette, 74, 1974, pp. 798-801.

SANDERSON, George.
"Fulfilment on the job: possible goal or impossible dream?" Labour gazette, 73, June 1973, pp. 385-391.

SARAN, D.
"Sick absentee: how American industry handles the problem." Industrial management, 9(8), Aug. 1970, pp. 33-38, 49.

SARAPATA, Adam.
"Motywacje i satysfakcje dyrektorow: studium porownawcze." /Motivation and satisfaction of executives; a comparative study./ Studia socjologiczne, 3, 1970, pp. 61-89.

SARAPATA, Adam, ed.
Problematyka i metody badań nad zadowoleniem z pracy. /The problems and methods of research on job satisfaction./ Wroclaw, 1973.

SCHEER, L.
"Comparison using perceptual indicators: job satisfaction." Social indicators research, 2(1), June 1975, pp. 1-8.

SCHMITZ, H.P.W.; LAENEN, G.; KOEKENBIER, H.A.J.
Onvrede en klachten van werknemers; een studie naar het ontstaan, de opvang en de oplossing van klachten van werknemers ten behoeve van het beleid. /Dissatisfaction and complaints of employees; a study on the cause, the appreciation and the remedy of complaints raised by employees in the interest of policy./ Utrecht, Stichting Wetenschappelijk Onderzoek Vakcentrales/ Instituut voor Aoegepaste Sociologie, 1975. 323 p.

SCHNEIDER, Benjamin; ALDERFER, Clayton p.
"Three studies of measures of need satisfaction in organizations." Administrative science quarterly, Dec. 1973, pp. 489-505.

SCHREINER, John.
" Why are more workers in a 'I hate my job' mood? Experts warn: find solutions, the problem is growing." Financial post, Mar. 31, 1973. p.7.

SCHULER, Randall; HULIN, Charles L.; SHEPARD, Jon M.
"Worker backgound and job satisfaction; comment." Industrial and labor relations review, 26(2), Jan. 1973, pp. 851-859.

SCHULTZ, James R.
"Blueprint for executive job satisfaction." Personnel, Jul.-Aug. 1964, pp. 8-18.

SCHWAB, Donald P.; CUMMINGS, L. L.
"Theories of performance and satisfaction." Personnel administrator. 18(2), 1973, pp. 39-46.

SCHWARTZ, A. P.; RONAN, W. W.; DAY, G. J.
"Individual differences and job satisfaction." Studies in personnel psychology, 6(9), Spring 1975, pp. 35-53.
The article reports on a survey of job satisfaction in the USA and presents results which demonstrate the effect of demographic factors on job satisfaction. (French abstract.)

SCOBEL, Donald N.
"Doing away with the factory blues." Harvard business review, Nov.-Dec. 1975, pp. 132-142.

SEASHORE, Stanley E.
"Job satisfaction: a dynamic predictor of adaptive and defensive behaviour." Studies in personnel psychology, 1973, 5(1), 7-20.

SEASHORE, Stanley E.
"Job satisfaction as an indicator of the quality of employment." Social indicators research, 1(2), Sept. 1974, pp. 135-168.
The author explains the importance attached to the measurement of the quality of employment by drawing attention to the fact that as work is prevalent and occupies a large part of the available time of adults its ramifications affect virtually all other aspects of the quality of life. He attempts to clarify conceptual issues that are basic to its effective assessment, comments

critically on the currently popular conceptions of the nature of job satisfaction and its role as a social indicator, suggests a broader view of the nature of job satisfaction and recommends priorities for research and action.

SEASHORE, Stanley E.
"Job satisfaction as an indicator of the quality of working life." In: PORTIGAL, Alan H., ed. Measuring the quality of working life. Ottawa, Canada Department of Labour, 1974, pp. 8-38.

SEASHORE, Stanley E.; TABER, Thomas D.
"Job satisfaction indicators and their correlates." American behavioral scientist, Jan.-Feb. 1975, pp. 333-368.
Presents an overview of the present position of research into the measurement of job satisfaction, summarizing considerations that bear upon the choice of approaches and operational methods. The known correlates of job satisfaction are reviewed so as to assess the value of its potential role as an indicator of the quality of employment and theoretical development priorities are outlined. The authors suggest that high priority should be given to longitudinal studies, to the accumulation of time series data archives and to the validation of causal propositions by experimentation.

SEEMAN, M.
On the personal consequences of alienation in work. Evian, 1966. 39 l.
Conference paper presented at the 6th world congress of sociology on the psychological aspects and the consequences of lack of job satisfaction - uses an industrial psychology case study of manual workers in Sweden as a basis, and covers motivation, communication, etc. Conf. Evian 1966 Sep. 4 to 11.

SEQUEIRA, C.E.
"Job satisfaction of supervisors in an Indian engineering undertaking." Personnel practice bulletin, June 1963, pp. 25-33.

SERVAN-SCHREIBER, J.L.
L'entreprise à visage humain. /A human face for the undertaking./ Paris, R. Laffont, 1973. 266 p.
The article considers the issues of job satisfaction and the humanisation of work and explores the questions of alienation and boredom among manual and non-manual workers and among the managerial staff, with special reference to France and the United States. Other subjects considered include hours of work, assembly-line work, worker participation and the social role of the enterprise.

SETHI, Narendra K.
"Job satisfaction: a managerial myth revisited." Industrial times, 1 Jan. 1970, pp. 21-22.

SHAPIRO, H. J.; STERN, L.W.
"Job satisfaction: male and female, professional and non-professional workers." Personnel journal, 54, 1975, pp. 388-389.

SHARMA, Baldev R.
"Absenteeism: a search for correlates." Indian journal of industrial relations, 5(3), Jan. 1970, pp. 267-289.

SHEPPARD, Harold Lloyd.
"Asking the right questions about job satisfaction." Monthly labor review, Apr. 1973, pp. 51-52.

SHEPPARD, Harold Lloyd.
"Discontented blue-collar workers: case study." Monthly labor review, 94, Apr. 1971, pp. 25-32.

SIASSI, Iradj; CORCETTI, Guido; SPIRO, Herzl R.
"Loneliness and dissatisfaction in a blue collar population." Archives of general psychiatry, 30, Feb. 1974, pp. 261-265.

SIASSI, I.; CROCETTI, G.; SPIRO, H.R.
"Emotional health, life and job satisfaction in aging workers." Industrial gerontology, 2(4), Fall 1975, pp. 289-296.
Article on the emotional and mental health, life and job satisfaction of older workers in the USA. Includes a comparison of psychological aspects of older and young workers.

SIMONETTI, S.H.; WEITZ, J.
"Job satisfaction: some cross-cultural effects." Personnel psychology, 25, 1972, pp. 107-118.

SINGH, Prabhakar.
"Study of differential job-expectations satisfaction and behaviour of the three-pro-management, pro-union and uncertain loyalty-groups of industrial workers." Indian psychological review, 5(2), Jan. 1969, pp. 210-211.

SINGHAL, Sushila.
"Measurement of job satisfaction on a three-dimensional plane. Indian journal of industrial relations, 9(2), Oct. 1973, pp. 263-279.
The article deals with the combination of personal, organisational and situational factors necessary to obtain job satisfaction. Based on a questionnaire survey of 88 industrial workers adaptation. It also considers employee attitudes and factors in the work environment.

SINGHAL, Sushila.
"Need-gratification, absenteeism and its correlates." Indian journal of industrial relations, 11(3), Jan. 1976, pp. 351-361.

SINGHAL, Sushila.
"Need-gratification and organisational behaviour of industrial employees." Indian journal of industrial relations, 10(4), Apr. 1975, pp. 487-502.

SINGHAL, Sishila; UPADHYAYA, H.S.
"Psychology of men at work: employee perception of job incentives." Indian journal of industrial relations, 8(1), Jul. 1972, pp. 17-30.
Results of a sample survey of the motivational aspects of job satisfaction among industrial workers and supervisors in India.

SINHA, Durganand.
"Job satisfaction and absenteeism." Indian journal of industrial relations, (1), 1965, pp. 189-199.
The author investigates the relationship between satisfaction with work and attendance. The study throws light on the operation of certain personal factors like age, education, ski marital status and size of family.

SINHA, Durganand; SARMA, Keshab C.
"Union attitude and job satisfaction in Indian workers." Journal of applied psychology, Aug. 1962, pp. 247-251.

SINHA, Durganand; SINGH, P.
"Job satisfaction and absenteeism." Indian journal of social work, 21, 1961, pp. 337-343.

SLOCUM, John W. Jr.
"Performance and satisfaction: an analysis." Industrial relations, 9(4), Oct. 1970, pp. 431-436.
Re-examines the Port and Lawler model of performance and job satisfaction in the light of the findings of an empirical study of two hundred middle and lower-level managers employed by a steelmill in Pennsylvania. Although the results tend to support the prediction that performance is related to the satisfaction of needs for autonomy and self-actualization, the author points out that his findings could also be used to support many other theories of the causal relationship between performance and satisfaction and suggests that further research is imperative.

SLOCUM, John W. Jr.; HAND, H.H.
"Prediction of job success and employee satisfaction for executives and foremen." Training and development journal, 25, Oct. 1971, pp. 28-36.

SLOCUM, John W.; TOPICHAK, Paul M.
"Do cultural differences affect job satisfaction?" Journal of applied psychology, Apr. 1972, pp. 177-178.

SLOCUM, John W. Jr.; MILLER, James D.; MISSHAUK, Micheal J.
"Needs, environmental work satisfaction and job performance." Training and development journal, 24, Feb. 1970, pp. 12-15.

SMART, John C.
"Environmental as reinforcer systems in the study of job satisfaction." Journal of vocational behavior, 6, June 1975, pp. 337-347.

SMITH, Patricia C., et al.
"Factor structure for blacks and whites of the job descriptive index and its discrimation of job satisfaction." Journal of applied psychology, 59, 1974, pp. 99-100.

SMITH, Patricia C., et al.
The measurement of satisfaction in work and retirement: a strategy for the study of attitudes. Chicago, Ill., Rand McNally, 1969. 186 p.

SOLEM, Allen R.
"On structure and process in work motivation." Human relations, 27, Oct. 1974, pp. 779-792.

SPILLANE, R.
"Intrinsic and extrinsic job satisfaction and labour turnover." Occupational psychology, 47, 1973, pp. 71-74.

SRIVASTAVA, A.K.; SINHA, M.M.
"Effect of socio-personal variables on the degree of job anxiety of blue-collar personnel." Indian journal of industrial relations, 9(3), Jan. 1974, pp. 397-405.

SRIVASTAVA, A.K.; SINHA, M.M.
"Morale of the blue-collar workers in relation to different degrees of job anxiety." Indian journal of industrial relations, 10(3), Jan. 1975, pp. 371-378.

STAGNER, Ross.
"Boredom on the assembly line; age and personality variables." Industrial gerontology, 2(2)., Winter 1975, pp. 23-44.
An industrial psychological survey of literature on the boredom or satisfaction of older assembly-line workers.

STAGNER, Ross; FLEBBE, D.R.; WOOD, E.V.
"Working on the railroad: a study of job satisfaction." Personnel psychology, Winter 1952, pp. 293-306.

STEERS, Richard M.
"Effects of need for achievement or the job performance: job attitude relationship." Journal of applied psychology, 60, Dec. 1975, pp. 678-682.

STEERS, Richard M.; PORTER, Lyman W., eds.
Motivation and work behavior. New York, McGraw-Hill, 1975, 585 p.

STOLLBERG, Rudhard.
Arbeitszufriedenheit: theoretische und praktische Probleme. /Job satisfaction: theoretical and practical problems./ Dietz, Berlin, DDR, 1968.

STOLLBERG, Rudhard.
Job satisfaction and relationship to work. Paper prepared for the VIII World Congress of Sociology, Toronto, August 1974.

STONE, Eugene F.
"Job scope, job satisfaction, and the protestant ethics: a study of enlisted men in the U.S. Navy." Journal of vocational behavior, 7, Oct. 1975, pp. 215-224.

SUKHAREVA, A.; BORISOVA, E.; SOLDATOVA, L.
"Nuzhen li profotbor dlia massovykh professii?" /Is manpower selection necessary for general occupations?/ Professional'no tekhnicheskoe obrazovanie, (11), Nov. 1972, pp. 59-61.
The article examines psychological and physiological factors (including job satisfaction) which have an impact on workers' adaptation and concludes that there is no need for manpower selection in respect to general occupation.

SWAAN, A. de.
Een boterham met tevredenheid? Gesprekken met arbeiders. /Is a piece of dry bread enough? Discussions with workers./ Amsterdam, van Gennep, 1972. 144 p.

SZURA, John P.; VERMILLION, Mary E.
"Effects of defensiveness and self-actualization on a Herzberg replication." Journal of vocational behavior, 7, Oct. 1975, pp. 181-187.

TANNENBAUM, Arnold.
"Rank, clout and worker satisfaction: Pecking order, capitalist and communist style." Psychology today, Sept. 1975, pp. 40-43.

TATA, Naval H.
"Consequence of absenteeism." Economic times, 12th Aug. 1975, p.5.

TAYLOR, James C.
Job satisfaction and quality of working life: a reassessment. Human Systems Development Study Centre, working paper No.76(4), April 1976.
The document deals with research and measurement of job satisfaction. The author states that there often is a discrepancy between the high levels of reported job satisfaction and actual fact (as is demonstrated by such indicators of decreasing worker commitment as strikes and absenteeism etc.) In order to prevent this he proposes the use of an action research approach comprising a model of measures designed by managers, workers and social scientists in the field of job satisfaction.

THOMPSON, Anthony Peter.
Subjective expectations and reinforcer predictability in job satisfaction; final report for Department of Labour-University Research Committee. London, Ont., 1975, 207 p.

TINGEY, S.; INSKEEP, G.
"Job satisfaction and mobility among scientific and engineering personnel." Journal of College Placement, 34, (2), 1974, pp, 58-64.

TOWERS, J. Maxwell.
"Job satisfaction among workers and supervisors: an American/Yugoslav comparison." Supervisory management, Spring 1976, pp. 24-26.

"Le travail en question." /Work is called into question./ Projet, (95), May 1975, pp. 502-564.
Compilation of articles on employees attitudes towards their jobs, with particular reference to the question of job satisfaction among young workers and industrial workers in France and covering such issues as boredom, working conditions and the humanisation of work.

TRIPARTITE STEERING GROUP ON JOB SATISFACTION, London.
Making work more satisfying. London, H.M.S.O., 1975. 22p.
Pamphlet on job satisfaction and job enrichment in the UK which includes some suggestions for management based on experimental programmes carried out in several enterprises.

UNITED STATES. DEPARTMENT OF NATIONAL AFFAIRS.
Turnover and job satisfaction. Washington, 1970. 26p.

UNITED STATES. DEPARTMENT OF HEALTH, EDUCATION, AND WELFARE.
Work in America; report of a special task force to the Secretary of Health, Education, and Welfare. Cambridge, Mass., MIT Press, 1972. xix, 269p.
Alternately criticised for its research methods and hailed as a breakthrough in the acceptance of public responsibility for the quality of working life, the Report presents an analysis of the problems of working in America and recommends some solutions. It defines work, analyses its functions in American society and indicates that there is a growing sense of alienation among both white and blue collar workers and suggests possible reasons for this. Special attention is paid to the problems of minority workers, young workers and women workers. The relationship berween work and retirement and work and health are explored. Suggested solutions to perceived problems include redesigning jobs, increasing worker participation and opportunities for self-fulfilment, massive worker re-training programmes and seven yearly sabbiticals for all workers. Concludes that the government has an important role to play in planning future strategies for the improvement of the working environment.

UNITED STATES. MANPOWER ADMINISTRATION.
Job satisfaction: is there a trend? Washington, G.P.O., 1974. vi, 52p. (Manpower research monograph, No. 30.)
Report on trends in job satisfaction in the USA including the research results of a 1972 to 1973 survey (which covers information according to occupation, sex, education level, age group, etc.) The article discusses the importance of job satisfaction from both the employee's and the employer's perspective, and considers strategies for increasing satisfaction, such as job enrichment, reassignment, etc.

URIS, A.
"Is your job really satisfying?" International management, 28, Apr. 1973, pp. 51-52.

VAID, K.N.
"On containing absenteeism." Indian journal of industrial relations, 6(1), Jul. 1970, pp. 69-74.

VAMPLEY, Clieve.
"Automated process operators: work attitudes and behavior." British journal of industrial relations, 11, Nov. 1973, pp. 415-430.

VAN CAUWELAEAT, C.; CORNIETTI, B.
"L'absentéisme, nouveau fléau économique." /Absenteeism, a new economic plague./ Personnel, (175), Jan. 1975, pp. 12-93.
An article on the phenomenon of absentees which covers the measures taken by a French enterprise to improve motivation and the work environment.

VAN MAANEN, John.
"Police socialization: a longitudinal examination of job attitudes in an urban police department." Administrative science quarterly, 20, June 1975, pp. 207-228.

VAUGHN, W.; DUNN, J.D.
"The problem of continuously monitoring job satisfactions in formal work organizations." NTSU business studies, 12, 1973, pp. 23-31.

VOLLMER, Howard N.; KINNEY, Jack A.
"Age, education and job satisfaction." Personnel, Jul. 1955, pp. 38-43.

WALKER, Kenneth F.; LUMSDEN, J.
"Employee job satisfaction and attitudes." Business review, Mar. 1963, pp. 3-12.

WALL, Toby D.; STEPHENSON, Geoffrey M.
"Herzberg's two-factor theory of job attitudes: a critical evaluation and some fresh evidence." Industrial relations journal, Dec. 1970, pp. 41-65.
The article reviews research projects based on Herzberg's two-factor theory and finds that they do not confirm Herzberg's contentions regarding "motivators" and "hygiene". They do, however, indicate that the respondants' desire to give the "socially acceptable" answer could falsify the results. The authors feel that while job enrichment can have a positive effect on job satisfaction, it is not identical with the factors of Herzberg's theory.

WALLER, R.J.
"Job satisfaction: the 'throwaway' society." Business horizons, 16, Oct. 1973, pp. 61-62.

WANOUS, John P.; LAWLER, Edward E.
"Measurement and meaning of job satisfaction." Journal of applied psychology, 56, 1972, pp. 95-105.

"Wanted: ways to make the job less dull." Business week, May 12, 1973, pp. 147-148.

WARRIAR, S.K.; PAPPACHAN, C.V.
"Case study on absenteeism." Industrial relations. 22(3), May-June 1970, pp. 156-161.

WEAVER, Charles N.
"Negro-white differences in job satisfaction." Business horizons, 17, 1974, pp. 67-72.

WEAVER, Charles N.
"Sex difference in job satisfaction." Business horizons, June 1974, pp. 43-49.

WEAVER, Charles N.; HOLMES, S.L.
"A comparative study of the work satisfaction of females with full-time employment and full-time housekeeping." Journal of applied psychology, 60, 1975, pp. 117-118.

WIENER, Yoash; HERZBERG, Frederick; KLEIN, Kenneth; VAITENAS, Rimantas.
"A new classification system for critical incidents: implications for the defensiveness hypothesis and white collar-blue collar job feelings." In: Human resources management publication, 1975, pp. 75-101.
The most recent criticism of motivation-hygiene theory is that the Herzberg classification system confuses events and agents and therefore produces artifactual results. A new classification system was developed by Schneider and Locke which classified separately by event and agent. Their event classification results did not support motivation-hygiene predictions, and the agent classification results indicated subject defensiveness. The present investigation showed that the Schneider and Locke criticism has not been substantiated theoretically or empirically. Their event classification system was not inclusive. Slightly modifying this system to include one missing event category, produced results supportive of motivation-hygiene theory. This modified system also showed that sources of good and bad job feelings were similar for white and blue collar workers. The agent results showed the same pattern of attribution of good and bad events to self and others by high and low defensiveness groups, refuting the defensiveness hypothesis.

WIENER, Yoash; HERZBERG, Frederick; VAITENAS, Rimantas.
"Social desirability, repression and sensitization as factors in the critical incidents method of motivation-hygiene theory." In: Human resources management publication, 1975, pp. 75-101.
A major criticism of motivation-hygiene (M-H) theory suggests that confirming results, obtained by the critical incidents method, are an artifact of defensive processes within individuals. The present study tested the defensiveness hypothesis by assessing the effects of both social desirability and repressive processes on critical incidents responses. Also, the effect of sensitization defensive processes was studied. Subjects produced critical incidents anonymously, in a written format, and completed the Marlowe-Crowne Social-Desirability Scale and the Byrne Repression-Sensitization Scale. Results did not support the defensiveness hypothesis. High social-desirability individuals conformed slightly less than low ones with M-H theory predictions in good events. Sensitizers confirmed more with these predictions than normals in good events. No other significant relationships were found.

WEIR, Mary, ed.
Job satisfaction: challenge and response in modern Britain. London, Fontana, 1976. 288p.
A comprehensive book of readings on various aspects of job satisfaction and other related issues. The book includes papers on topics such as the quality of working life, the history and theory of job satisfaction, the experience of work, current thought on job satisfaction, and case studies on job improvement. Also included are 15 case studies from Europe and America and 13 shorter summaries of each study reports. Among the most distinctive articles are those by British writers containing explicit or implicit criticism of much Q.W.L. work from the trade unions and other points of view.

WEITZ, Joseph; NUCKOLS, Robert C.
"Job satisfaction and job survival." The journal of applied psychology, Aug. 1955, pp. 294-300.

WERNIMONT, Paul F.
"A system view of job satisfaction." Journal of applied psychology, Apr. 1972, pp. 173-176.

WHISENAND, P.M.
"Work values and job satisfaction: anyone interested?" Public personnel review, 32, 1971, pp. 228-234.

WIDICK, B.J., ed.
Auto work and its discontents. Baltimore, Md., Johns Hopkins University Press, /n.d./
Five academics who have worked in the auto industry examine the dissatisfactions of the modern auto worker. They consider such problems as boredom on the assembly line, injustices within the system, lack of opportunity, inequalities in hiring and firing and the general feeling of dehumanisation.

WILD, Ray, et al.
"Job satisfaction and labour turnover amongst women workers." Journal of management studies, 7, 1970, pp. 78-86.

WILLIAMSON, J. R.; KARRAS, E. J.
"Job satisfaction variables and female clerical workers." Journal of applied psychology, 54, 1970, pp. 343-346.

WINPISINGER, William W.
"Blue collar blues of young workers overrated." AFL-CIO Free Trade Union news, Feb. 1973, p.8.

WINPISINGER, William W.
"Happiness on the job: is it possible?" RWDSU record, Mar. 1973, p.11.

WINPISINGER, William W.
"Job satisfaction: a union response." The American federationist, 80(2), Feb. 1973, pp. 8-11.

WOFFORD, J. C.
"The motivational bases of job satisfaction and job performance." Personnel psychology, 24, 1971, pp. 501-518.

WOLF, M.G.
"Need gratification theory: a theoretical reformulation of job satisfaction/dissatisfaction and job motivation." Journal of applied psychology, 54, 1970, pp. 87-94.

WOOL, Harold.
"What's wrong with work in America? A review essay." Monthly labor review, Mar. 1973, pp. 38-44.

"Workers are still satisfied, but...." Personnel, 52, 1975, pp. 6-7.

"World of work." Dialogue, 7(4), 1974, pp. 3-52.
Compilation of articles on employees' attitudes and society's expectations in respect of job satisfaction, humanisation of work, and other aspects of the work environment in the USA.

YOUNGBERG, Charles F.X.; HEDBERG, Raymond; BAXTER, Brent.
"Management action recommendations based on one versus two dimensions of a job satisfaction questionnaire." Personnel psychology, Summer 1962, pp. 145-150.

III. NEW FORMS OF WORK ORGANISATION

"Adapting jobs to human needs."
In: INDUSTRIAL RELATIONS RESEARCH ASSOCIATION. Proceedings, Dec. 1972. Nadison, Wis., 1973, pp. 121-165.
Includes papers on: national and international developments in the field of the quality of working life; selected issues relevant to the quality of working life and government approaches to the humanisation of work.

AGER, B.
"Work organization in sawmills: for the individual."
In: Proceedings of IUFRO Joint Meeting, Div 3 and 5, Ergonomics in Sawmills and Woodworking Industries, Symposium in Sweden, Aug, 26-30, 1974. Stockholm, Arbetarskyddsstyrelsen, 1975, pp. 295-300.

AGERSNAP, Flemming, et al.
"Danish experiments with new forms of cooperation on the shop-floor." Personnel review, 3, 1974, pp. 34-50.

AGERVOLD, MOGENS.
"Sweden experiments in industrial democracy." In: DAVIS, Louis E., CHERNS, Albert B. The quality of working life. New York, Free Press, 1975.

AGURÉN, Stefan; HANSSON, Reine; KARLSSON, K.G.
Volvo Kalmarverken. Erfarenheter av nya arbetsformer. /Volvo Kalmar Plant. Experiences with new forms of work organisation./ Stockholm, Kugel Tryckeri AB, 1976. 56 p.
Study of Volvo's experience with group production methods in the newly designed Kalmar plant. Concludes that workers can influence their work to a greater extent than in conventional assembly-line car production; quality of production is as good as that of other Volvo plants but more adjustment work was needed than was expected. The physical work environment of the Kalmar plant is experienced as favourable but dissatisfaction is expressed with some work positions and with ventilation. Production efficiency appears to be as high as that of the conventional Swedish Volvo plants. Instalment cost of the Kalmar plant is 10% higher than the others. However at full capacity production, it is believed that the entire extra investment cost would be offset. Production advantages, such as a smaller number of supervisors, ease of altering production and lower absenteeism and turnover are also experienced.

ALDERFER, Clayton P.
"Job enlargement and the organizational context." Personnel psychology, Winter 1969, pp. 418-426.

ALEXANDRE, Roger.
"Trois expériences de démocratie dans l'atelier." /Three experiments with shopfloor democracy./ L'expansion, (85), May 1975, pp. 100-105.

ALGERA, S.B.
"Ervaringen en inzichten met betrekking tot werkoverleg." /Experience with and insight into work consultation./ Management facetten, 25 (6), June 1975, pp. 130-136.

ALLEGRO, J.T.
"Experience of advances in work organisation: Bamshoere." In: ORGANISATION FOR ECONOMIC CO-OPERATION AND DEVELOPMENT. Advances in work organisation; proceedings of an International Management Seminar, Paris, Apr. 1973. Paris, 1974.

ALLEGRO, J.T.
Organisatie-ontwikkeling van onder af; naar een grotere betrokkenheid in de werksituatie. /Organization development starting at the bottom; to a greater involvement in the work situation./

ALTENHENNE, Harald; VÖLKEL, Brigitte.
"Zur Planung der Arbeits-und Lebensbedingungen." /On the planning of conditions of work and life./ Sozialistische Arbeitswissenschaft, 7, 1976, pp. 499-508.
Analyses new scientific forms of work organisation and their importance for improving the conditions of life in the context of rational five year plans. Includes indicators for planned improvements at both enterprise and national level.

"L'amélioration des conditions de travail: résultats de l'enquête." /The improvement of working conditions: results of an inquiry./ Entreprise et progrès, June 1973, 33 p.
A survey of a sample of 1,254,250 wage earners in which workers listed the improvements in working conditions they felt were most necessary in order of importance. Overall, the restructuration of tasks was placed third, after hygiene and security and the physical environment.

ANDERSON, G.
"The quality of work life: South Australian development." In: Seminar on Worker Participation in Australia, University of Melbourne, 1975: proceedings. Parkville, Vic., Department of Legal Studies and Industrial Relations Programme, University of Melbourne and Melbourne Chamber of Commerce, 1975, pp. 16-24.
The author states that a great deal is happening in South Australia in the field of improving the quality of work life, especially in the policy area. To explain this he outlines the background and work of the "Unit for the Quality of Work Life" (later Unit for Industrial Democracy) which is now part of the Premier's Department in South Australia. He says that methods such as job enrichment and joint consultative councils are not totally effective because they rest on assumptions about industry which he feels are not totally correct. Trade

union reactions to schemes of worker participation are discussed.

ANDERSON, John W.
"The impact of technology on job enrichment." Personnel, Sept.-Oct. 1970, pp. 29-37.

ANDERSON, John W.
"Limites technologiques de l'enrichissement des tâches. /Technological limits to job enrichment./ Synopsis (Bruxelles), July.-Aug. 1971, p. 9.

ANDLAVER, P.; FOURRE, L.
"Aspects ergonomiques du travail en équipes alternantes." /Ergonomic aspects of work on alternate shifts./ Revue médicale de l'assurance maladie, (1), 1974, pp.5-12.

ANDREATTA, A.J.
"Job enrichment through autonomous groups." Personnel practice bulletin, 30(1), Mar. 1974, pp. 9-13.
An Australian case study is used to demonstrate that autonomous work groups provide employees with the opportunity to participate and to develop responsibility in relation to their work, thereby acquiring a sense of achievement, of interest and of job satisfaction. The author notes that under such circumstances involvement and productivity generally increase while absenteeism declines.

ANDREATTA, Helen; RUMBOLD, Bronwen.
"Building effective work teams." Work and people, 1(3), Spring 1975, pp. 3-9.
Article on current trends in Australia with respect to the introduction of team work in job enrichment schemes.

ANDREATTA, Helen; RUMBOLD, Bronwen.
Organisation development in action. Melbourne, Productivity Promotion Council of Australia, 1974. 64 p.
Reports the findings of research undertaken by the Human Relations Branch of the Department of Labour and Immigration on advanced organisational practices being used in Australian industry in 1973-74. The booklet looks at the way firms have used a variety of techniques and strategies based on behavioural science theories but tailored to the needs of their own particular organisations. It aims to demonstrate and give guidance on the implementation of such programmes as team building, job redesign, and communication exercises, goal setting and planning for change and strategies for diagnosing organisational problems.

ANOIULH, Gilles.
"Weg vom Fliessband zurück zum Menschen." /Away from the assembly-line back to man/. Europäische Gemeinschaft, 4, 1973.

"Après l'accord conclu avec Ford, l'industrie automobile aux Etats-Unis s'oriente vers la semaine de travail de quatre jours." /After the agreement reached with Ford, the US automobile industry orients itself towards a four-day week."/ Le Monde, 16 Oct. 1976, p. 40.

ARBEITGEBERVERBAND SCHWEIZERISCHER MASCHINEN- UND INDUSTRIELLER.
INDUSTRIELLER.
Neue Arbeitsformen. /New forms of work organisation./ /N.p./, 1975.
The paper contains an analysis of employers' view of and experiences with new production methods and presents some case studies on various types of production. The author contends that new forms of work organisation make production and work itself more flexible and cites studies in Switzerland and elsewhere in support of the argument that they also improve both productivity and job satisfaction. He feels that the most important phases of work reorganisation are the introduction of the new work form and the education of the workers concerned. He concludes that to be effective the new forms of work organisation have to be adapted to meet different organisational needs.

Arbeidets tilpassing til mennesket. Rapport fra seminar for arbeidsformidlingens tjensestemenn i de nordiske land. /Adjustment of work to men./ Stockholm, Nordiska Rådet, 1975.

Arbeitshygiene. /Work hygiene/ Berlin, Verl. Volk und Gesundheit, 1973. 508 p.
The article looks at job design and work organisation from the point of view of industrial medecine. It deals with the working conditions which endanger and with the toxicity of many industrial tools and suggests preventative measures.

ARCHER, J.
Towards a more satisfactory work group: a case study of a sheltered experiment at the Aluminum Company of Canada. Waterloo, University of Waterloo, 1972.

ARENDT, Walter, et al
Humanisierung des Arbeitslebens. /Humanisation of work./ Frankfurt, Rationalisierungs. Kuratorium der Deutschen Wirtschaft 1974.
The authors deal with reorganisation of work. They argue that the extreme division of work causes physical and mental stress and limits the worker's autonomy and that it should therefore be replaced with new forms of cooperation (such as small groups) in order to improve job satisfaction and thereby productivity.

ARQUIE, D.; NEBENHAUS, D.; NORECK, J. P.
"Expériences étrangères: pour une nouvelle organisation des tâches." /Experiences in foreign countries: towards a new organisation of tasks./ Enseignement et gestion, (6), Nov. 1973, pp. 12-13. (Expèriences NOBO et PHILIPS.)

ARQUIE, D.; NEBENHAUS, D.; NORECK, J. P.
Quelques expériences de nouvelle organisation des tâches en milieu industriel." /Some experiments in new forms of work organisation in an industrial setting./ Jouy-en Josas, CESA-HEC, /n.d./ (Mimeo.)

"Aspects concrets de la participation dans l'entreprise." /Concrete aspects of participation in the undertaking./ Bulletin Acadi, (Paris), June 1975.

"Assuring a successful job enrichment project." Industrial and commercial training, June 1975, pp. 240-245.

ASTROP, A. W.
"Group technology as a way of life." Machinery, 126(3241), 1975.

ASZÓDI, J.; SZAKÁTS, I.
A tudományos szervezés lényege, tartalma, a szervezési egységek tevékenysége, helye, kapcsolatai a vállalati szervezetben. /Essence, contents of scientific organisation; activity, place and relations of organisational units in the organisation of an enterprise./ Budapest, Ministry of Labour, Research Institute for Labour, 1976. (Target study.)
Discusses the essence of scientific organisation, the general and special basic principles of its contents and provides a practical justification for it. Emphasises the importance of the planning of the regular organisational work and takes a stand on the types, classification and tasks of organisational activity. Defines, within the hierarchy of the enterprise the "directing" level where the establishment of an organisational apparatus is required with a view to the efficient performance of tasks. By discussing the above questions the study performs a timely task because of the variations and dispersions which manifest themselves currently on determining the place of organisation and its tasks.

ASZTALOS, T.; ASZÓDI, J.; SZAKÁTS. I.
A tudományos munkaszervezés tervezésének módszerei. /Methods for planning scientific work organisation./ Budapest, Ministry of Labour, Research Institute for Labour, 1976. (Target study. Manuscript.)
Covers the forms and methods of the planning activity of organisational work. In Hungary, the planning of organisational activity as an industrial enterprise obligation is presently in the making. It is therefore necessary to determine methods of developing organisations and forming a uniform planning attitude with wide acceptability. Considers also basic principles involved in elaborating plans for organisational development and defines the content and order of tasks to be performed in this connection.

Gives a practical example with detailed explanations on activities concerned, covering the steps of organisational planning and the fulfilment of measures.

AUDIBERT, Dominique.
"Peugeot: L'enrichissement des tâches au banc d'essai." /Peugeot: job enrichment on trial./ Les informations, (1521), Jul. 1974, pp. 47-48.
The reduction of absenteeism and the improvement of the quality of production are positive results of the Peugeot automobile company's programme for the improvement of working conditions which has been under way since 1972. However, two important problems have emerged, namely: the higher cost and the larger space requirements implied by enriched work and the creation of autonomous work groups.

BAGLIONI, M.
"Sindacati e nuova organizzazione del lavoro." /Trade unions and new forms of work organisation./ Prospettiva sindicale, 5(1), Apr. 1974, pp. 79-95.
An analysis of some experiments in new forms of work organisation in Holland, Sweden and Great Britain. The author considers mainly the role played by trade unions in the introduction of changes in the organisation of work.

BALDRIDGE, J. Victor; BURNHAM, A.
"Organizational innovation: individual, organizational, and environmental impacts." Administrative science quarterly, 20, June 1975, pp. 165-176.

BANKS, Tony.
"Autonomous work groups." Industrial society, Jul.-Aug. 1974, pp. 10-12.

BARKING, Solomon.
"Retraining and job redesign: positive approaches to the continued employment of older persons." In: SHEPPARD, Harold L., ed. Toward an industrial gerontology. London, Schenkman Publishing Co., 1970, pp. 17-30.

BARRADOS, Maria.
Autonomy in work. 2d ed. Ottawa, Queen's Printer, 1970. 38 p.

BARRITT, R. O.
New forms of work organisation. London, Department of Employment, 1975. (Work Research Unit Paper, No. 3.)
This is a short English summary of a longer report (in Swedish) by the Swedish Employers Federation which discusses that country's experience with new forms of work organisation. The report discusses shop-floor cooperation, new leadership roles, continuity and changes in piecework incentive schemes, effects of group work organisation on management and the characteristics of new types of factories. It distinguishes the factors which were described as being of importance to either the success or the failure of various experiments.

BARTÖLKE, L.; GOHL, J.
A critical perspective on humanization activities and ongoing experiments in Germany. Wuppertal, 1976. (Gesamthochschule Wuppertal. Fachbereich Wirtschaftswissenschaft, Arbeitspapiere, No. 16.)

BELL, D. Wallace.
"The participation debate: a new dimension." Industrial participation, (555), Summer 1974, pp. 9-13.
The analysis of employee attitudes towards participation shows that most employees include this area in job enrichment and work restructuring schemes. For many trade unionists too, changing the pattern of control of industry has become more important than the extension of public ownership. The author examines the different reasons for this change in union attitude and states that the present trade union policy calls for some form of supervisory board structure with 50% employee representation elected through trade union channels.

BERG, C.; MUZUCZAK, B.
"Autonome Arbeitsgruppen als neue Form der Arbeitsorganisation - ein Bericht über die Erfahrungen eines schwedischen Unternehmens." /Autonomous work groups as a new form of work organisation: a report on the experiences of a Swedish enterprise./ Wirtschaftswissenschaftliches Studium, 1975/4 (4), 1975, pp. 190-194.

BERG, Harald.
Organisationsutveckling för ökat medinflytande i tjänstemannaföretag. Delrapport 1: Försök med chefslösa grupper inom Skandia. /Organisational development for increased workers influence - industrial democracy in a white collar enterprise. Report 1: experiments with autonomous groups at Skandia (insurance)/. Stockholm 1975. 85 p. (Nya former för de anställdas inflytande i företagen. 6.) (PA -rådets rapport nr 0068 75.)

BERG, N. von.
"Selbstbestimmung am Arbeitsplatz." /Autonomy in the work place./ Liberal, 17(2), Feb. 1975, pp. 122-130.
Humanisation of work and self-determination at the workplace as topics for reflexion towards a policy of the German liberal party.

BERNASSE, J.
"Conditions de vie au travail et nouvelles méthodes d'organisation." /Conditions of working life and new forms of work organisation/ Personnel A.N.D.C.P., (189), Jul.-Aug. 1976, pp. 24-29.

BERNOUX, Philippe; RUFFIER, J.
Les groupes semi-autonomes de production: étude monographique sur la mise en place d'une nouvelle forme d'organisation du travail. /Semi-autonomous work groups: a monograph on the establishment of a new form of work organisation./ Caluire, Economie et Humanisme, 1974. 267 p.

BERNOUX, Philippe; MOTTE, Dominique; SAGLIO, Jean.
Trois ateliers d'O.S. /Three plants of semi-skilled workers./ Paris, Ed. Ouvrières, 1973. 215 p.

BERTAUX, M.
"Evolution ou révolution des structures? Les tendances nouvelles de l'organisation des entreprises sur le plan social." /Evolution or change in structures? New tendances in the organisation of enterprises on the social level./ Travail et méthodes, (286), Feb. 1973, pp. 6-9.

BHATTACHARYA, K.P.
"A motion and time study experiment: usefulness for redesigning work place layouts and observer reliability." Journal of psychological researches, 5, 1961, pp. 63-69.

"Big firms start to talk job enrichment." Industry week, Jul. 9, 1973, pp. 42-46.

BIGGANE, James F; STEWART, Paul A.
"Job enlargement: a case study." In: DAVIS, Louis E.; TAYLOR, James C. Design of jobs. Harmondsworth, Penguin, 1972, pp. 264-276.

BIHL, G.
Von der Mitbestimmung zur Selbstbestimmung; das skandinavische Modell der selbststeuernden Gruppen. /From participation to auto-determination: the Scandinavian model of autonomous work groups./ München, 1963.

BINEAU, R.
Pratique de l'enrichissement des tâches à l'atelier. /Methods of job enrichment at the plant level./ Paris, Entreprise Moderne d'Edition, 1974. 106 p.
Monograph on job enrichment concepts and methodology which covers industrial psychological considerations and the use of preliminary work studies, with particular reference to the situation in factories in France.

BINOIS, R.
Conséquences structurelles et sociales des nouvelles organisations du travail dans les ateliers." /Structural and social consequences of new forms of work organisation at the enterprise level./ Hommes et techniques, 31(372), Oct. 1975, pp. 576-582.
Article on the consequences of job enrichment and the humanisation of work for the enterprise and the industrial structure in France.

BINOIS, R.; CAIRE, G.; CARRAUD, M.
"Nouvelles formes d'organisation du travail." /New forms of work organisation./ Sociologie du travail, 18(1), Jan.-Mar. 1976, pp. 1-109.
Compilation of articles on concepts and experiences in job enrichment and the restructuration of assembly-line work in western Europe. The authors discuss group work, polyvalence, and the effects of new forms of work organisation on motivation and labour relations.

BINOIS, R.; LANSELLE, B.; PRESTAT, C.
"La place des réunions dans le fonctionnement des groupes de travail semi-autonomes." /The place of group discussion in the functioning of semi-autonomous work groups./ Sociologie du travail, 18(1), Jan.-Mar. 1976, pp. 51-82.
An article analysing the impact of group discussion on the evolution of employees' attitudes and behaviour in job enrichment and other innovational experiments in the context of group work.

BIRCHALL, D.W.
"Job design." In: BOWEY, A.; LUPTON, T., eds. Handbook of salary and wage administration. London, Gower Press, 1975.

BIRCHALL, D.W.
Job design; a planning and implementation guide for managers. London, Gower Press, 1975. 141 p.
Manual on job enrichment processes and their effects on employees attitudes, behaviour and job satisfaction containing some case studies of experiments concerning industrial and office workers in developed countries.

BIRCHALL, D.W.
New Criteria for job design. Document prepared for the 21st Annual Conference of the West of England Employers' Federation, 4-5 October 1974.

BIRCHALL, D.W.; WILD, R.
"Autonomous work groups." Journal of general management, 2(1), 1974.

BIRCHALL, D.W.; WILD, R.
"Work groups." In: WEIR, M., ed. Job satisfaction in UK. /London/ Fontana, 1975.

BISHOP, Ronald C.; HILL, James W.
"Effects of job enlargement and job change on contiguous but non-manipulated jobs as a function of worker status." Journal of applied psychology, 55, 1971, pp. 175-181.
Studies the effects of job change and job enlargement using data from 48 persons in a workshop for the rehabilitation of the mentally and physically handicapped. The effects of job enlargement were not differentiated from those of job change and both resulted in reduced worker tension and an increase in perceived status.

BJÖRK, Lars.
"An experiment in work satisfaction." Scientific American, Mar. 1975, pp. 17-23.

BJÖRK, L., HANSSON, R.; HELLBERG, P.
Försök med ändrad arbetsutformning och arbetsorganisation på en avdelning vid Atlas Copco MCT AB. /Experiments with different forms of work organisation at Atlas Copco./ Stockholm, 1975. 47 p. (Nya former för de anställdas inflytande i företagen. 5. PA-rådets rapport nr 0067 75.)

BLACKER, F.H.M.; BROWN, C.A.
"The impending crisis in job redesign." Journal of occupational psychology, 48(3), 1975, pp. 185-193.

BLASSEL, H.; LETRON, M.
"Les groupes autonomes de production." /Autonomous production groups./ CFDT aujord'hui, (16), Nov.-Dec. 1975, pp. 59-72.
The authors outline the psychosociological theories of group production and consider management strategies and some problems arising from the introduction of new forms of work organisation.

BLUESTONE, Irving.
Democratizing the work place. /N.p./, International Union, United Automobile, Aerospace & Agricultural Implement Workers of America, 1972.

BLUM, A.A.; MOORE, M.L.; FAIRY, B.P.
"Effect of motivational programs on collective bargaining." Personnel journal, 52(7), Jul. 1973, pp. 633-641.
An article which considers the effect of the lack of contractual clauses concerning "job enrichment" in collective agreements. Originating from a rare union interest in this field the paper is based on the results of the analysis of various agreements.

BLUM, Fred H.
Toward a democratic work process: the Hormel-Packinghouse workers' experiment. New York, Harper, 1953. 229 p.

BOLWEG, J.
Job design and industrial democracy: the case of Norway. Leiden, Martinus Nijhoff, 1976.

BONAZZI, G.
In una fabbrica di motori. /In an automobile factory./ Milano, Feltrinelli, 1975.
A sociological analysis of an unsuccessful experiment of introduction of autonomous work groups.

BOMBAY LABOUR INSTITUTE.
Report of the Seminar on floor level leadership: a survey of proceedings of the two day seminar held by the Institute on Aug. 1965. Ed. by R.D. Joshi, Bombay, 1967.

BORZAIX, A.; CHAVE, D.
Réorganisation du travail et dynamique des conflits. /The re-organisation of work and the dynamics of conflict./ Paris, Conservatoire National des Arts et Métiers, 1975.

BOWERS; HAUSSER; SPENCER.
District office organizational development experiment. East Lansing, University of Michigan, 1976. (Organizational Development Research Program.)

BRITISH STEEL CORPORATION.
Work restructuring exercise: Bilston Finishing and Dispatch Department; report of development group. London, 1975.

BROKMANN, W.
"Arbeitsneustrukturierung bei Ford." /Work restructuring at Ford./ Mitteilungen. Institut für Angewandte Arbeitswissenschaft (Köln), (54), Sept. 1974, pp. 3-26.

BRYAN, E.J.
"Work improvement and job enrichment: the case of Cummings Engine Co." In: DAVIS, L.E.; CHERNS, A.B. The quality of working life. New York, The Free Press, 1975, T.2, pp. 315-329.

BUCKINGHAM, G.L.; JEFFREY, R.G.; THORNE, B.A.
Job enrichment and organizational change; a study in participation at Gallaher Ltd. Epping, Gower Press, 1975. x, 161 p.
Monograph on a job enrichment programme undertaken at Gallaher Ltd. in the UK. The study covers the theory and implications of organisational development and job design. It also describes the implementation of job restructuring at various management levels.

BUCKLOW, M.
"A new role for the work group." In: DAVIS, L.E.; TAYLOR, James C. Job design. Harmondsworth, Penguin Books, 1972, pp. 199-212.

BUDD, M.
"Employee motivation through job enrichment." Journal of systems management, 25(8), 1974, pp. 34-38.

BUITENDAM, A.
Deverticalisation in production organizations. Eindhoven, 1968.

*BURBIDGE, John L.
Group production methods and humanisation of work: the evidence in industrialised countries. Geneva, 1976. 18 p. (International Institute for Labour Studies. Research series, No. 10.)
Based on a study of the effects of group production methods on the humanisation of work undertaken by the Turin International Centre for the International Labour Organisation, this paper considers the relationship between the new methods of group production now being undertaken and the humanisation of work. A survey of 477 enterprises and a detailed study of 54 selected enterprises provided evidence that group production methods not only make a major contribution to the humanisation of work but also have important economic advantages.

BURBIDGE, John L.
Group technology. Paper prepared for the Symposium on the Effects of Group Production Methods on the Humanisation of Work, Turin, July 1975. Turin, International Centre for Advanced Technical and Vocational Training, 1975. 12 p.

BURBIDGE, John L.
Introduction of group technology. London, Heinemann, 1975. vii, 267 p.
A management development textbook on the introduction of group technology and the necessary modification of factory organisation. It outlines the advantages of the system, and covers such topics as production control and planning, production flow analysis, loading, plant layout in groups, and personnel management.

"Le bureau de demain: interview de G. Patrix." /The Office of tomorrow./ Architecture française, (392), Aug. 1975, p.94.

BUSCH, R.
Gruppenfertigung. /Group production./ Graz, Institut für Industriebetriebslehre und Wirtschaftstechnik, 1974.

BUTERA, F.
"Partecipazione operaia nella progettazione dell'organizzazione del lavoro e gruppi autonomi di lavoro." /The participation of workers, the planning of work organisation and autonomous work groups./ La critica sociologica, (30), 1974, pp.23-48.

BUTERA, F.
"Contributo all'analisi di variabili strutturali del mutamento dell'organizzazione del lavoro: il caso Olivetti." /Contribution to the analysis of the structural variables of changes in the organisation of work: the case of Olivetti./ Studi organizzativi, (1), 1973.
An extended analysis of the phenomenology, causes and effects of the change in the Olivetti assembly lines.

BUTERA, F.
"Environmental factors in job and organization design: the case of Olivetti." In: DAVIS, Louis E.; CHERNS, Albert B. The quality of working life. New York, The Free Press, 1975, T.2, pp. 166-200.

BUTERA, F.
"Organizzazione del lavoro e professionalitá nell'industria." /Organisation of work and professionalism in industry./ Quaderni di formazione, (17), Jul. 1975, pp. 1-74.
Compilation of articles on the theorètical aspects of job enrichment, polyvalence, professionalism and training in the context of the innovative trends in factory organisation in Italy.

*BUTTERISS, Margaret.
Job enrichment and employee participation; a study. London, Institute of Personnel Management, 1971. 71 p.
A booklet on workers' participation and its effect on job satisfaction, with particular reference to the UK. Covers such topics as workers' representation, job reassignment and enrichment, management by objectives, decision-making powers and effects on labour relations.

BUTTERISS, Margaret.
A strategy for job enrichment; a summary of the Hackman and Oldham reports Nos. 3, 4 and 6. London, /n.d./ (Great Britain. Department of Employment. Work Research Unit, No. 6.)
Summarises a less well known theoretical development in approaches to job enrichment. Outlines other theories on job design and their weaknesses and lays out a strategy for introducing job enrichment based on set procedures for assessing its need. Develops step-by-step 'Job Diagnosis Survey' which takes full account of the individual employee and proposes diagnostic tools to monitor the results of each stage of the strategy.

CAMERON, C.R.
"Modern technology, job enrichment and the quality of life." Journal of industrial relations, 14(4), 1972, pp. 361-378. A statement of Australia's future labour policy expressing the views of the Socialist Party with regard to employment policy, approaches to technological change, job enrichment and the humanisation of work.

CAMPBELL, Bonnie.
"How to implement the humanizing process; extracts from speeches given at 10th Annual Conference of IRRI, Queen's University, Kingston, 1973." Labour gazette, Aug. 1973, pp. 522-524.

CANADA. DEPARTMENT OF LABOUR.
Job enrichment. Prepared by Paul Lampkin. Ottawa, 1975. 1 v.

CANADA. DEPARTMENT OF LABOUR.
The Kingston works: Alcan, the machinists and the steelworkers. Ottawa, /n.d./

CANADA. MINISTRY OF LABOUR.
A case study in job enrichment: Canadian Industries Ltd. Paints Division, Vaughan Centre. Toronto, Ont., 1974. (Its: Employment information series, No.8.)

CANNON, Martin J.; POOLE, Brian, A.; PRANGLEY, Robert E.
"Involuntary job rotation and work behavior." Personnel journal, June 1972, pp. 446-448.

CARNALL, C.A.; BIRCHALL, D.W.
Work group autonomy on the shop floor. Paper presented to British Association Conference, 28 August 1975. Henley-on-Thames, England, Administrative Staff College, 1975.

CARNALL, C.A.; BIRCHALL, D.W.; WILD, R.
The design of jobs: an outline strategy for diagnosis and change. Henley-on-Thames, England, Administrative Staff College, /n.d./

CARNALL, C.A.; WILD, R.
The location of variable work stations and the performance of production flow lines. Henley-on-Thames, England, Administrative Staff College, /n.d./.

CARPENTIER, J.
"Organisational techniques and the humanisation of work." International labour review, 110(2), Aug. 1974, p. 93 et seq.
The growing feelings of dissatisfaction and alienation that are finding expression, in many industrialised societies, in the questioning of established patterns of life and work, in poorer workmanship, spreading absenteeism and labour disputes obviously call for a searching reappraisal of the way production is organised: hence the current emphasis on research and experimentation in an attempt to discover some way of reinvesting factory work with meaning and appeal. After analysing the conceptual basis of work organisation and the historical factors that encouraged the development of mass production, the author examines the present situation and the various means by which work may be humanised, particularly through revised organisational techniques.

CARPENTIER, J.
La restructuration du travail. /The restructuring of work./ /n.p./ Centre de Productivité de l'Isère, 1972.

CARRAUD, M.
"Experiences de restructuration d'entreprise en vue d'enrichir les tâches." /Experiments in restructing the enterprise to attain job enrichment./ Sociologie du travail, 18(1), Jan.-Mar. 1976, pp. 36-50.
Article on a job enrichment experiment in an industrial enterprise in France which necessitated the restructuring on assembly-line work. The author describes the in-plant training required by the changed factory organisation and its effects on the polyvalence of the skilled workers and on the communication systems.

CARRE, Henri.
"L'élargissement des tâches à l'usine IBM-France de Corbeil-Essonnes." /Job enlargement at the IBM-France factory in Corbeil-Essonnes./ Etude du travail (Paris), (176), sept. 1966, 14 p.

CARROLL, Archie B.
"Conceptual foundations of job enrichment." Public personnel management, Jan.-Feb. 1974, pp. 35-38.

CELLA, G.P.
Divisione del lavoro e iniziativa operaia. /The division of labour and workers initiatives./ Bari, De Donato, 1972. 208 p.
Monograph on the behavioural implications of job enrichment in modern factory organisation, with particular reference to industrial workers on assembly-line work in Italy. Discusses political and sociological aspects, trade union policies and social implications. Also considers job satisfaction, motivation, group work and the effects of automation on job requirements and occupational qualifications.

CENTRALE DES METALLURGISTES DE BELGIQUE.
"Conditions de travail." /Conditions of work./ C.M.B. inform, (7), Jan. 1975, pp. 17-29.
An article assessing current experiences and trends in Belgium with regard to the improvement of working conditions and the humanisation of work. Covers such topics as assembly-line work, job enrichment and group work and flexible hours of work, etc.

"La chaîne brisée? L'enrichissement des tâches." /The broken chain? Job enrichment."/ CNPF. Patronnat, (355), Jan. 1975, pp. 6-13.

CHAMPAGNE, Jean.
"Adapting jobs to people: experiments at Alcan." Monthly labor review, 96(4), Apr. 1973, pp. 49-51.

CHARY, Asha; DASTUR, Zarin.
The new technology of work in the Indian banking industry. /N.p./ National Institute of Bank Management, /N.d./ (Unpubl. report.)
The paper, based on research experience in redesigning the technology of work in the commercial banks in India, deals with such issues as perspective of the banking industry in India, technological changes, the process of such change and the methodology adopted, socio-technical elements of work technology, and the implications of the change in work technology.

CHATTERJEE, S.K.
"Few thoughts on job evaluation and job enrichment and their problems." Industrial relations (Calcutta), 23(1), Jan.-Feb. 1971, pp. 18-22.

CHAUMETTE, P.
A quelle condition et sous quelles formes se développe la restructuration des tâches? /Under what condition and in what forms does job restructuring take place./ Paris, Entreprise et Personnel, 1975. (Roneogr.)

CHAVE, D.
"Neotaylorisme ou autonomie ouvrière? Réflexion sur trois expériences de réorganisation du travail." /Neotaylorism or worker autonomy? Reflections on three experiments in work reorganisation./ Sociologie du travail, 18(1), Jan.-Mar. 1976, pp. 3-14.
Article describing three job enrichment experiments in assembly-line work in France - examines the labour relations and social change effects.

CHIAROMONTE, N.
"Come si ristruttura la fabbrica." /How to restructure manufacturing./ I consigli, (20-21), Feb. 1976, pp. 23-26.
An analysis of the basic line taken by managements of enterprises in the area of the organisation of work and the unions response to it.

CLERC, Jean-Marc.
Expériences en vue d'une organisation plus humaine du travail industriel. Compte rendu d'un colloque international qui s'est tenu à Paris les 26 et 27 janvier 1973. /Experiments in humanising the organisation of industrial work. Report of an international symposium, Paris, 26 and 27 January 1973./ Paris, Librairie Armand Colin, 1973. 114 p.
The work consists of three sections. The first covers the experiment with integrated work units undertaken by the Italian enterprise Olivetti. The second considers aspects of social policy in the USSR and looks at the improvements in the working conditions of automation workers. The third section traces the stages of the experiments in the upgrading of work undertaken by the French firm BSN since 1955.

CLERC, Jean-Marc.
"Experiments in humanising the organisation of industrial work: some points from a symposium." International Institute for Labour Studies, Bulletin, (11), 1975, pp. 15-20.

CLUTTERBUCK, D.
"Faiveley opens its doors to shop-floor management." International management, May 1975, pp. 22-26.
A description of the management patterns in a 600-employee French engineering firm in which the board has an equal number of representatives from among shareholders, managers and workers. The structure of the organisation ensures that information is readily available to those who need it. Consultation takes place at all levels including the shop-floor level and covers both day-to-day decision-making and planning for the future and a training programme for every level of employee is available.

"CMA talks about job enrichment." Labour gazette, Aug. 1969, pp. 453-454.

COCH, L; FRENCH, J.R.P.
"Overcoming resistance to change." Human relations, 1, 1948.

CODILLA, L.R.
"Job enrichment: the key to motivation." Cost and management, Jul.-Aug. 1968, p. 38 et seq.

COLLINS, D.C.; RAULBOLT, R.R.
"A study of employee resistance to job enrichment." Personnel journal, 54(4), Apr. 1975, pp. 232-235.
On the basis of results of empirical research, the authors contend that age, seniority and the number of years an employee still has to work before retirement are important elements in the resistance to job enrichment experiments.

CONANT, E.H.; KILBRIDGE, M.D.
"Une analyse interdisciplinaire de l'élargissement des tâches : ergonomie, technologie, coûts et réaction des travailleurs." /An interdisciplinary analysis of job enlargement, ergonomics, technology, costs and reactions of workers./ Personnel, (117), Jul.-Aug. 1968.

CONANT, E.H.; KILBRIDGE, M.D.
"An interdisciplinary analysis of job enlargement: technology, costs and behavioral implications." Industrial and labor relations review, 18, 1965. pp.377-395.

"Conditions de travail: aspects des recherches et des expériences américaines." /Conditions of work: aspects of american research and experiments./ Intersocial, (17), June 1976.
To systematic job enrichment of the kind experimented with in Europe more flexible formulae are preferred, laying stress on self-expression and the development of communications, which may go as far as labour-management co-operation. Above all, pragmatic solutions are sought.

"Conditions de travail: le Taylorisme en question." /Working conditions - Taylorism challenged./ Sociologie du travail, (4), Oct.-Dec. 1974, pp. 337-444.
Covers job content and workload, employers' job enrichment policies, Taylorism and anti-Taylorism and semi-autonomous work groups. Poses the question of an universal model for organisational structures.

"Conditions de travail: les expériences de la Régie Renault." /Working conditions: the experience of Renault./ Liaisons sociales, série R 71/73, Aug. 1973, 6 p.

"Conditions de travail: une priorité, la restructuration des tâches." /Conditions of work: a priority, the restructuring of tasks./ L'usine nouvelle, (44), Oct. 1975, p. 98.

"Conditions de travail et automation chez I.B.M. /Conditions of work and automation at IBM./ Production et gestion, (267), Dec. 1974, pp. 46-54.
The article reviews experiments in job enrichment and the

satisfaction of work in the three highly automated branches of IBM in France and the Federal Republic of Germany. It also evaluates the effects of these measures on the job satisfaction of assembly-line workers.

CONLON, J.A.; VAN OOSTEROM, C.
Administrative implications of teamwork. Canberra, Department of Police and Customs, 1975. 38 p.
Prepared as a discussion paper for the Royal Commission on Australian Government Administration, the document provides a proposal for changes to the present Australian Public Service administrative system to allow for the introduction of "teamwork" (semi-autonomous groups).

CONSIGLIO, M.
"Un nuovo modo di lavorare in fabbrica : mito o realità?" /The new form of work in manufacturing: myth or reality./ Il Mulino, 24(237), Jan.-Feb. 1975, pp. 96-111.

COOPER, Cary L.
Theories of group processus. London, John Wiley, 1975.
From the point of view of the behavioural sciences and socio-technical systems the author considers the role of the individual in the organisation, the impact of group processes on personal and organisational development, strategies for the humanisation of the work environment and the influence of economic factors, techniques on organisational life.

COOPER, R.
Job motivation and job design. London, Institute of Personnel Management, 1974. 140 p.
Monograph on motivation and job satisfaction which discusses behavioural response to job design and the implications of job enrichment programmes composed of planning, execution and control modules.

COOPER, R.; FOSTER, P.M.
"Socio-technical systems." American psychologist, 26, 1971, pp. 467-474.
The paper defines the concept of a socio-technical system and describes its framework in a typical industrial system, examining the supports and constraints of the technical environment which determine the socio-psychological factors that will be salient in a given production system. The authors consider the implications of the socio-technical theory for task organisation and conclude that its value will become increasingly apparent as technology advances.

*COTGROVE, S.; DUNHAM, J.; VAMPLEW, C.
The nylon spinners: a case study in productivity bargaining and job enlargement. London, G. Allen and Unwin, 1971.

CRAVEN, F.W.
Human aspects of group technology. Paper presented at the Symposium on the Effects of Group Production Methods on the Humanisation of Work, Turin, July 1975. Turin, International Centre for Advanced Technical and Vocational Training, 1975. 22 p.
A description of the introduction of group technology in a

British tool manufacturing plant which examines the methods and problems of introduction and the technological and human benefits that accrue from it. The author notes that group technology permits enlightened managements to develop a workshop environment that allows for greater responsibility and involvement (and, therefore, greater contentment) on the part of the workers. He suggests however that the success of such efforts depends largely on the flexibility of management and on its willingness to allow the changing worker/management relationship to evolve rather than be engineered.

CROCE - SPINELLI, J.
"La formation gestuelle des O.S.: une étape vers le job enrichment." /Management training of unskilled workers: a step towards job enrichment./ Entreprise et formation continue, Dec. 1972.

DAIMLER BENZ, A.G. ARBEITSKREIS GESTALTUNG MENSCHLICHER ARBEIT.
Dokumentation über menschengerechte Arbeitsgestaltung in den Werken der Daimler-Benz AG. /Documentation on humanised work places in the factories of Daimler - Benz. A.G./ /N.p./, 1973.

DAIMLER - BENZ, A.G. ARBEITSKREIS NEUE ARBEITSSTRUKTUREN DER DEUTSCHEN AUTOMOBILINDUSTRIE.
Gestaltung der menschlichen Arbeit: Beispiele aus der deutschen Automobilindustrie. /Designing human work: examples from the German automobile industry./ /N.p./, 1976.

DANIEL, W.W.
Beyond the wage-work bargain. London, Political and Economic Planning, 1970.

DANIEL, W.W.
"Changing hierarchies at work." Listener, (7), Sept. 1972, pp. 300-302.

DANIEL, W.W.; McINTOSH, Neil.
The right to manage? A study of leadership and reform in employee relations. London, Political and Economic Planning, 1972, vii, 217 p.
Political and Economic Planning (P.E.P.) has had for many years an established reputation in U.K. and elsewhere as an independent, policy-oriented research institute. The first section of the book provides a background of examples, misunderstandings and some conclusions about job enrichment. The second section discusses worker involvement in decision making and representation in which the main example is in the United Kingdom in a fully unionised plant. The third section discusses the reform of systems of payment and job evaluation. The authors accept that a high proportion of jobs are meaningless; that workers generally lack opportunity for a constructive say over work place decisions; and that industrial relations are beset by irrational and inequitable systems of payment. They make an attempt to evaluate the scope and possibilities of change in relation to these problems.

DAUTOVIĆ, M.
Development of work organization in Yugoslav theory and practise paper presented at the Symposium on Work Organization in Self-Management Relations, Zagreb, 1970.

DAVIS, Louis E.
"The sign of jobs." Industrial relations, Oct. 1966, pp. 21-45.

DAVIS, Louis E.
"Developments in job design."
"In: WARR, Peter B., ed. Personnel goals and work design. London, J. Wiley, 1975.
The review focusses on recent developments in job design or, more accurately, role design and work systems design. The author considers it very necessary to develop demonstration experiments in work design so as to generate a continuous learning process which will ensure that research in this area remains relevant in the face of the changing needs of western societies. Such experiments would permit the study of worker behaviour in settings that are free from the constraints and dogma inherent in the organisations of the industrial era. He concludes that it is more important to consider the development of roles and work systems than job design per se.

DAVIS, Louis E.
Evolving alternative organization designs: their socio-technical bases. Los Angeles, Institute of Industrial Relations, University of California, 1976.
This review of alternative organizations indicates that new organizations are evolving that are characterized by being systemic. An examination of all the attributes and characteristics described reveals that they are interrelated, one supporting another. Rewarding individuals for knowledge and competence has a bearing on adaptability. Team ownership of work process has a bearing on control of critical variances, etc.

The author thinks that there is widespread applicability for these alternative organizations. They are proving themselves to be suitable not only to new demands and conditions, but they provide the beginnings for examining long-standing issues regarding industrial and business organizations in democratic societies.

DAVIS, Louis E.
"Restructuring jobs in social goals." Manpower, Feb. 1970, pp. 2-6.
The author examines the relationship of the organisation to the social system in which it operates and acknowledges that a socio-technical interchange must influence the concept of job restructuring. He argues that any programme for job restructuring must define its social objectives with respect to organisation, the individual and society.

DAVIS, Louis E.; CANTER, R.R.
"Job design research." Journal of industrial engineering, 1956.

DAVIS, Louis E.; CANTER, R.R.; HOFFMANN, J.
"Current job design criteria." In: DAVIS, Louis E.; TAYLOR, James C., eds. Design of jobs. Harmondsworth, Penguin Books, 1972, pp. 65-82.

DAVIS, Louis, E.; ENGELSTAD, P.N.
Unit operations in socio-technical systems. London, Tavistock Institute, 1966. (Doc. T894.)
A basic paper in socio-technical understanding. It gives some basic concepts and definitions which make it possible to give comparable descriptions of different technological processes.

*DAVIS, Louis E.; TAYLOR, James C., eds.
Design of jobs. Harmondsworth, Penguin Books, 1972. 477 p.
A collection of reprints whose first five papers on "Evolution of job Design in Industrial Society" range from 1835 to 1962. The second section on "The Current Condition" introduces questions about job design criteria, white-collar automation, the man-machine relation in automated systems, and concludes with a 1966 paper, by Hans van Beinum, on "The Relation Between the Role of the Trade Union in Modern Society and the Attitudes of Workers". The third section consists of six papers on "Recent Theoretical Trends". The fourth and fifth sections cover "Job Design Cost Criteria" and "Job-Centered Studies" and the sixth section illustrates and clarifies the meaning of "Work-System Studies". The final section of the book deals with future possibilities in the area.

*DAVIS, Louis E; TAYLOR, James C.
Technology, organisation and job structure. Paper prepared for the International Conference on the Quality of Working Life, Arden House, New York, August 1972.

*DAVIS, Louis E.; TRIST, E.L.
"Improving the quality of work life: experience of the socio-technical approach." In: O'TOOLE, James, ed. Work and the quality of life. Cambridge, Mass., M.I.T. Press, 1974.
This summarising and synoptic volume is based on the use and experience of the concept of the socio-technical system. It begins with a brief history of the origin and development of this idea, and goes on to use specific case experiences in terms of their contribution in seven different areas of concern: production technologies of the first industrial revolution; production technologies of the second industrial revolution; the maintenance function; supervisory roles; the service and professional area; corporate strategies for socio-technical change; and socio-technical change at the national level. There is a brief note on other developments in the U.S. and elsewhere, and a final section on "What Has Been Learned", on four particular topics: autonomy, personal growth and participation; systemic properties; implications for management, unions and government; and action requirements.

DAVIS, Louis E.; VALFER, E.S.
"Intervening responses to changes in supervisor job designs." Occupational psychology, 39, 1965, pp. 171-189.
A relatively technical description and discussion of a project involving alteration of supervisory jobs.

DAVIS, Louis E.; VALFER, E.S.
"Supervisor job design." Ergonomics, 8, 1965.

*DE Nitish R.
Country report on India as a part of the Project Comparative Study on New Forms of Work Organisations, a report submitted to Conditions of Work and Life Branch, Working Conditions and Environment Department, International Labour Office, Geneva, 1976.
This report reviews the work carried out in India since A.K. Rice's pioneering work in a textile factory in 1953. It considers the progress of new forms of work organisation in Indian environments, and discusses strategies of diffusion. It also looks at the development of a network of action-researchers in India who are committed to the Quality of Working Life movement and the prospect of a regional network in Asia. The report also highlights the potentially positive role that the International Council for the Quality of Working Life and International Labour Organisation can play in concretising Quality of Working Life movement in developing countries.

DE, Nitish R.
"Diffusion of work system re-design on participative design in a large complex engineering factor." To be published in National Labour Institute bulletin.
The author, as an action researcher, involved management, trade unions and shop-floor workers in exploring the possibility of bringing about a positive change in the Quality of Working Life in a factory employing 10,000 employees. With the concurrence of the parties concerned, the experiment started with two shops manufacturing condenser units of thermal equipment plants and then gradually diffused to the other shops in the plant. Essentially, a composite task force developed in each shop consisting of workers, technicians and managers who, on the basis of continuous dialogue with the concerned workers, redesigned the work system by introducing "multi-skilling", an operation based on group norms.

DE, Nitish R.
"Spontaneous work system innovation in two shops of Heavy Boiler Equipment Plant of a large public section organization." To be published in National Labour Institute Bulletin.
After attending two seminars on work re-design and participative management, two managers initiated action in the Drum Shop and the Header Shop of the plant redesigning the work system with the active involvement of small work groups. There was substantial improvement in quality of product, higher productivity and higher level of machine utilisation. Gradually, each work team around an activity centre began to undertake weekly production planning, scheduling and reviewing activity thereby releasing the supervisors to concentrate on higher level boundary maintenance functions.

DE, Nitish R.
"Training strategy for required attitudinal change." National Labour Institute bulletin, (1), 1976, pp. 13-28.
The author considers the context and dynamics of attitudinal change and presents a model of the role of social systems design in this area based on his theoretical formulation. This theoretical model proposed by the author could serve as a useful guide for attitudinal change programmes for work redesign

in "struggling" countries. The paper then presents four case-studies (three in India and one in Somalia) to illustrate the way in which attitudinal change training strategies lead to the reorganisation of the work system at both micro and macro levels.

DEDERING, H.
Personalplanung und Mitbestimmung. /Personnel planning and participation./ Opladen, 1972.

DE HEER, B.
"Het Bello-project van Hoogovens." /The Bello project of 'Hoogovens'./ Bedrijfsvoering, 23(10), Oct. 1974, pp. 178-181.

DELAMOTTE, Yves.
Recherches en vue d'une organisation plus humaine du travail industriel. Rapport établie à la demande de M. Fontanet, Ministre du Travail, de l'Emploi et de la Population. /Rearch on the more humanised organisation of industrial work. Report made to Mr. Fontanet, Minister of Labour, Employment and Population./ Paris, La Documentation Française, 1972. 96 p.
After a brief look at various theories of work organisation such as those of Taylor and at the work of Herzberg and the Tavistock Institute, the author considers the upgrading of individual tasks, giving as examples the Olivetti experiment of 1959 and the case of Fiat where the redesign of jobs is included in enterprise-level collective agreements. He then describes the composition of work groups and analyses two experiments at Philips and one at Olivetti. Finally, he considers the Norwegian experiments with semi-autonomous work groups. In the last chapter he presents some general abservations about the experiments described, the reactions of the managers of enterprises, the problems solved by the restructuring of jobs and the attitude of the trade unions.

DELAMOTTE, Yves.
L'amélioration des conditions de travail en Suède; législation et expèriences. /The improvement of working conditions in Sweden: legislation and experiments./ Paris, Agence Nationale pour l'Amelioration des Conditions de Travail, 1975. 20 p.
Pamphlet on job enrichment, workers' participation and other measures to improve working conditions in Sweden. It comments on labour legislation and on the experiences of various enterprises.

DELAMOTTE, Yves.
"L'enrichissement des tâches, les groupes semi-autonomes." /Job enrichment: semi-autonomous work groups./ Personnel Mar.-Apr. 1975.

DELAMOTTE, Yves.
"Vers de nouvelles formes d'organisation du travail." /Towards a new form of work organisation./ Prospectives, (4), Mar. 1975, pp. 63-74.
The author points out that many experiments with new forms of work organisation are interrupted for a variety of reasons including the attitudes of trade unions towards them. In this article he considers the utility of the application of socio-technical systems in the reorganisation of work.

DEL LUNGO, S.
I mutamenti nell'organizzazione del lavaro. /Changes in work organisation./ Roma, Studio Staff - Intersind, 1975. (Roneogr.) Exploration of several cases of planned and unplanned change in the state-owned industries.

DEMUS, H.
Soziometrische Methoden zur Beurteilung der Gruppenstruktur bei alternativen Fertigungsprinzipen. /Sociometric methods to judge group structures with alternative production principles./ Darmstadt, Institut für Arbeitswissenschaft, 1974. (Studiearbeit)

DEMKO, P.
Základy vedeckej organizácie práce vo výrobnom procese. /Basic principles of scientific organisation work in the production process./ Bratislava, Práca, 1966. 299 p.

DEN HERTOG, F.J.
Das Experiment der Philips Fernsehenfabrik: Vom Fliessband zur selbständigen Gruppe. /The experiment in the Philips television factory: from the assembly line to the autonomous group./ Vereinigung schweizerischer Betriebsingenieure, Eidgenössische Technische Hochschule. Zürich, 1973.

DEN HERTOG, F.J.
Werkstrukturering; ervaringen met alternatieve werkorganisaties binnen het Philips bedrijf. /Work structuring; experience with alternative work organizations within the Philips concern./ Eindhoven, Gema, 1975. 170 p.(Proefschrift Techn. Hogeschool Delft)

DEN HERTOG, F.J.
"Work structuring: Philips' Gloeilampenfabrieken." Industrial psychology, Aug. 1974.

DEN HERTOG, F.J.; KERKHOFF, W.H.C.
Experiment work structuring television receiver factory Eindhoven, Part II. Eindhoven, 1973.
Evaluation of the social psychological effects of autonomous task-oriented production groups, Philips.

DEN HERTOG, F.J.; KERKHOFF, W.H.C.
"Vom Fliessband zur selbständigen Gruppe." /From the assembly line to the autonomous group./ Industrielle Organisation, 43(1), 1974, pp. 21-24

DEN HERTOG, F.J.; VOSSEN, H.
"Werkstructurering in een lampenfabriek." /Work structuring in a bulb factory./ Mens en Onderneming, 29(6), Nov.-Dec. 1975, pp. 320-333.
Report of the objectives of the experiment of work reorganisation at Philips' including independence and responsibility of the workers, education and development possibilities.

DEN HERTOG, F.J.; VOSSEN, H.P.
Organizational renewal. Terneuzen "special miniature" project - evaluation of the technical and social objective of a work structuring experiment. Eindhoven, 1974.

DESCOMBES, A.
"Conditions humaines et sociales du travail en groupes autonomes. /Human and social working conditions in autonomous groups./ Hommes et techniques, 31(374), Dec. 1974, pp. 761-765.
Article on the promotion of autonomous group work as a job enrichment measure in France.

DETTELBACK, W.W.; KRAFT, P.
"Organization change through job enrichment." Training and development journal, Aug. 1971, pp. 2-6.
Report of the successful enrichment of typists' jobs at Bankers Trust, with the emphasis on the "spin-off" effects of job enrichment on other sectors of the organization.

*DEVELOPMENT COUNCIL FOR COLLABORATION QUESTIONS.
Participation in thirty-five Swedish companies. Stockholm, 1975. 45 p.
The booklet contains case studies of participation and consultation activities in Swedish companies of varying sizes and in different industries. The experiments are concerned with practical participation at the level of the work place and the descriptions cover such subjects as changes in work organisation, project groups, consultation, changing supervisory roles and the development of information activities. While it does not present standard solutions or suggest the exportability of the Swedish experience the booklet hopes to "provide ideas and stimuli" in this field.

DHOME, N.
"L'enrichissement du travail humain dans le groupe Volvo." /The enrichment of work at Volvo./ Revue française des affaires sociales, 30(2), Apr.-June 1976, pp. 221-250.
Article describes the job enrichment and humanization of work experiments in the Volvo factories in Sweden and comments on the evolution of labour legislation in that country.

DICKSON, Paul.
The future of the workplace; the coming revolution in jobs. New York, Weybright and Talley, 1975. 378 p.

"The diffusion of new work structures: explaining why success didn't take." Organizational dynamics, 3(1), Winter 1975, pp. 2-22.

DONALDSON, Lex.
"Job enlargement: a multidimensional process." Human relations, 28(7), Sept. 1975, pp. 593-610.
Reports the results of a study of job enlargement on a group of female assemblers in a Scottish plant of a large multinational electronics firm. Comparison between the experimental and control groups indicated the achievement of the expected increases in satisfaction associated with greater work variety, novelty and perceived use of capabilities. However, decreased social interaction and increased effort of work suggest that there is a greater need for behavioral science analysts and practitioners to conceptualize job enlargement as a phenomenon involving multiple variables and outcomes in order to produce a better understanding of the effects of job enlargement programmes.

*DORAY, Bernard.
"Participation, intensification du travail et usure des hommes." /Participation, intensification of work and debilitation of men./ Economie et politique, (218), Sept. 1972.

DÖRKEN, W.
"Formen der Arbeitsstrukturierung." /Forms of work structuring (organisations)./ In: Leistung und Lohn. Köln, Bundesvereinigung der Deutschen Arbeitsgeberverbände, 1975.

DOUARD, Henri.
"Job enrichment, équipes autonomes, nouvelles perspectives dans la restructuration du travail." /Job enrichment, autonomous groups and new perspectives in the restructuring of work./ Entreprise et personnel, Feb. 1972.

DOUARD, Henri.
"L'enrichissement des tâches ou la restructuration du travail." /Job enrichment or the restructuring of work./ Direction et gestion des entreprises, Nov.-Dec. 1973.

DOUARD, Henri.
'Innovation industrielle et changement social: Volvo et Fiat." /Industrial innovation and social change: Volvo and Fiat./ Esprit, (7-8), Jul.-Aug. 1975, pp. 23-33.
An article on job enrichment and humanisation of work in the Volvo and Fiat factories in Sweden and Italy.

DOUARD, Henri.
"Restructuration des tâches." /Restructuring of jobs./ Entreprise et personnel, 1973.

DOUARD, Henri.
"Restructuration des tâches et formation."/Job restructuring and training./ Actualité de la formation permanente, (20), Nov.-Dec. 1975, pp. 5-12.
An article on the correlation between job enrichment and training needs, with particular reference to the influence of the educational system in France.

DOUGLAS, Merrill E.; JOHNSON, T. Stephen.
"Successful job enrichment: a case example." Altanta economic review, Nov.-Dec. 1974, pp. 9-12.

DOWLING, William F.
"Job redesign on the assembly line: farewell to blue-collar blues?" Organizational dynamics, Autumn 1973, pp. 51-67.

"The drive to make dull jobs interesting." U.S. news and world report, July 17, 1972, pp. 50-59.
Results from job enrichment programs and reported for several companies: Corning Glass Works at Midfield, Massachusetts; Donnelly Mirrors of Holland, Michigan; Monsanto Textiles of Pensacola, Florida; two General Electric plants; and the Gaines Pet Food plant at Topeka, Kansas.

DUBREUIL, H.
"L'organisation du travail et le système des équipes autonomes." /The organisation of work and the system of autonomous groups./ Revue internationale du travail, Oct. 1951, 20 p. (Also published in English.)

DUBROWSKI, J.N.
The systems of notions of categories of scientific work organisation. Moscow, Economica, 1973. 118 p. (In Russian.)
Describes the substance of the scientific organisation of work, its place and role in the system of social production forms, and methods of organisation of working people's activities within the limits of the personnel of enterprises. The author considers such ideas as the "basis of the scientific organisation of work", "principles of the scientific organisation of work", "elements of the scientific organisation of work" and others. Includes a short bibliography.

DUBROWSKI, J.N.
Wissenschaftliche Arbeitsorganisation. /Scientific organisation of work./ Berlin, Die Wirtschaft, 1976.

DUFFANY, Bruce.
"Beyond job enrichment." Journal of humanistic management, 2(1), 1974, pp. 22-27.

DÜLFER, E.
Die Auswirkungen von Gruppenfertigungsmethoden auf die Humanisierung der Arbeit. /Effects of group production methods on the humanisation of work./ Bericht über eine Internationale Tagung des ILO. Turin, 1975.

DUMONT, Jean-Pierre.
"Les innovations pour améliorer les conditions de travail." /Innovations for the improvement of working conditions./ Le Monde, 11 May 1976, p. 20. (Expérience CHAUSSON, expériences VOLVO et ASTRA.) (Experiments at CHAUSSON VOLVO and ASTRA.)

DUMONT, Jean-Pierre.
"L'expérience des Pompes Guinard: une usine artisanale à la campagne et sans 'petit chef'." /The experiment of Pompes Guinard: a small-scale factory in the country without 'small bosses'/ Le Monde, 12 Oct. 1976, p. 23.

DUMONT, Jean-Pierre.
"Amélioration des conditions de travail: dans le domaine de l'élargissement des tâches, Renault va plus loin que FIAT." /Improvement of working conditions: in the area of job enlargement, Renault goes further than FIAT./ Le Monde, 10 July 1973.

DUMONT, Jean-Pierre.
"A nouvelles usines, meilleures conditions de travail." /New factories, better working conditions./ Le Monde, 8 June 1976.

DUNAJEWSKI, H.
Note sur la choix de la technique améliorant les conditions de travail. /Note on the choice of technology for the improvement of working conditions./ Aix-en-Provence, Laboratoire d'Economie, et de Sociologie du Travail du CNRS, 1971. 6 p.(Roneogr.)

DURAFOUR, M.
"La revalorisation du travail manuel." /The upgrading of manual work./ Production et gestion, (276), Oct. 1975, pp. 38-40.

DURAND, Claude
"Les politiques patronales d'enrichissement de tâches." /Employer policies regarding job enrichment./ Sociologue du travail, (4), 1974, pp. 358-373.

ECKARDSTEIN, D. von.
"Job rotation." Management Enzyklopädie, (München), Bd. 3, 1970, pp. 774-778.

ECONOMIC DEVELOPMENT COMMITTEE FOR MECHANICAL ENGINEERING, London.
Why group technology? London, 1975. ii, 36 p.
Pamphlet aiming to encourage the introduction of group work into batch engineering production in the UK.

EDGREN , Jan.
With varying success - a Swedish experiment in wage systems and shop floor organization. Stockholm, SAF, 1974.

EDGREN , Jan.
"Swedish experiments in work organization." Personnel management, 6, June 1974, pp. 25-27.
Discusses new arrangements for joint problem-solving, delegation of decision-making, new types of production system designs, new wage systems. Most of the experiments show positive results in job-satisfaction and productivity.

EDMONDS, Norman D.
"Implementation methods of job enrichment." Journal of humanistic management, 2(1), 1974, pp. 32-41.

EDWARDS, G.A.B.
"Group technology: a technical answer to a social problem?" Personnel management, Mar. 1974, pp. 35-39.

EDWARDS, G.A.B.
Readings in group technology - cellular systems. /N.p./, Machinery Publishing Co. 1971.
Deals with the management of firms which manufacture engineering products. The purpose of this book is to identify some of the problems of these firms and to produce a framework around which a management information system can be developed. Examines various methods of proceeding to group technology and gives some practical applications.

EGGENS, Jean-Baptiste.
"Introduction critique au job enrichment." /Critical introduction to job enrichment./ Le management, Oct. 1971.

EGGENS, Jean-Baptiste.
"Peut-on enrichir le travail à la chaîne?" /Can assembly-line work be enriched./ Le management, Oct. 1971.

ELBING, Alvar; GORDON, John.
"Self-management in the flexible organization." Futures, Aug. 1974, pp. 319-328.

ELLIOTT, T.H.
"Work enrichment for Singapore?" Free labour world, Mar. 1973, pp. 11-14.

*EMERY, Fred E.
"Characteristics of socio-technical systems." In: DAVIS, L.E.; TAYLOR, J.C., eds. Design of jobs. Harmondsworth, Penguin Books, 1972, pp. 177-198.

EMERY, Fred E.; EMERY, Messelyn.
A choice of futures. Leiden, Martinus Nijholf, 1976. 213 p.

EMERY, Fred E.; EMERY, Messelyn.
Participative design. Canberra, ANU, Centre for Continuing Studies, 1974.

*EMERY, Fred E.; MAREK, J.
"Some socio-technical aspects of automation." Human relations, 15, 1962, pp. 17-25.
The authors use case studies of the introduction of automation to illustrate the problems of (i) the need for a radical change in the supervisor's job in the face of the increasing responsibility of the operator and (ii) reduction in employment due to automation. The authors feel that the latter issue is not a problem for a reasonably competent management as many social mechanisms exist through which this can be handled without disruption of morale.

*EMERY, Fred E.; THORSRUD, E.
Democracy at work: the report of the Norwegian industrial democracy programme. Oslo, Tanum Press, 1970.
A description of the implementation and results of projects in several Norwegian companies, aimed at the testing of alternative organisational forms and their impact on employee particiaption at different levels of the companies involved. Major emphasis is placed on the concrete conditions for personal participation including technological factors structuring the tasks, the work roles and the wider organisational environment of workers. In the course of experiments semi-autonomous work groups came to be accepted as an important alternative form of work organisation.

*EMERY, F.E.; TRIST, E.L.
"Socio-technical systems." In: CHURCHMAN, C.W.; VERHULST, M., eds. Management sciences, models and techniques. Oxford, Pergamon Press, 1960, T.2, pp. 83-97. (Reprinted in: EMERY, F.E., ed. Systems thinking. Harmondsworth, Penguin Books, 1969, pp. 281-296, and FRANK, H.E., ed. Organization structuring. London, McGraw-Hill, 1971, pp. 41-53.)

"Emploi et conditions de travail." /Employment and the conditions of work./ Dirigeant, (61), May, 1975, pp. 2-15.
Article on problems of job enrichment and humanisation of work in France. Presents the views, experience and activities of trade unions, employers' organisations and a government agency.

"Employee attitude, job enrichment, and the work ethic." In: INDUSTRIAL RELATIONS RESEARCH ASSOCIATION. Proceedings 1973. Madison, Wisc., 1974, pp. 201-223.

ENGELSTAD, P.
"Socio-technical approach to problems of process control." In: DAVIS, Louis E.; TAYLOR, James C., eds. Design of jobs. Harmondsworth, Penguin Books, 1972, pp. 328-356.

Enrichir le travail humain dans les entreprises et les organisations. /Enriching work in enterprises and organisations./ Paris, Dunod, 1975.

"L'enrichissement des tâches et l'expérience Volvo." /Job enrichment and the experience at Volvo./ Monde du travail libre, (271), Jan. 1973, pp. 4-8.

"L'enrichissement des tâches est-il déjà démodé?" /Job enrichment, is it already out-dated?/ In: Harvard l'expansion, (1), Summer 1976, p. 93.

"L'enrichissement des tâches: motiver ou produire plus?" /Job enrichment: to motivate or to produce more?/ Entreprise, (1024), Apr. 1975, pp. 69-71.
Examines how labour conditions can be improved without deterioration of productivity. The author concludes that a wide area of choice must be left for the adoption of adequate solutions ranging from old to new production methods.

"L'enrichissement du potentiel humain - management horizon 80." /The enrichment of the human potential - management horizon 80./ Personnel, (160), May 1973. (Special issue.)
The prospective reflections of four enterprises presented during a Congress of the ICG - "Management 1980". The arrangement of hours of work, job enrichment, the creation of autonomous work groups were among the measures envisaged for the reinforcement of the social ethic and the economic success of the enterprise.

EPHLIN, Donald F.
"The union's role in job enrichment programs." In: INDUSTRIAL RELATIONS RESEARCH ASSOCIATION. Proceedings of the 26th Annual Winter Meeting, New York, 1973. Madison, Wisc., 1974, pp. 219-223.

"Les équipes autonomes d'entreprises et l'amélioration des conditions de travail." /Autonomous work group and improvements of labour conditions./ Travail et méthodes, (308), Dec. 1974, pp. 3-68.

ESPE, P.
"Abschied vom Fliessband?" /Goodbye to the assembly line?/ *Personalführung*, 6(9), 1973, pp. 207-210.

EUROPÄISCHER VERBAND FÜR PRODUCTIVITÄTSFÖRDERUNG.
Arbeitsmotivierung unf Partizipation; 11. Konferenz vom 9.-12. Mai 1972 in Stresa." /Work motivation and participation./ *Das Mitbestimmungsgespräch*, (6), 1972, pp. 100-101.

"European Commission proposals on the reform of the organisation of work." *European industrial relations review*, (30), June 1976, pp. 6-7.

*EUROPEAN COMMUNITIES. COMMISSION.
Report of the Conference on Work Organisation, Technical Development and Motivation of the Individual. Brussels, 1974. Conference on work organisation, technical progress and human motivation held on the 5-7th Nov. 1974 at Brussels. Contains reports of groups studies on work reorganisation and special seminars in the sectors of the car industry, manufacturing industry, metallurgy, services and automation.

EXECUTIVE STUDY CONFERENCE, Inc.
Job enrichment: theory and practice. Proceedings of the Executive Study Conference, April 28 and 29, 1970. (Copies available from John F. Bullard, Caterpiller Tractor Co., Peoria, Illinois.)

"Expériences de restructuration du travail dans une usine de construction électrique." /Experiments in the restructuring of work in an electrical construction factory./ *U.I.M.M. Documentation étrangère*, (336), Dec. 1976, p. 5.

"L'expérience de S.A.A.B., la chaîne condamnée." /Experience of S.A.A.B. An assembly-line condemned./ *Les informations*, 5 Mar. 1973, pp. 38-41.

"Expérimentations d'entreprises." /Experiments of enterprises./ *Dirigeant*, (63), Aug.-Sept. 1975, pp. 20-25.

"Experiments in job reform in Norway." *European industrial review*, (32), Aug. 1976, pp. 14-15.

FAIRFIELD, Roy, P., ed.
Humanizing the workplace. Buffalo, N. Y., Prometheus Books, /1974/. 265 p.

FAURE, C.
"Les unités de montage intégrées chez Olivetti." /Integrated assembly units (autonomous workgroups) at Olivetti./ *Production et gestion*, (285), Jul.-Aug. 1976, pp. 49-51.

*FAZAKERLEY, G.M.
"Group technology." Production engineer, Oct. 1974, pp. 383-386. Views group technology as a socio-technical system, considering both its benefits such as increased worker involvment and the reduction of frustration and monotony and its problems including resistance to change and problems encountered by foremen. Suggests that too much reliance should not be placed on the favourable first reactions of workers.

FEIN, Mitchell.
"Job enrichment: a revaluation." Sloan management review, Winter 1974, pp. 69-88.

FEIN, Mitchell.
"Job enrichment does not work." Atlanta economic review, Nov.-Dec. 1975, pp. 50-55.

FEIN, Mitchell.
"The myth of job enrichment." Humanist, Sept.-Oct. 1973, pp. 30-32.

FEIST, Rudolf. et al. (eds)
Wissenschaftliche Arbeitsorganisation. /Scientific organisation of work./ Grundsätze, Aussagen, Erfahrungen, Berlin, 1975.

FOEGEN, J. H.
"Reading at the work station: job enrichment." Training and development journal. 28(2), Feb. 1974, pp. 3-5.

FOLKER, D. A.
"Does the industrial engineer dehumanize jobs?" Personnel, 50(4), 1973, pp. 62-67.

FONDATION NATIONAL POUR L'ENSEIGNEMENT DE LA GESTION.
"L'amélioration des conditions de travail." /The improvement of conditions of work./ Enseignement et gestion, (10), Jan. 1975, pp. 41-52.
Considers new forms of work organisation and describes French experiments in the areas of the content of work and semi-autonomous work groups. The author looks breifly at certain theories of work organisation, considers the difficulties in evaluating the experiments and analyses some of the obstacles encountered during the experiments.

FONDATION NATIONALE POUR L'ENSEIGNEMENT DE LA GESTION.
Documents du colloque sur les nouvelles formes d'organisation du travail. /Documents of a symposium on new forms of work organisation./ Royaumont, 1974. (Roneogr.)

FONTIJNE, J.
"Experimente mit kleinen autonomen produktorientierten Gruppen." /Experiments with small autonomous production groups./ Mitteilungen. Institut für Angewandte Arbeitswissenschaft,(Köhn), (41), Sept. 1973, pp. 33-47.

FONTIJNE, J.
Neu-Gestaltung der Arbeit in einer Fernsehapparatefabrik von Philips. /New structuring of work in a television set factory at Philips./ IfaA, Rodenkirchen, 1973.

FORD, Robert N.
"Job enrichment lessons from AT&T." Harvard business review, 51(1), Jan.-Feb. 1973, pp. 96-106.
Discussion of an effort to redesign work undertaken by AT&T in the field of job enrichment.

FORD, Robert N.
"Motivating people." American Telephone and Telegraph Co. Bell telephone magazine, Jul.-Aug. 1968, pp. 4-9.

FORD, Robert N.
Motivation through work itself. A report. New York, American Management Association, 1969.
Description of studies performed by AT&T during the 1960's. Motivated by high annual turnover of personnel and lack of interest on the part of workers the efforts at improving work through job enrichment proved successful.

FORD, Robert N.; GILLETTE, Malcolm B.
A newer approach to job motivation: improving the work itself. /N.p./, American Telephone and Telegraph Company, 1965. 28 p. (Restricted.)

FORSBERG, L.; HANSSON, R.; PÅRSSON, J.
Försök med ändrad arbetsutformning och arbetsorganisation på en avdelning vid Perstorp AB. /Experiments with new forms of work organisation at PERSTORP./ Delrapport 2: Beskrivning av försöksförloppet. Stockholm 1974. 95 p.
(Nya former för de anställdas inflytande i företagen. 2. - PA-rådets rapport Nr 0064 74.)

FOULKES, Fred K.
Creating more meaningful work. /New York/, American Management Association, /1969/ 222 p.

FOY, N.
"Industrial democracy at Norsk Hydro." European business, (36), 1973.

FRANK, L.L.; HACKMAN, J.R.
"A failure of job enrichment: the case of the change that wasn't." Journal of applied behavioral science, (4), 1975, pp. 413-436.
Analysis of an unsuccessful job enrichment project, focusing on aspects of the implementation process that can cause a project to fail.

FRICKE, Werner.
Arbeitsorganisation und Qualifikation. /Work organisation and qualification./ Ein industrie-soziologischen Beitrag zur Humanisierung der Arbeit. Bonn, Verlag Neue Gesellschaft, 1975.
The study reviews existing data on the subject of the humanisation of work, considering especially its impact on the social aspects of the conditions of work which matter more than the technical aspects. In his analysis the author distinguishes between "static" propositions for improvements in working conditions (these concerned mainly with technological improvements) and dynamic ones (which concern themselves with professional qualification, work organisation, etc.).

*FRIEDMANN, Georges.
The anatomy of work. New York, The Free Press of Glencoe, 1961.
Chapters III and IV provide descriptions of (and commentaries on) early job enlargement experiments conducted in the U.S. and in Britain.

*FRIEDMANN, Georges.
"Towards job enlargement. A. American experiments. B. British investigations." In: The anatomy of work; the implications of specialization. London, Heinemann, 1956, pp. 40-67.

GABARRO, John; LORSCH, Jay W.
Northern Electric Company. /N.p./, Intercollegiate Case Clearing House, Harvard Business School, 1968. 14 p.

GAKKHAR, Subhash C.
"Organisation innovation with employee participation: case of Tiruchirapalli Heavy Boiler Plant of Bharat Heavy Electricals Ltd." To be published in National Labour Institute bulletin.
The author carried out an intensive study on the introduction of various innovations in the organisation over a period of 10 years, essentially on the philosophy of employee participation in resolving industrial disputes and differences. The innovation process was a comprehensive one including offices, shop floor and technological departments.

GAKKHAR, Subhash C.; NILAKANT, V.
"Post office reorganisation." National Labour Institute bulletin, (11), Nov. 1975, pp. 35-41.
A paper reporting the reorganisation of work system in a small post office in northern India. The reorganisation was based on a sociotechnical design and was implemented in participative design manner. The reorganisation consists of formation of semi-autonomous work groups to carry out a total task, such as Mail Despatch and Sub-Accounts Group, Reception/Enquiries Group, Delivery Group, Public Services Group, etc.

GALLIENNE, G.
"Une expérience d'enrichissement des tâches." /An experiment in job enrichment./ Pour, (47/48), March-Apr. 1976, p. 40.

GANGULI, T.
"Group participation as an effective technique to improve the industrial workers' attitude and morale: an experiment." Indian journal of psychology, 33, 1958, pp. 25-36.

GANNON, M.J.; POOLE, B.A.; PRANGLEY, R.E.
"Involuntary job rotation and work behavior." Personnel journal, 51(6), 1972, pp. 446-448.

GARDNER, Neely D.
Group leadership. Washington, National Training and Development Service Press, 1974. 41 p.

*GAUGLER, Edward; KOLB, Meimulf; LING, Bernard.
Humaniserung der Arbeitswelt und Produktivität. /Humanisation of work and productivity./ München, 1976.
A study conducted for the Bavarian Ministry of Labour and Social Affairs. Surveys relevant literature (more than 900 titles); analyses practical experiments, especially from the F.R. of Germany, and makes recommendations to the social partners, government and academics. Includes a lithography mainly of German literature in this field.

GENERAL FOODS COOPERATION.
Organization of a manufacturing plant to fit business and people's needs. Topeka, Kansas, Gaines Pet Foods. 1973.

"Germany's work humanization program aims at major advances in work reform." World of work report, May 1976, pp. 3-7.

GERSHENFELD, Walter J.
"Work enrichment and productivity bargaining: a critique of the issues." In: NEW YORK UNIVERSITY. CONFERENCE ON LABOR. Proceedings, No. 27. New York, M. Bender, 1975, pp. 289-306.

Gestaltung menschlicher Arbeit in der Daimler-Benz AG. /Humanised work design at Daimler-Benz./ Dokumentation über menschengerechte Arbeitsgestaltung in der Werken der Daimler-Benz AG. /N.p./, 1973.

GIBSON, Charles H.
"Volvo increases productivity through job enrichment." California management review, Summer, 1973, pp. 64-66.

GIFFORD, John B.
"Job enlargement." Personnel administration, Jan.-Feb. 1972, pp. 42-45.

GINNOLD, Richard E.
"Comment: urban-rural differences in job satisfaction." Industrial and labour relations review, Apr. 1976, pp. 420-422.

GINZBERG, E.
"Work structuring and manpower realities." In: DAVIS, Louis E.; CHERNS, Albert B. The quality of working life. New York, Free Press, 1975, T.1, pp. 368-377.

GIORDANO, J.L.; SUQUET, J.C.
Aide à la décision en matière d'organisation d'atelier: compromis entre les composantes humaines et économiques. Cas d'une chaîne. /Decision-aids for the organisation of plants: compromises between human and economic elements. The case of an assembly line./
Develops a methodology for interlinked decision-making. It is applied then to the reorganisation of an assembly line for workers in a big car factory.

GLASER, Edward M.
Improving the quality of worklife ... and in the process, improving productivity. Los Angeles, Human Interaction Research Institute, 1975.
An analysis of more than 25 cases of improvement of the quality of working life which involved the redesign of jobs or work systems.

GÖLTENBOTH, H.
"Praktische Arbeitsstrukturierung in einem Fotowerk." /Practical work structuring in a camera factory./ In: Arbeitsstrukturierung in der deutschen Metallindustrie. (3), Köln, IFAA, 1975.

GÖLTENBOTH, H.
"Vom Fliessband zur Gruppenarbeit." /From the assembly-line to group work./ REFA-Nachrichten, Heft. 5, 1975.

GOMEZ, Luis R.; MUSSIO, Stephen J.
"An application of job enrichment in a civil service setting: a demonstration study." Public personnel management, 4(1), Jan.-Feb. 1975, pp. 49-55.

GOODING, J.
The job-revolution, Walker and Company, New York, 1972.

GOTTSCHALL, D.; RÜSMANN, K.H.
"Job enrichment: the long road to utopia." Manager magazine, Dec. 1974, p. 193 et seq.

GRANDJEAN, E.
Die Bedeutung von Aufgabenerweiterung und Arbeitswechsel." /The significance of job enrichment and job rotation./ Industrielle Organisation, (43), 1974, pp. 9-14.

GRANEL, M.
Gruppenarbeit in der PKW-Motorenmontage. /Group production methods in automobile engine assembly./ Fachtagung Arbeitsgestaltung in der Produktion '76 des Instituts für Produktionstechnik und Automatisierung. /N.p./, IPA, 1976. (Vortrag, No. 10.)
Report on experiments with new forms of work organisation at Wolkswagen, Germany.

GRANEL, M., ed.
Vergleich von Arbeitsstrukturen. /Comparison or work structures./ Frankfurt, Rationalisierungs-Kuratorium der Deutschen Wirtschaft (RKW), 1976.

GRANSTEDT, I.; DOUARD, H.
"L'outil contre l'autogestion: de la chaîne au groupe autonome." /A measure against self-management: from the assembly to the autonomous work group./ Esprit, (7-8), Jul.-Aug. 1975.

*GREAT BRITAIN. DEPARTMENT OF EMPLOYMENT. WORK RESEARCH UNIT. Improving satisfaction at work by job redesign. London, H.M.S.O., /n.d./ (Its: Report, 1.)
A broad summary of developments in the theory and practice of methods to improve job satisfaction. It considers various aspects of job rotation, job enlargement and job enrichment and discusses the socio-technical systems approach to job redesign with particular attention to the Norwegian experience. Covers the problem of measuring the effectiveness of change programmes. 12 case studies in the UK, USA, Norway and Sweden are also presented.

*GREAT BRITAIN. DEPARTMENT OF EMPLOYMENT. WORK RESEARCH UNIT. Job satisfaction and job design; by Gilbert Jessup. London, H.M.S.O., /N.d./. (Its: Paper, 1.)
An introduction to the field of job satisfaction and current changes in attitudes and perceptions. Considers the functioning of autonomous work groups at Saab-Scania and of a job enrichment scheme at ICI. Outlines implications of change programmes and the sort of approach required.

*GREAT BRITAIN. DEPARTMENT OF EMPLOYMENT. WORK RESEARCH UNIT. Making work more satisfying. London, H.M.S.O., 1975.
Booklet published for the Tripartite Steering Group on Job Satisfaction. Outlines problems that can point to the need to redesign certain jobs and the benefits that can accrue both to employees and employers. What to go for in job redesign and what to avoid. Contains six case histories as examples of what can be achieved and shows need for cautious approach and full involvement of all concerned and their unions.

*GREAT BRITAIN. DEPARTMENT OF EMPLOYMENT. WORK RESEARCH UNIT. Work restructuring projects and experiments in the U.K. London, H.M.S.O., /N.d./. (Its: Report, 2.)
Gives details of 111 examples of work restructuring, describing reasons for change, techniques used and human and economic results of each, and analysing the examples, listing industrial classification, types of employees involved, reasons for introducing job restructuring and the results.

GREEN, R.G.; HEGLAND, D.E.
"Production engineer's dilemma; can mass-production survive job enrichment?" Automation (Cleveland), May 1975, pp. 74-80.
Article on strategies for alleviating the conflict between job enrichment and assembly-line work in the USA.

GREENBLATT, Alan D.
"Maximizing productivity through job enrichment." Personnel, 50(2), Mar.-Apr. 1973, pp. 31-44.

GRIEW, Stephen.
Job re-design. Paris, Organisation for Economic Co-operation and Development, 1964.

GROENEVELD, A.
Job enrichment; a case history. Den Haag, 1971.

GROTE, Richard C.
"Implementing job enrichment." California management review, 15(2), Fall 1972, pp. 16-22.

GROTHUS, H.
"Motivation durch Arbeitsbereicherung." /Motivation through job enrichment./ Industrial engineering, (2), 1972.

GROTHUS, H.
"Job enrichment: nur eine neue Masche?" /Job enrichment - just a fashion?/ Plus, (4), 1972.

GROTHUS INSTITUT FÜR SOZIOTECHNIK.
Motivierende Arbeitsgestaltung in der Praxis - menschengerecht und produktiv. /Motivating work design in practice - human and productive./ Gruppendynamisches Management-Seminar, Düsseldorf, 11. - 12. Dezember 1974. Dorsten, 1974. (Verfügbar bei: Bücherei und Archiv der Carl-Backhaus-Stiftung.)

GÜLDEN, Klaus; KRUTZ, Wolfgang; KRUTZ-AHLRING, Ingrid.
Humanisierung der Arbeit? Ansätze zur Veränderung von Form und Inhalt industrieller Arbeit. /Humanisation of work: proposals for the changing of the form and context of industrial work./ Berlin, Verlag Die Arbeitswelt, 1973. 141 p.
A theoretical evaluation of the propositions to changes of industrial work as a discussion basis for system-changing political trade union concerned group work.

GULOWSEN, Jon.
"Democratizing organizational design in industry: towards a socio-technical approach." Personnel review, 1973.

GULOWSEN, Jon.
Kriterier for autonomie o betingelser for selfstyrte arbeidsgrupper. /Criteria for autonomy and prerequisites for self-guided working groups./ Oslo, Arbeidsforskningsinstitute, 1968.

GULOWSEN, Jon.
" A measure of work-group autonomy." In: DAVIS, Louis E.; TAYLOR, James C., eds. Design of jobs. Harmondworth, Penguin Books, 1972, pp. 374-390.

GULOWSEN, Jon.
Selvstyrte arbeidsgrupper. /Selfmanaging work groups./ Oslo, Tanum, 1971.

*GUNZBERG, Doron, ed.
Bringing work to life: the Australian experience. Melbourne, Chesire in association with the Productivity Promotion Council of Australia, 1975. 195 p.
A collection of articles on various aspects of work organisation and job satisfaction. Includes discussions of alternative forms of work organisation, participative work design, semi-autonomous work groups and case studies of job enrichment and job redesign attempts.

GYLLENHAMMAR, P.G.
"Changing work organisation at Volvo." Industrial participation, (554), Spring 1974, pp. 5-10.
Conference paper on the accomplishments of the Volvo automobile industry firm in Sweden in providing a job enrichment programme covers work structuring and planning, employee motivation the importance of workers participation.

GYLLENHAMMAR, P.G.
"Participation at Volvo." Journal of general management, Summer 1974, pp. 34-47.
Discusses the policies introduced by the Volvo car plants in Sweden in the areas of job enrichment and worker participation, dealing in particular with environment, production-team organization and the new consultative procedures. Includes a description of the production and personnel systems of the new Kalmar and the modernized Skövde plants.

GYLLENHAMMAR, P.G.
"Volvo's project in human engineering." In: FORD, G.W., ed. Searchlight. Sydney, Wiley, 1973, pp. 75-81.

GYLLENHAMMAR, P.G.
"Volvo's solution to the blue collar blues." Business and society review innovation, Autumn 1973, pp. 50-53.

HACKMAN, J. Richard.
"Is job enrichment just a fad?" Harvard business review, 53, Sept.-Oct. 1975, pp. 129-138.

HACKMAN, J. Richard; OLDHAM, G.; JANSON, R., et al.
New strategy for job enrichment." California management review, 17(4), Summer 1975, pp. 57-71.
Article on job enrichment strategies in the USA.

HAIDER, M.; POPPER, L.
Arbeitsbeanspruchung im modernen Betrieb. Bericht ueber Untersuchungen bei taktgebundener u. freier Arbeit, 1958-1963. /Working stresses in the modern enterprise. Report on studies of work with imposed tempo and of work without such constraints./ Unter Mitarbeit v. E. Groll. Wien, Arbeitsgemeinschaft z. Studium d. Arbeitsbelastung, 1963.

HAMMOND, Brian.
"La chaîne condamnée, l'expérience de Saab." /The assembly line condemned, the Saab experience./ Les informations économie-actualité (Paris), (1451), Mar. 1973, pp. 38-41.
Before Volvo, Saab-Scania started experiments of new work organisation. Today the assembly line has gone after a 4½-year programme of experiments and reforms. It is followed by a general upgrading of responsibility.

HARMAN, Sidney.
"The transforming influence of a work quality programme." Advanced management journal, 41(1), Winter 1976.
Description of an experiment with work groups in a plant in Bolivar, Tenn., where teams of workers determine among themselves the distribution of work, work breaks, vacation schedules, etc. Joint meetings of the teams with management are held regularly to discuss work improvements. While the author feels that programmes of this nature could transform the American business system and enhance life outside the workplace, he notes that two conditions are essential to the success of such experiments. They are: the systematisation of the programme and the willingness to take risks.

HARTMANN, Karl.
Wissenschaftlich-technischer Fortschritt - Intensivierung - Initiative. /Scientific and technical progress - intensification - initiative./ Einheit (Berlin), 30(12), 1975, p. 1380.

HASSENKAMP, A.
Quality of working conditions, problems and approaches to a solution. Geneva, International Institute for Labour Studies, 1975. 13 p. (International Educational Materials Exchange.)
Paper on the improvement of the quality of working conditions through job restructuring, the introduction of flexible working hours and the amelioration of conditions of work.

HAUG, G.
"Fliessband Kontra Gruppenarbeit?" /Assembly-line versus group work./ REFA-Nachrichten, 26(6), 1973, pp. 399-401.

HAUG, H.
"Ansätze zur Arbeitsbereicherung durch Ausweitung der Gruppenarbeit." /Proposals for job enrichment by enlargement of group work./ Mitteilungen. Institut für Angewandte Arbeitswissenschaft. (Köln), (42), Sept. 1973, pp. 14-22.

HEDBERG, M.
Changes in work organisation; summary of trial activities in Sweden. Stockholm, Swedish Council for Personnel Administration, 1972.
A discussion of the preliminary research results of several on-going projects in workers' participation and job enrichment.

HEINER, Peter; MANN, Werner E.; MUTZ, Heinrich.
"Technisch-organisatorische Voraussetzungen zur Realisierung von Gruppenarbeit in der Produktion." /Technical-organisational conditions for the implementation of group work in production./ In: Arbeitsstrukturierung in der deutschen Mettallindustrie, Köln, 1975. IFAA, 1975.

HELFERT, M.
"Gesellschaftliche Bedingungen der Arbeit und Humanisierung der Arbeit setzt Demokratisierung voraus." /Social working conditions and humanisation of work presupposes democratisation./ Die Neue Gesellschaft, (4), 1974, p. 299 et seq.; (5), 1974, p. 391 et seq.

HEPWORTH, Andrew; OSBALDESTON, Michael.
The introduction of autonomous work groups in a small manufacturing company. Berhamsted, Ashridge Management Research Unit, 1975.

HEPWORTH, Andrew; OSBALDESTON, Michael.
Restructuring the motor insurance section, eastern zone. Berhamsted, Ashbridge Management Research Unit, 1975.

*HERBST, P.G.
Alternatives to hierarchies. Leiden, Martinus Mijhoff, 1976.
Discusses different approaches to development of alternatives to hierarchies types of organisation and suggests three types of non-hierarchic organisation; the composite autonomous group, the matrix group and the network group. He also discusses and evaluates diffusion strategies against the background of the Norwegian projects in this area.

HERBST, P.G.
Autonomous group functioning: an exploration in behaviour theory and measurement. London, Tavistock Publications, 1972. 271 p.
A quantitative case study technique is developed for the study of work group functioning. Based on a continuous 3-month record of activities and interactions, of a group of men in the coal mining industry. The men were given complete responsibility for the organization and performance of their task.

HERBST, P.G.
Demokratiseringsprosessen i arbeidslivet. /Democracy in working life./ Oslo Universitetsforlaget. 1971. 203 p.

HERMANN, C.
Organization development at Philips Radio A/S, Copenhagen. Copenhagen, 1973.

HERMANN, C.
Some experience gained with autonomous groups at Philips Radio A/S Copenhagen.
Copenhagen, 1973.

HERZBERG, Frederick.
"Job enrichment - Ogden style." In: UNITED STATES. DEPARTMENT OF COMMERCE. Productivity enhancement in logistical systems. 1975.

HERZBERG, Frederick.
"Job enrichment: sometimes it works." Wall Street journal, Dec. 1971.

HERZBERG, Frederick.
"Job enrichment's father admits: disparity between promise and reality." Industry week, Nov. 25 1975.

HERZBERG, Frederick.
"Making a job more than a job." Business week, Apr. 19, 1969, p. 88.

HERZBERG, Frederick.
"New approaches in management organization and job design." Industrial medicine and surgery, 31, 1962.

HERZBERG, Frederick.
"One more time: how do you motivate employees?" In: DAVIS, Louis E.; TAYLOR, James C., eds. Design of jobs. Harmondsworth, Penguin, 1972, p. 113 et seq.

HERZBERG, Frederick.
"Types of job enrichment." In: Proceedings of First International Congress of Labor and Psychology. Mexico, Asociación de Psicologos Industriales, 1976.

HERZBERG, Frederick; JO, Paul, W.J.; ROBERTSON, K.B.
Workshop structuring, a summary of experiments at Philips: 1963-1968. Eindhoven, Socio-economic Department, Personnel and Industrial Relations Division, N.V. Philips Gloeilampen Fabrieken, 1969.

*HERZBERG, Frederick; PAUL, William; ROBERTSON, Keith B.
"Job enrichment pays off." Harvard business review, Mar.-April 1969.

HERZBERG, Frederick; RAFKO, Edmund A.
"Efficiency in the military cutting costs within orthodox job enrichment." Personnel, Nov.-Dec. 1975.
Trying a package of modern organisational techniques, the Ogden Air Logistics Center (ALC) has adopted an effective programme of orthodox job enrichment in order to create an impact on areas of fragmented job and heavy workload requirements. Two task groups were organised: one for implementation, the other co-ordination. The data shows positive results.

HERZBERG, Frederick; WALTERS, Roy; GRIGALIUNAS, B.
Job enrichment; coordinator guide. Vols. I and II. Elk Grove Village, Ill. Advanced Systems, 1974.

HIERONYMUS, George H.
Job design: meeting the manpower challenge. Washington, Society for Personnel Administration, 1958.

HILL, P.
Towards a new philosophy of management. New York, Barnes and Noble, 1972.

*HILL, S.
"Norms, groups and power; the sociology of workplace industrial relations." British journal of industrial relations, 12(2), July 1974, pp. 213-235.
Article on labour relations at the enterprise level in the United Kingdom, covering shop-floor behaviour and action and the power of work groups.

HINSKEN, Hans-Georg.
Grenzen und Möglichkeiten der Selbstbestimmung am Arbeitsplatz. /Limits and possibilities of self-determination at the workplace./ Essen, 1975, 320 p. (Diplomarbeit.)

HINTZE, H.-U.
"Gestaltung der menschlichen Arbeit bei Daimler-Benz." /Design of human work at Daimler-Benz./ Mitteilungen. Institut für Angewandte Arbeitswissenschaft (Köln), (49), June 1974, pp. 1-38.

HOLDEN, J.
"Le Groupe ACEK." In: ORGANISATION FOR ECONOMIC CO-OPERATION AND DEVELOPMENT. Compte rendu de séminaire patronal international sur les progrès dans l'organisation du travail. /The ACEK group, report of an international employer seminar concerning progress in work organisation./ Paris. 1973, 14 p.

HOLLIER, D.
"Job enrichment at IBM." Business administration, Oct. 1974, pp. 37-39.

HOSTAGE, G.M.
"Quality control in a service business." Harvard business review, 53(4), Jul.-Aug. 1975, pp. 98-106.
Article on quality control in the hotel industry illustrated by a case study of job enrichment and management development programmes developed in a large hotel corporation in the USA.

HOYER, H.
Frühe sozialwissenschaftliche Ansätze zur Organisation der Industriearbeit in Gruppen. /Early sociological proposals for the organisation of industrial works in groups./ Hamburg, 1975. (Diplomarbeit.)

HOYOS, Liberto.
"Structure socio-technique de gestion par les équipes d'entreprise et les conseils de fonction à la Fonderie Leroy-Somer, Angoulème." /Socio-technical structure of the management by teams and production councils at the boundries of Leroy-Somer./ Bulletin d'information et de coordination du Comité Hyacinthe Dubreuil, (3), Mar. 1976.

HUBERT, J.
"Mise en pratique des équipes autonomes d'entreprise." /Putting autonomous work groups into effect./ Travail et méthodes, (308), Dec. 1974, pp. 11-20.

HUG, M.; DELILE, G.
Organiser le changement dans l'entreprise: une expérience à Electricité de France. /Organising changes in the enterprise: an experiment at French Electric./ Paris, Dunod, 1975.

HULIN, Charles L.; BLOOD, Milton R.
"Job enlargement, individual differences, and worker responses." Psychological bulletin, Jan. 1968, pp. 42-55.

Humanisierung der Arbeitswelt und menschengerechte Arbeitsgestaltung. /Humanisation of work and humanised work organisation./ Köln, Bund-Verlag, 1975.
(Arbeits- und betriebskundliche Reihe 32. Nachdruck aus dem Mitbestimmungsgespräch 5 bis 8/1974.)

Humanization of the workplace, the Swedish experience: proceedings of a seminar on the quality of working life, 8 October 1974. Los Angeles, Institute of Industrial Relations, University of California. /1974?/. 67 p.
Papers presented at a one-day seminar, sponsored by the Institute of Industrial Relations in cooperation with the Graduate School of Management, UCLA, and the Swedish Embassy, Washington, D.C.

IMBERMAN, A.A.
"Assembly line workers, humbug job enrichment." The personnel administrator, 18(2), Mar.-Apr. 1973, pp. 29-35.

Industrial democracy in state-owned companies: some issues. /Stockholm?/ Swedish Delegation for the State-owned Companies, 1970 (In Swedish.)

Initiative und ihre Leitung in der Wirtschaft. /Guiding initiatives in the economy./ Schriften zur sozialistischen Wirtschaftsführung. Berlin, DDR, Dietz Verl., 1975. 202 p.
Describes conditions and forms for the development of the creative initiatives of workers, which is seen as an important concern of socialist efficiency.

INSTITUT FÜR ANGEWANDTE ARBEITSWISSENSCHAFT, Köln.
Expériences de restructuration du travail chez Philips, Eindhoven. /Experiments with work restructuring at Philips, Eindhoven. Paris, Union des Industries Métallurgiques et Minières, 1974. 30 p.
Report on some experiments in the humanisation of work and improvement of job satisfaction in assembly-line work carried out by Philips' Gloeilampenfabrieken at Eindhoven. Covers employees' attitudes towards group work.

INSTITUT FÜR ANGEWANDTE ARBEITSWISSENSCHAFT, Köln.
Fortschrittliche Arbeitsgestaltung. /Progressive work design./ Report of a meeting of the Bavarian employers' association. (Munich, 1976.) (Its: Schriftenreihe Nr. 6.)

*INTERNATIONAL CENTRE FOR ADVANCED TECHNICAL AND VOCATIONAL TRAINING.
Final report on a study of the effects of group production methods on the humanisation of work. By J. Burbidge, Turin, 1975.
Surveys experiments in group production methods, analysing the different forms of reorganisation and considering the degree of job satisfaction achieved or claimed as a result. Information for the study was obtained with a questionnaire sent to over 800 companies and research institutes in 57 countries. In addition on-the-spot investigations of 54 companies in 11 countries were undertaken. Concludes that although the change to group production is a technological one, usually undertaken for economic reasons, there is some subjective evidence that workers prefer the resulting work organisation which allows for greater shopfloor participation.

INTERNATIONAL CENTRE FOR ADVANCED TECHNICAL AND VOCATIONAL TRAINING.
Study of the effects of group production methods on the humanisation of work; interim report. Turin, 1974. 1 v.
Progress report on a study of the effects of group work on the humanisation of work - includes an inventory of 388 group production methods in 32 different countries.

INTERNATIONAL CHRISTIAN UNION OF BUSINESS EXECUTIVES.
Quality of life in the business firm: a report on five experiments being carried out in four European countries. Brussels, 1974. 54 p.
A conference report on experiments in the humanisation of work (including job enrichment, assembly-line work and labour-relations experiments) in five enterprises in four Western European countries.

JACOBS, Carl D.
"Job enrichment of field technical representatives, Xerox Corporation." In: DAVIS, Louis E.; CHERNS, Albert B. The quality of working life. New York, The Free Press, 1975, T. 2, pp. 285-289.

JANSON, Robert H.
"Job design for quality." Personnel administrator, Oct. 1974, pp. 14-17.

JANSON, Robert H.
Job enrichment: challenge of the 70's." Training and development journal, June 1970, pp. 7-9.

JARDILLIER, P.
Organisation humaine du travail. /The humanised organisation of work./ Paris, Presses Universitaires de France, 1973. 122 p.

JENKINS, David.
"Beyond job enrichment: workplace democracy in Europe." Working papers for a new society, Winter 1975, pp. 51-57. (Coll. "Que sais-je?" No. 125.)

JENKINS, David, ed.
Job reform in Sweden: conclusions from five hundred shopfloor projects. Stockholm, Swedish Employers' Confederation, 1975. 130 p.
Seen as a "progress report" on the course of development in job reform, the book presents the conclusions of more than five hundred experimental projects introduced under everyday operating conditions in manufacturing industries in Sweden since 1969. Describes experiments in worker participation, autonomous work groups, job design, job rotation, job enlargement and enrichment, and discusses the factors leading to their success or failure. Attention is also drawn to innovations in supervisory roles and wage systems. Organizational innovations in seven new Swedish factories are also discussed. The authors recognise the value of the opinions and suggestions of lower level workers in these fields and conclude that workers can and should be given greater influence over matters directly concerning them.

"The job blues: who wants to work?" Newsweek, 81 (13), Mar. 1973, pp. 37-38, 40-43.
Discusses attempts being made by American managers to dispel the alienation, frustration and boredom of industrial workers by introducing job enrichment programmes designed to change the work situation and to give workers a sense of satisfaction and achievement. In view of the favourable results of many ongoing job enrichment programmes it is suggested that those methods will be used increasingly to combat worker alienation and the resultant problems of high turnover and absence rates, poor morale and low productivity.

"Job enlargement: the Saab-Scania experiment." European industrial relations review, (4), Apr. 1974, pp. 2-5.
Analysis of the experiment of work reorganisation in the Saab-Scania automobile factory based on a system of assembly groups.

"Job enrichment and the 'Volvo experiment'." Free labour world, Jan. 1973, pp. 4-7.

"Job enrichment at Eamshoeve." European industrial relations review, (23), Nov. 1975, pp. 14-17.
A socio-technical approach to job enrichment: job redesign in a textile factory in Netherlands.

"Job enrichment at Hoogovens." European industrial relations review, (19), Jul. 1975, pp. 20-22.
Characteristics of experiments of work reorganisation made in the most important metallurgical enterprise in Netherlands.

"Job enlargement at Ladybird." European industrial relations review, (22), Oct. 1975, pp. 9-13.

"Job enrichment at Télémecanique." European industrial relations review, (21), Sept. 1975, pp. 17-20.
Experiment of job enrichment at an electromechanic French enterprise.

"Job enrichment at the Eaton Corporation." European industrial relations review, (25), Jan. 1976, pp. 10-13.
The innovation in the field of work organisation introducted at the Eaton Corporation in the USA in order to reduce absenteeism, turnover and the workers alienation.

"Job enrichment at United Biscuits." European industrial relations review, (11), Nov. 1974, pp. 2-5.
Experiment of job enrichment in four enterprises of the "United Biscuit" in Great Britain.

"Job enrichment in Aer Lingus." European industrial relations review, (12), Dec. 1974, pp. 5-7.
Deals with the job enrichment experiment carried out by the Irish State Airlines.

"Job enrichment in France: a company study." European industrial relations review, (18), June 1975, pp. 5-8.
Experiment of job enrichment in the French company Guilliet which produces industrial machines.

"Job enrichment in General Foods USA." European industrial relations review, (11), Nov. 1974, pp. 16-18.
New work organisation systems in the company of "General Foods" of Topeka (USA).

"Job enrichment in IBM Berlin." European industrial relations review, (6), June 1974, pp. 3-5.
The recent work organisation based on a reduced assembly line in the establishment IBM of Berlin.

"Job enrichment in the Netherlands." European industrial relations review, (17), May 1975, pp. 8-9.
Attempts to improve the working conditions in Dutch enterprises. Different theoretical approaches and union and management attitudes.

"Job monotony becomes critical." Business Week, 9 Sept. 1972.

"Job redesign: some case histories." Manpower, May 1973, pp. 15-20.

"Job reform in France: the CIAPEM scheme." European industrial relations review, (33), Sept. 1976, pp. 9-11.

JOHANSSON, S-Å.B.; MARKING, C.
Utveckling av samarbets former för planering av produktionen vid AB Åkers Styckebruk. Delrapport 2: Beskrivning av försöksförloppet. /Development of forms of cooperation for production planning at AB Åkers Styckebruk; description of the experiment./ Stockholm, 1974. 253 p. (Nya former för de anställdas inflytande i företagen. 9. PA-rådets rapport nr 0071 75.)

JONSON, B.
Man at work: changing patterns in the quality of working life; some social, economic and technical implications: Volvo. /Stockholm?/ Volvo, /N.d./. 17 p. (Roneogr.)

JØRGENSEN, Sten Martini.
Kommunale samarbejdsudvalg. En undersøgelse af samarbejdet mellem ledelsen og de ansatte på 14 arbejdspladser under Københavns kommune. /Municipal joint committees. A study of cooperation between management and employees at 14 places of work under the Municipality of Copenhagen./ Copenhagen, 1971. 166 p. (Socialforskningsinstituttet. Publikation, No. 50.) (With an English summary.)

KAHN, R.L.
"The work module: a tonic for lunchpail lassitude." Psychology today, 6 (9), 1973, 35-39, 94-95.
The establishment of work modules -- "...a time-task unit -- the smallest allocation of time that is economically and psychologically meaningful" -- is suggested as a means of humanizing work.
The author feels that the establishment of a system of work modules would increase worker satisfaction "self-utilization (use of one's skills and abilities) and self-development (acquisition of new skills and abilities)" and would improve the fit between the individual and his job.

KANAWATY, G.
"Labour - management co-operation in work organisation: cases and issues." Management and productivity, (38), 1973, pp. 24-29.
Article describing a participative model of job enrichment illustrating an experimental application of joint consultation in the field of job design.

KAPLAN, H. Roy; TANSKY, Curt; BHOPINDER, S. Bolaria.
"Job enrichment." Personnel Journal, Oct. 1969.

KARLSSON, L.E.; SÖDERLUND, J.
Lägesrapport från Arvikaprojektet. Företagsdemokratidelegationen. /Partial report on the Arvika project: a case study of industrial democracy at the Swedish Tobacco plant./ Stockholm, Svenska Tobaks AB., 1971,

KERN, H., ed.
Neue Formen betrieblicher Arbeitsgestaltung. /New forms of work organisation in the enterprises./ Gottingen, Soziologisches Forschungsinstitut, 1975.
An analysis of experiments in Great Britain, Italy, Norway and Sweden.

KETCHURER, L.
"General Foods." In: ORGANISATION FOR ECONOMIC CO-OPERATION AND DEVELOPMENT. Compte-rendu du séminaire patronal international sur les progrès dans l'organisation du travail. /General Foods, report of an international employers seminar concerning progress in work organisations./ Paris, 1973, 11 p.

KHANDELWAL. G.K.; NILAKANT, V.
"Work re-organisation in State Bank: a preliminary report." National Labour Institute bulletin, 11(7), Jul. 1976, pp. 249-258.
The paper describes the re-organisation of work system in the Personal Banking Segment of a medium-sized branch of the State Bank of India. The genesis and the process of change have been documented. It is essentially a socio-technical approach to work system design based on participative design principles i.e. the design has been worked out by the employees themselves.

KHETAN, O.P.
"Workers' participation in management: a study of Rourkela Steel Plant." Indian manager, 11(9), Sept. 1972.

KILBRIDGE, Maurice D.
"Do they all want larger jobs? Supervisory management, Apr. 1961, pp. 25-28.

KING, Albert J.
"Management's ecstacy and disparity over job enrichment." Training and development journal, Mar. 1976, pp. 3-8.

KIRCHNER, J.H.
"Einige kritische Bemerkungen zur Teamarbeit." /Some critical comments on teamwork./ Fortschrittliche betriebsführung, 21(3), 1972, pp. 208-209.

KLEIN, Lisl.
New forms of work organisation. Cambridge, Mass., Cambridge University Press, 1976. 102 p.
This is a lucid and well-informed conspectus of developments in Europe, originally produced for the Kommission für wirtschaftlichen und sozialen Wandel, and for the Bundesministerium für Forschung und Technologie in Bonn. She discusses: the importance of work organisation; assumptions, values and responses in work organisation; new thinking in work organisation, e.g. organisational choice and industrial democracy; current developments in work organisation; and 'the next generation of issues'. A first appendix is from a critique by R.F. Hoxie of Taylor's approach - a critique first published in 1915. A second appendix contains "Some Policy Suggestions"; and there is a selected list of fifty-four references.

*KLEUSER, B.
"Mitarbeiter motivieren durch job-enrichment." [Motivating collaborators through job-enrichment.] Rationeller Handel, 16(3), 1973, p. 42 et seq.

KOBAYASHI, Shigeru.
"The creative organization; a Japanese experiment." Personnel, 47(6), 1970.

KOENIGSBERGER, R.; EDWARDS, G.A.B.
"Group technology, machine tools and the cell system." Journal of the Institution of Production Engineers, Jul.-Aug. 1973.

KOICHI, Yoshida
"Design of jobs as organization development." Labor relations study (Roum-kenkyu), Jan. 1973; Feb. 1973; Mar. 1973.

KOSTELEZKY, Helmut.
"Moderne Arbeitsgestaltung - Ein Rückblick auf 12 Jahre praktischer Anwendung von MTM." [Modern work organisation - a retrospective of the practical application of MTM.] In: Arbeitsstrukturierung in der deutschen Mettindustrie. Köln, IFAA, 1975.

KRAFT, W.P.
"Job enrichment for production typists; a case study." In: MAHER, J.R. New perspectives in job enrichment. New York, van Nostrand-Reinhold, 1971.

KREMEN, Bennett.
"Lordstown: searching for a better way of work." New York Times, S.9, 1973, Section 3, p. 1, 4.

KRIEG, W.
"Autonome Arbeitsgruppen - selbsterfahrene Montagestationen - erweiterter Computereinsatz im Werkstattbereich." /Autonomous work groups - autonomous assembly stations - enlarged computer use in the plant./ Industrielle Organisation, 44(1), 1975, pp. 3-8.
A report on experience at Volvo-Kalmar.

KROUPA, V.
"Směr inovace." /The direction of innovation./ Podniková organizace, 28(7), 1974, pp. 2-3.

KRUGMAN, Herbert E.
"Just like running your own store... use of job enlargement by a variety store chain." Personnel, Jul. 1957, pp. 46-50.

KUHS, William P.
"Let's talk about job enrichment." Bell Telephone magazine, May-June 1973, pp. 16-23.

*LADNER, O.
"Job enlargement im Bürobereich." /Job enlargement for office work./ Industrielle Organisation, 43(1), 1974, pp. 25-29.

LANDIER, H.; VIEUX, N.
Le travail posté en question. /Shift work challenged./ Paris, Cerf, 1976.
An economist and an industrial doctor analyse shift work and propose practical solutions to the problems it engenders.

LASHER, Harry J.; VERNEY, Glenn H.
"There is no humbug in job enrichment." Personnel administrator, Jul.-Aug. 1973, pp. 42, 44-47.

LASSERE, G.
"Le régime juridique du travail en équipe autonome." /Legal status of group work./ Droit social, (2), Feb. 1975, pp. 96-101.
Article commenting on the present legal status and possible future of group work in France from the viewpoint of labour relations and labour legislation.

LATTMANN, C.
Das norwegische Modell der selbstgesteuerten Arbeitsgruppe. /The Norwegian model of autonomous work groups./ Bern, 1972. (Betriebswirtschaftliche Mitteilungen, Band 56.)

LAWLER, Edward E. III.
"Job design and employee motivation." Personnel psychology, Winter 1969, pp. 426-435.

LAWLER, Edward E. III.
"Motivation and the design of jobs." ASTME vectors, Aug. 1968.

LAWLER, Edward E. III; HACKMAN, J.R.; KAUFMAN, S.
"Effects of job redesign: a field experiment." Journal of applied social psychology, 3(1), 1973, pp. 49-62.
Description of a job enrichment programme involving thirty-nine female employees of a telephone company. Although the changes made increased both variety and autonomy in the job, there were no changes in work motivation, job involvement or growth need satisfaction. There was instead a significant negative impact on interpersonal relationships, with older employees reporting less satisfaction in this area. Supervisors whose jobs were affected reported less job security and reduced interpersonal satisfaction.

LAWRENCE, Susanne.
"The team road to success." Personnel management, June 1974.

LEBELT, J.
"Aufgaben bei der Ausbildung der Lehrlinge in den sozialistischen Arbeitskollektiven." /Tasks of training apprentices in the socialist work collectives./ Berufsbildung, 28(10), Oct. 1974, pp. 449-452.
Article on problems of in-plant training of apprentices in group work in socialist collective enterprise in the German Democratic Republic.

LEFEBVRE, C.
"Restructuration des tâches et formation dans le secteur tertiaire." /Job redesigning and training in the services sector./ Education permanente, (32), Jan.-Feb. 1976, pp. 35-47.
Article on current trends and requirements with regard to training and job enrichment for office workers in service industries in France.

LEFEBVRE, H.
"La motivation des travailleurs." /Worker motivation./ Travail et méthodes, (301), May 1974, pp. 49-58.
Worker motivation with reference to Herzberg's theory and job enrichment.

LEFORT, Paul.
"Les nouvelles formules d'organisation du travail; l'apparence et réalité." /New forms of work organisation: appearance and reality./ Communisme, (Paris), Oct. 1973.

LEGENDRE, Michèle.
La restructuration des tâches en milieu administratif. /Job restructuring in administration./ Paris, 1975. (Paris. Université. Thèse.)

LEICH, D.N.
"Shell UK and the Shell Company of Australia." In: ORGANISATION FOR ECONOMIC CO-OPERATION AND DEVELOPMENT. Advances in work organisation; supplement to the final report of an International Management Seminar, Paris, Apr. 1973. Paris, 1974, p. 5 et seq.

LEVITAN, Sar A.
"Les limites à restructuration et à l'enrichissement des tâches." /The limitations of restructuring and job enrichment./ Problèmes économiques, 7 Nov. 1973.

LEVITAN, Sar A.; JOHNSTON, William B.
"Changes in work: more evolution then revolution." Manpower, Sept. 1973, pp. 3-7.

LEVITAN, Sar A.; JOHNSTON, William B.
"Job redesign, reform, enrichment: exploring the limitations." Vocational guidance quarterly, Nov. 1975, pp. 172-180.
Noting that interest in the quality of managerial professional and high-level sales jobs has more recently been extended to other white-collar workers, the authors consider some of the limitations on job reform. They also look into the question of whether wide spread job reform is either possible or necessary.

LEVITAN, Sar A.; JOHNSTON, William B.
"The limits of job reform." Dialogue, 7 (4), 1974, pp. 28-35.
Considers American experiments to improve working conditions. Feels that their number seems limited and diminishing because of the requirements of technology.

LIBERTINI, L.
"Nuove tendenze nell'organizzazione industriale." /New trends in industrial organisations./ Politica ed economia, 5, (2-3), Mar. 1974, pp. 43-49.
Reviews the main changes which have taken place in the organisation of work and production in the major Italian industries.

LINDESTAD, H.; KVIST, A.
Volkswagen report; a new payments system and new work organisation. Stockholm, Swedish Employers' Confederation, 1975. 56 p.
Report on a job enrichment experiment conducted in a Volkswagen repair shop in Sweden. It describes changes in work organisation and in the wage payment system, the introduction of team work and wage incentives, and examines the effect of the changes on productivity and labour turnover.

*LINDESTAD, H.; NORSTEDT, Jan-Peder.
Autonomous groups and payment by results. Stockholm, S.A.F., 1973.
The authors note that job security depends to some extent on a firm's ability to adapt to the changing demands of the market. They feel that group work provides greater scope for work variation and a greater sense of involvement than is the case with sharply demarcated individual assignments. Group norms and relations are also important to work motivation. Efficiency functioning groups may also be an important resource in adapting easily to change and may therefore safegurad job security

LINDHOLM, Rolf.
Advances in work organisation: four Swedish cases. Stockholm, Swedish Employers' Confederation, 1973.
Four case studies of development in factory organisation and assembly-line work and of innovations in production which resulted in the humanisation of work and in increased productivity.

LINDHOLM, Rolf.
"Neue Wege in der Arbeitsorganisation schwedischer Unternehmen." /New approaches to work organisation in Swedish enterprises./ *Mitteilungen. Institut für Angewandte Arbeitswissenschaft*, (Köln), (46), Apr. 1974, pp. 4-15.

LINDHOLM, Rolf; NORSTEDT, Jan-Peder.
The Volvo report. Stockholm, Swedish Employers' Confederation, 1975. 92 p.
A "progress report" on Volvo's multifaceted work reform efforts focussing on some of the new ideas put into action at ten of the company's plants. These include shop-floor participation, innovative job design, job rotation, decentralisation of responsibility, the creation of new technology and new plant design.

LINDNER, E.
"Plandzten zur Arbeitsstrukturierung in einen Büromaschinenwerk." /Indicators for the planning of work restructuring in a factory producing office machinery./ *In*: INSTITUT FÜR ANGEWANDTE ARBEITSWISSENSCHAFT, Köln, *Arbeitsstrukturierung in der deutschen Metallindustrie*. Köln, 1975.

LITTLE, Allen; WARR, Peter.
"Who's afraid of job enrichment?" Personnel management, Fall 1971, pp. 34-37.

LITTON, Walter, M.
Werken in groepsverband. /Working in teams./ Utrecht-Antwerpen, Het Spectrum, 1965. 281 p.

LIU, Michel; BECCUART, Georges.
Enrichissement des tâches et des rôles et actions de formation en situation de travail. /Job enrichment and the role of on-the-job training job activities./ Paris, Université de Paris, 1972. 1 v. (Thèse.)

LOBOS, J.
"Enriquecimento occupational." /Occupational enrichment./ Revista de administracão de empresas, 15(4), Jul.-Aug. 1975, pp. 35-41.
Article comprising a literature survey on the theory and practice of job enrichment including cost.

LÖHLEIN, G.
"Die Gruppe entscheidet." /The group decides./ Die Zeit, 12. Mar. 1974, p. 28.

LONDON, Manuel.
"Effects of shared information and participation on group process and outcome." Journal of applied psychology, 60, Oct. 1975, pp. 537-543.

LUCAS, A.
"L'amélioration des conditions de travail: justification, définition, illustration." /Improved working conditions: justification, definition and illustration./ Management France, (516), May-June 1975, pp. 21-34.
Achievements at the Renault Factory.

LUCAS, Yvette.
"L'automation au coeur de la révolution scientifique et technique." /Automation at the heart of the scientific and technological revolution./ Economie et politique, (211), Feb. 1972.

LUCAS, Yvette.
L'automation et les travailleurs industriels. /Automation and industrial workers./ /Paris?/ Centre Européen de Recherches et de Documentation en Science Sociales, 1975.

*LUPTON, Tom.
"Efficiency and the quality of worklife: the technology of reconciliation." Organizational dynamics, 4(2), Aut. 1975, pp. 68-80.
A joint attempt by social scientists and engineers to increase business efficiency and the quality of working life by designing a new manufacturing system. Six alternative production systems were proposed and their job characteristics were measured according to their variety, autonomy, responsibility, interaction and completeness of task. The system finally selected tried fairly successfully to balance automation with worker autonomy. However, while its goals included high volume output at low cost, safe and pleasant working conditions, job enlargement and enrichment and greater mechanisation, some jobs with a low quality of work life were, nevertheless, necessary.

LUTHANS, Fred; REIF, William E.
"Job enrichment: long on theory, short on practice." Organizational dynamics, Winter 1974, pp. 30-38.

*MACCOBY, Michael.
Changing work; The Bolivar Project: A report by the Harvard Project on Technology, work and character. Washington, /1975?/
An experiment with shop-floor democracy at an unionised plant of an automobile mirror factory in Bolivar (Tennessee). The employees and management of the plant introduced the experiment with the collaboration and active assistance of the United Automobile Workers of America, a Harvard University project team and a Norwegian specialist in the field - Dr. Einar Thorsrud. Over a one and a half year period the workers themselves developed work improvement techniques, job rotation, self-control and supervision and demanded that the experiment be diffused over the entire plant. The project also had an important effect on the union officials involved and on the middle management whose security appeared to be threatened by the changes.

MacCOWN, Steve.
"Job enrichment experiments in the Air Force Logistics Command." Journal for humanistic management, 2(1), 1974, pp. 72-74.

MacKENZIE, Eileen.
"Job redesign in an industrial democracy." Management review, Dec. 1971, pp. 32, 42-43.

MacKENZIE, Eileen.
"Employees redesign their jobs in Norway." International management, Aug. 1971, pp. 38-39.

MacSWEEN, Jim.
"Manpower, job enrichment, the work ethic and welfare reform." The labour gazette, 73(3), Mar. 1973, pp. 156-162.

McCULLOUGH, G.E.
"The effects of changes in organizational structure: demonstration projects in an oil refinery." In: DAVIS, Louis E.; CHERNS, Albert B., eds. The quality of working life. New York, The Free Press, 1975.

McNULTY, Louise A.
"Job enrichment: how to make it work." Supervisory management, Sept. 1973, pp. 7-15.

MAHER, J.R., ed.
New perspectives in job enrichment. New York, Van Nostrand-Reinhold, 1971. 226 p. (Frontiers in management series)
Chapters in the book describe in some detail successful job enrichment projects, mostly authored by individuals who were personally involved in the change activities. Includes bibliographies.

MAIWALD, Friedrich-Karl.
Humanisierung der Arbeitswelt. [Humanization of work.] Stuttgart, Landesvereinigung Baden-Württembergischer Arbeitgeberverbände, 1975.
Study on humanization of work experiments in five countries: France (CIAPEM at Lyon), Italy (FIAT at Torino, OLIVETTI at Ivrea and Scarmagno), Sweden (VOLVO), Netherlands (UNILEVER, PHILIPS), and Germany (BOSCH; DAIMLER-BENZ).

MAIWALDOVÁ, J.
"Interakěni ehování ělenů malé skupiny přířesení spolěcné experimentální úlohy." [The interaction behaviour of small group members in the solution of a common experimental task.] Psychologie v ekonomické praxi, (2), 1973, pp. 100-105.

MAMET, C.
"Les nouvelles formes d'organisation du travail." [New forms of work organisation.] Pour, (47-48), Mar.-Apr. 1976, p. 19.

MANCHEKAR, D.S.
"Workers' participation in management; a co-operative model." Labour chronicle, (Bombay), 5(3), Aug. 1972, pp. 13-14.

MANN, W.E.; SCHÄFER, D.; METZGER, H.
"Auf dem Weg zu neuen Arbeitsstrukturen." /On the way to new work structure./ Heft Stand, 9, 1976.

MAREK; LANGE; ENGLESTAD.
Wire Mill of the Christiana Spegerverk. Trondheim, Institute for Industrial Social Research, 1964.

MARGERISON, Charles J.
"Group development: a question of consulting strategy." Journal of European training, 3(3), 1974, pp. 247-261. The author notes that group work as a training method is becoming increasingly popular and describes in detail four such methods; namely: the technically centred, the person centred, the work-role centred and the attitude centered groups. Notes that each kind of group has a different objective and evokes different behaviour from the trainees. Discusses the widening of the role of the training executive beyond the confines of the traditional training course and his evolution into a resource person or process consultant.

MARGERISON, Charles J.
Managing effective work groups. London, McGraw-Hill, 1973. 88 p.
Management development textbook on the management of group work which examines managerial leadership and authority, motivation, decision making and behavioural factors.

MARGULIES, N.
"Organizational culture and psychological growth." Journal of applied behavioural science, 5 (4), 1969, pp. 491-508.
An experiment with four departments of Non-Linear Systems which explored the degree to which sociotechnical systems influence individual psychological growth. The experiment involved replacing assembly-line with small cohesive work groups in two of the four departments concerned. The other two departments functioned as control groups. The data, which were collected in a variety of ways, indicated that there was a positive relationship between value-orientation and self-actualisation and that higher self-actualising groups exhibit more awareness of the interconnectedness between task achievement and social needs satisfaction. Futhermore the behaviour of the more self-actualising groups is less determined by formal structures, role prescription or authority and that of self-actualising individuals is determined more by internalised values than formal authority or group ideology.

MEADOWS, Ian S.G.
Innovative work arrangements: a case study in job enrichment: Canadian Industries Limited - CIL - Paints Division, Vaughan Centre. Toronto, 1974. 16 p. (Ontario. Ministry of Labour. Research Branch. Employment information series, No. 8.)

MEADOWS, Ian S.G.
Innovative work arrangements; a case study in job enrichment: Miracle Food Mart-subsidiary of Steinberg's Limited-Personnel Services. Toronto, 1975. 16 p. (Ontario. Ministry of Labour. Research Branch. Employment information series, No. 14.)

MECOZZI, A.
"Le 'isole' e il resto." /The 'islands' and the rest./ I Consigli, (3), Feb.-Mar. 1974, pp. 14-15.
Report of the congress of FIAT delegates on work organisation held by FLM in Turin.

MEIGNANT, A.
"Formation et division du travail." /Training and the division of labour./ Education permanente, 26, Nov.-Dec. 1974, pp. 5-25.
An analysis of the relationship between job enrichment, training and humanisation of work in industrial undertakings in France.

MELANGE, D.
"La restructuration du travail." /Work restructuring./ Annales de sciences économiques appliquées, (4), 1974-1975, pp. 63-83.
Article on current trends in work study methods to bring about job enrichment of industrial tasks. Contains three case studies of changes in a textile industry plant in the UK, an office machine manufacturing plant in Italy and an electronics industry plant in Belgium. Examines theoretical concepts, the motivation of job satisfaction and the impact of greater decision-making authority on group work. (English abstract)

MEYER, H.O.
Erfahrungen bei der Einführung neuer Arbeitsformen in der Montage von Haushaltsgeräten. /Experience with the introduction of new forms of work organisation in the assembly of household appliances./ Fachtagung Arbeitsgestaltung in der Produktion '76 des Instituts für Produktionstechnik und Automatisierung. /N.p./, IPA, 1976. (Vortrag, No. 19.)

MEYER, H.O.
"Erfahrungen mit Gruppenmontage-Plätzen am Beispiel eines Elektrogerätewerkes." /Experience with group assembly workplaces: the example of an electrical appliance factory./ In: INSTITUT FÜR ANGEWANDTE ARBEITSWISSENSCHAFT, Köln. Arbeitsstrukturierung in der deutschen Metallindustrie. Köln, 1975, pp. 55-62.

MICHELI, S.; ROUVERY, L.
"Orientamenti per una strategia di cambiamento dell'organizzazione del lavoro." /Guidelines for a strategy of change in work organisation./ Impresa e società, 1 (8-9), Sept. 1975, pp. 3-11.
Discussion of the conceptual lines of development emerging from analysis of the situation in Italian undertakings where work organisation experiments have been carried out.

MILLAR, J.
"Motivatoral aspects of job enrichment." Management international review, 16(2), 1976, pp. 2-3, 37-46.
Reviews some developments in motivation theory and practice. The Maslow-Herzberg models are criticised and three new theories are discussed in the light of their advantages and weaknesses. The author concludes that until the present only very tentative alternatives to the Maslow-Herzberg models have been advanced.

MILLBANK. NATIONAL ECONOMIC DEVELOPMENT OFFICE. MECHANICAL ENGINEERING DEVELOPMENT COMMITTEE.
Why group technology? London, 1975.

MILLER, Eric J.
"Social factors in setting up a new works." In: ASSOCIATION OF BRITISH CHEMICAL MANUFACTURERS. Proceedings of Joint Conference on Human Factors and Productivity, Brighton, April 1964. London, 1964. pp. 15-35.
The case history of building a new steelworks is used to illustrate the applications of a conceptual framework (which advocates the analysis of the processes involved in setting up new institutions in terms of interacting systems of activity). If used in the planning stages, such a framework could reduce the unpredictability of institution-building.

MILLER, Eric J.
"Socio-technical systems in weaving, 1953-1970: a follow-up study." Human relations, 28(4), pp. 349-386.
A follow-up study of a 1953-54 experiment in work organisation (semi-autonomous groups) in automatic and non-automatic loom sheds of an Indian textile mill. Findings demonstrated that, while work organisation and levels of performance remained largely unchanged in the non-automatic loom shed, considerable regression had occurred in the automatic one. The author feels that the regression could be explained in terms of a failure to maintain the necessary boundary conditions for group working in the face of progressive technological and market changes and that the persistance of the group system in the non-automatic shed confirms the assumptions of Rice's original experiment.

MILLER, Eric J.
"Technology, territory and time." Human relations, 12(3), 1959, pp. 243-272.
A basic paper in socio-technical design describing the way in which, with the growth of an organisation, there is some differentiation in the organisation by the formation of sub-systems with discrete whole sub-tasks. This differentiation usually takes place along one or more of three dimensions: technology, territory and time. Roles and role relations cluster around these differentiated sub-tasks and the main managerial system task is to compensate for all these discontinuities by reintegration of the sub-systems.

MILLER, Thomas E.
"Building teamwork in organizations." Personnel administration, Sept.-Oct. 1972, pp. 37-45.
The author discusses teamwork which he describes as the successful union of people and purpose. He considers the barriers to teamwork, the need to improve our understanding of the dynamics of organisational life and the communication skills necessary to the successful application of teamwork.

MILLS, T.
"Human resources, why the new concern?" Harvard business review, 53(2), Mar.-Apr. 1975, pp. 120-134.
Article on humanization of work and job enrichment strategies for improving job satisfaction in the USA also contains definition of key terms.

MITCHELL, M.R.
"New forms of work organisation." Work study and management services, 19(11), Nov. 1975, pp. 402-407.
Discusses new forms of organisation of work in Sweden (job enlargement, production group etc.) their diffusion and their impact on the remunerative system. Considers also the significance of such experiments and their possibilites of development in Great Britain.

MONCZKA, Robert M.; REIF, William E.
"A contingency approach to job enrichment design." Human resource management, 12, Winter 1973, pp. 9-17.

MONNIN, Pierre.
Comment revaloriser le travail administratif. /How to upgrade administrative work./ Paris, Dunod 1975. 106 p.
Covers three aspects of the subject, viz
(a) A theoretical reflection on administrative work,
(b) An analysis of the possibilities and preconditions of autonomous work groups, and
(c) A comprehensive review of techniques for the measurement and the improvement of the efficiency of administrative work.

MONTIRONI, M.
"L'organizzazione del lavoro: esperienze di transformazione." /Work organisation: one experience of its transformation./ Il lavoratore elettrico, 25(5), June-Jul. 1975, pp. 12-14.
Analyses the Swedish experiments in work organisation with special reference to job rotation and job enrichment.

MONTIRONI, M.
"L'organizzazione del lavoro: un'esperienza concreta." /Work organisation: a concrete experiment./ Il lavoratore elettrico, 25(7), Sept. 1975, pp. 15-17.
Examines a concrete experiment of work restructuring in a clothing factory in the south of Italy.

MONTMOLLIN, M. de.
"Aspects de l'organisation du travail en Chine populaire." /Aspects of the organisation of work in the People's Republic of China./ Production et gestion, (281), Apr. 1976, pp. 16-37.

MONTMOLLIN, M. de.
"Organisation du travail en Chine populaire." /Work organisation in the People's Republic of China./ Personnel, (183), Nov.-Dec. 1975, pp. 31-38.
Industrial policies and work organisation in China with reference to enterprises of different size and location.

MOORS, S.; VANSINA, I.; VERBORGH, E.
Etude des groupes semi-autonomes dans une enterprise d'électronique. /Study of semi-autonomous groups in an electronical enterprise./ /Bruxelles?/ Office Belge pour l'Accroissement de la Productivité, 1976. (Also publ. in Dutch.)
Analyses the possibilities and difficulties of the transformation of assembly-line work to work in semi-autonomous groups. Concludes that the success of group work requires a realistic definition of the tasks of the group, the establishment of rules between management and the respective departments of the enterprise, and finally, creativity to achieve optimal work structures.

MOORS, S.; VANSINA, I.; VERBORGH, E.
Restructuration des tâches et machines automatiques de production. /Restructuring of tasks and automatic production machinery./ /Bruxelles?/ Office Belge pour l'Accroissement de la Productivité, 1976. (Also publ. in Dutch.)
Analysis of the introduction of group work in a electrotechnical enterprise. Fragmentation of tasks is replaced by the production of a semi-finished article.

MORALDO, H.
"Suède: où en est la démocratie dans l'entreprise." /Where do we stand with enterprise democracy in Sweden./ L'usine nouvelle, 21, May 1975, pp. 64-65.
Deals with the success of new work structures in Saab-Scania's Södertälje factory. All 4500 production workers should be organised in production and development groups by 1976 and the extension of the system also to the 2000 office workers is being studied.

MORSE, John J.
"Contingency look at job design." *California management review*, 16(1), Fall 1973, pp. 67-75.
Article on management techniques for job design, with particular reference to the elements of motivation and job satisfaction in the job enrichment approach.

MÜLLER-HAGEN, Dorothee.
"Arbeitsmotivierung und Partizipation." /Work motivation and participation./ *Das Mitbestimmungsgespräch*, (6), 1972, p. 100.

MUKHERJEE, P.K.
The effects of group production methods on humanisation of work. Paper presented at the Seminar on the Effects of Group Production Methods on the Humanisation of Work, July 1975. Turin, International Centre for Advanced Technical and Vocational Training, 1975.
This study is an extension of the classical work of A.K. Rice (of the Tavistock Institute, London) at Calico Mills, Ahmedabad. on the introduction of group methods of production following the socio-technical system concept. The paper describes the historical background of the experiment and spells out in detail the methods of introducing group systems and the advantages that can be obtained from doing so. Some economic advantages are shown by illustrative comparisons of various workers and their basic wages in the group system vis-a-vis the traditional system.

MUMFORD, E.
"Strategy for the redesign of work." *Personnel review*, 5(2), Spring 1976, pp. 33-39.
Article on a strategy for job enrichment based on diagnosis of workers' job satisfaction needs and problems.

MURRAY, H.
An introduction to socio-technical systems at the level of the primary work group. London, 1970.

MYERS, M. Scott.
"Every employee a manager." *California management review*, Spring, 1968, pp. 9-20.
A prelude to the book with the same title, this article presents a model for defining the characteristics of meaningful work and develops a framework through which employees can "manage their jobs".

MYERS, M. Scott.
Every employee a manager: more meaningful work through job enrichment. New York, McGraw-Hill, 1970. 233 p.
A book for laymen explaining how theories of human effectiveness can be translated into practical managerial styles and management systems geared towards the achievement of job satisfaction through job enrichment. This last is defined as a process for developing employees to think and behave like managers and as a process for redefining the job and the role of the job incumbent so as to make such development feasible. Techniques and examples of job enrichment are presented and the changing roles of management and the role of the personnel function are dealt with in this context.

NATIONAL PLANNING ASSOCIATION, Washington.
Upgrading low-level employment; a major national challenge. Washington, 1975. 23 p.
Pamphlet outlining employment policy goals, manpower planning objectives and job enrichment strategies with respect to low income and unskilled worker occupations in the USA.

NATIONAL TECHNICAL COMMITTEE, Budapest.
The adjustment of manpower to the new technology. Budapest, 1976.
The study presents the long-term predictions, calculations and conclusions of a number of experts regarding automation and manpower. It analyses the results of automation in Hungary from the technical point of view as well as the professional and moral attitudes of the workers involved and the effect on working conditions, production relations and structures. On this basis it traces the anticipated paths of technical development (easing of heavy manual work, emphases on certain branches of industry, etc.), the need to change the contents of trade training, social tasks resulting from women's entry to employment, creation of the conditions for permanent education, improvement of health and welfare facilities for workers (hospitals, holidays homes, etc.), leisure and culture in general and the high level organisation of leisure time.

NETHERLANDS INSTITUTE FOR EFFICIENCY.
Werkoverleg; rapport van de studiegroep werkoverleg. /Work consultation report of the study group work consultation./ Den Haag, 1972. 186 p. (Its: Publikatie 534.)

Neuerbewegung - Arbeiterinitiative zur sozialistischen Rationalisierung. /Innovators movement. The workers' initiative for socialist rationalisation./ Berlin, Staatsverl. der DDR, 1975. 330 p.
For more than three years the "regulations about the promotion of the activities of innovators and rationalisers in the innovative movement" has been successfully applied in practice. The book provides a summary of developments, tasks and the organisation of the innovators movement together with indications on the legal aspects of innovations.

"New work experiments in Swedish car industry are trade union initiatives." ICF bulletin, May-June 1972, pp. 40-42.

NIELSEN, P.W.
Developing effective worker participation. Amsterdam, Urwick International Ltd., 1975.

NILAKANT, V.
"Work redesign and work commitment." National Labour Institute bulletin, 1(9), Sept. 1975, pp. 9-13.
This paper tries to clarify certain issues discussed at the 4th Seminar of work redesign and work commitment at the National Labour Institute in July 1975. The different seminar groups redesigned the socio-technical system in a banking enterprise, a chemical processing enterprise, a mining enterprise, a machine tools enterprise and a drilling rig.

NOLEPA, Gerda; STEITZ, Lilo.
Wissenschaftlich-technischer Fortschritt - Arbeiterklasse - Schöpfertum. /Scientific and technical progress - working class creativity./ Berlin, Verl. Dietz, 1975. 185 p.
Determines the notion "creative content of work" as a process which strengthens the combination of mental and material activity of production workers. The characteristics of this process are work for the socialist community, collaboration in the tasks of socialist rationalisation and the various forms of the innovator movement in the socialist competition.

NOORDHOF, Dirk.
"Work structuring and consultation at Philips." Industrial participation, (555), Summer 1974.
Recognition of changing technological and social needs led to the introduction of work structuring and work consultation at Philips. An experiment with autonomous work groups, based on job rotation and longitudinal and vertical job enlargement was undertaken at Eindhoven and vertical job enlargement (delegation of responsibility, consultation, special training etc.) was introduced at Blackburn. The study demonstrates that the highest value was placed on greater freedom, increased involvement in company activities and greater possibilities for problem-solving.

NORSTEDT, J.P.
Work organisation and payment system at Orrefors Glasbruk. Stockholm, Swedish Employers Confederation, 1970. 21 p.
A report on an experiment in increasing productivity through the introduction of job enrichment and wage incentive schemes in a glass industry enterprise.

NORSTEDT, J.P.; AGUREN, S.
Saab-Scania report; experiment with modified work organizations and work forms; final report. Stockholm, Svenska Arbetsgivareföreningen, 1973. 50 p.
Final report on an experiment, conducted at the Saab-Scania factory in Södertälje, involving the reorganisation of the work environment to allow greater job satisfaction - describes the experimental elimination of assembly-line work and the formation of production groups.

"Nouvelle ligne de montage de camions Scania." /New assembly line for lorries at the Scania factory./ U.I.M.M. documentation étrangère, (331), p. 3.

"Les nouvelles formes d'organisation du travail." /New forms of work organisation./ Sociologie du travail, (1), Jan.-Mar. 1975, 115 p.

"Nouvelles formes d'organisation du travail et négociation." /Bargaining and new forms of work organisation./ Liaisons sociales, 9 June 1975.

NOVARA, Francesco.
"Job enrichment in the Olivetti Company." International labour review, 108(4), Oct. 1973, pp. 283-294.
The article discusses changes in work organisation undertaken by Olivetti under the pressure of technological, commercial, and social developments, within and outside the company, which could not be dealt with by conventional bureaucratic approaches. The author contends that the changes which were introduced have resulted in greater job satisfaction and interest on the part of the workers - a fact which is reflected in the reduction of absenteeism and reported nervous disorders - and a very much higher quality of work. He suggests that only a new form of organisation based on an open-minded, imaginative approach and new criteria with which to appreciate and fashion it, can hope to formulate an adequate response to social and technological pressures facing industry today.

NUTTALL, J.
"Job enrichment and organizational development." Occupational psychology, 46(2), 1972, pp. 105-110.

OATES, D.
"Team concept brings job satisfaction." International management, 28, Feb. 1973, pp. 33-36.

ÖDEGAARD, L.A.
Direct forms of workers' participation; new trends in organizational change and their implications. Paper prepared for an International Management Seminar on Workers' Participation convened by the OECD, Versailles, Mar. 1975.

OLDANI, B.
"Neue Lösungen der Arbeitsorganisation bei Landis und Gyr." /New solutions to work organisation at Landis and Gyr./ Mitteilungen. Institut für Angewandte Arbeitswissenschaft, (Köln), (56), May 1975, pp. 7-17.

OLSSON, A.
"Gruppstyrd arbetsplats i Norge." /Group managed working places in Norway./ Fabriksarbetaren, (Stockholm), (7), 1968, pp. 16-27.

OPITZ, S.H.; WIENDAHL, H.B.
"Group technology and manufacturing systems for small and medium quantity production." International journal for production research. 9, 1970, p. 181 et seq.

"Organisatieverandering." /Changes in the organisation./ Bedrijfskunde, 48(2), pp. 98-126.

ORGANISATION FOR ECONOMIC CO-OPERATION AND DEVELOPMENT.
Prospects for labour/management cooperation in the enterprise; final report of a regional Joint Seminar, Paris, Oct. 1972. Paris, 1974.

Organizzazione del lavoro in fabrica: ricerche e proposte innovativo. /Organisation of work in the factory: research and proposed innovations./ Rome, Arpes Spa, 1974.

"L'organizzazione del lavoro operaio in fabbrica." /Organisation of production work in the factory./ Quaderni di formazione ISFOL, (9), Nov. 1974, pp. 7-130.
State of art and trends in production work organisation in Italy. New forms of work organisation. Findings of a research study carried out by ARPES for the Ministry of Labour and Social Welfare.

ORTSMANN, Oscar.
"Le cas de la Shell anglaise." /The case of Shell in the United Kingdom./ Direction et gestion, Nov. 1973.

OSBALDESTON, M.D.
"Skandia insurance group; restructuring the work and enriching the job." Management international review, 16(2), 1976, pp. 1-2, 9-22.
Article on job enrichment in an insurance enterprise in Sweden. (Abstracts in French, English and German.)

O'TOOLE, James, et al.
"Pour une redéfinition des emplois." /Redesigning jobs./ Dialogue, 6(3), 1975, p. 16.

OWEN, T.B.
"Experiences of advances in work organisation." In: ORGANISATION FOR ECONOMIC CO-OPERATION AND DEVELOPMENT. Advances in work organisation; International Management Seminar, Paris, Apr. 1973. Paris, 1974, p. 19.

PALMER, D.
"Saab axes the assembly line." Financial times, 23 May 1972, p. 17.

PARKE, E.L.; TAUSKY, C.
"The mythology of job enrichment: self-actualisation revisited." Personnel, 53(5), Sept.-Oct. 1975, pp. 12-21.
The authors criticize the assumption that job enrichment provides the primary incentive for improvement of on-the-job performance, increasing productivity and decreasing absenteeism and turnover. They feel it is more plausible to argue that the desired employee behaviour is elicited by increased accountability and by rewarding job performance that meets expressed standards. Several studies are reviewed to demonstrate the fact that while more interesting work may be psychologically gratifying, workers still expect to be compensated for increased responsibility, discretion and complexity in their work.

PATINKA, Paul J.
"Productivity bargaining and job enrichment: what it takes to make it work." In: NEW YORK UNIVERSITY. INSTITUTE OF LABOR RELATIONS. Proceedings of the 27th Annual Conference on Labor, 1974. New York, M. Bender, 1975, pp. 307-323.

PAUL, William J.
"Des expériances vécues d'enrichissement des fonctions." /Experiences with job enrichment./ Direction et gestion, Sept. 1972.

PAUL, William J.; ROBERTSON, K.B.
L'enrichissement du travail. /Job enrichment./ Paris, Entreprise Moderne d'Edition, 1974. 120 p.

PAUL, William J., ROBERTSON, K.B.
Job enrichment and employee motivation. London, Gower Press, 1970. 119 p.

PAUL, William J.; ROBERTSON, K.B; HERZBERG, F.
"Job enrichment pays off." Harvard business review, 47, 1969, 61-78.
Description of five experimental case studies in a British chemical company (ICI). The experiments aimed at the achievement of economic improvement through job enrichment. The article deals with overall findings in the field of job enrichment, its feasibility and the consequences of the changes required. The authors conclude that job enrichment may be applied to a large number of jobs in spite of occasional obtacles and that if experiments are successful the gains are significant.

PAULING, T.P.
"Job enlargement; an experience at Philips Telecommunications of Australia, Ltd." Personnel practice bulletin, 24(3), Sept. 1968, pp. 194-196.

PAULING, T.P.
"Job enlargement in Australia; an experience with longer job cycles." Philips personnel management review, Apr. 1968, pp. 20-23.

PELISSIER, R.F.
"Successful experience with job design." Personnel administration, 28, 1965, pp. 12-16.
Brief descriptions of experiments conducted in three federal agencies.

PENZER, William N.
"After everyone's had his job enriched, then what?" Administrative management, Oct. 1973, pp. 20-22, 76, 78.

PENZER, William N.
"Job development works big in small companies." Personnel administrator, May-June 1973, pp. 34-37.

PERLAKI, I.
"Vliv struktury organizačních jednotek na jejich inovativnost." /The influence of the structure of organisational units on innovation./ Sociologický časopis, 10(1), 1974, pp. 56-67.

PERLAKI, I.
"Zvyšovanie socioekonomickej efektívnosti pracovných skupin socialistických organizácií." /The augmentation of the socio-economic effectiveness of work groups in Socialist organisation./ Československá psychologie, 19(3), 1975, pp. 249-253.

PETER, H.
"Designing human work: a new challenge." Work and people, 1(1), 1975, pp. 3-9.

PHILIPS A.G.
Autonomous group. Eindhoven, 1972. (Internal doc.)

PHILIPS A.G.
Workstructuring; a summary of experiments at Philips, 1963 to 1968. Eindhoven, 1968.

PHILIPS A.G.
Workstructuring; content and tasks. Eindhoven, 1972. (Internal doc.)

PIEROTH, Elmar.
"Von der Fliessbandmonotonie zum modernen Arbeitsplatz." /From the monotony of the assembly-line to the modern work place./ Berliner Rundschau, 29 Aug. 1974.

PIORE, M.
"Union rules and the changing character of work." Social policy, 4(1), Jul.-Aug. 1973, pp. 10-15.
Discusses the negative effects of some union rules on the diffusion of job enrichment in the USA. Includes some perceptions on the contractual level - for example the clauses referring to job security.

"Plant that 'doesn't need it' tries job enrichment." Industry week, 16 Jul. 1973, p. 52.

PLASHA, Frank.
"Job enrichment: evangelist or carpetbagger of the 70's?" Personnel administrator, Jul.-Aug. 1973, pp. 43, 48-51.

PODESCHWIK, K.
Arbeitsgestaltung in der Montage unter dem Aspekt der Höherqualifizierung. /Work design in assembly under the aspect of higher qualifications./ Fachtagung Arbeitsgestaltung in der Produktion '76 des Instituts für Produktionstechnik und Automatisierung. /N.p./, IPA, 1976. (Vortrag, No. 28.)

PONSIOEN, G.A.M.
"The workstructuring experiment." Part. I-II. Announcer, Mar. 1971, pp. 5-9; Apr. 1971, pp. 27-31.

POULSEN, K.
"Sadilin & Holmblad." In: ORGANISATION FOR ECONOMIC CO-OPERATION AND DEVELOPMENT. International Management Seminar, Paris, 3-6 Apr. 1973. Paris, 1974, 11 p.

"Pour développer l"expression des salaires: la réunion d'échange." /Self-expression for wage earners: meetings for exchange of views./ Entreprise et progrès, June 1976, 67 p.

POUSSET, André.
"Le groupe de travail; animation et participation." /The working group; activation and participation./ L'entreprise et l'homme, (5), May 1976, pp. 215-223.

POWERS, J.E.
"Job enrichment: how one company overcame the obstacles." Personnel, May-June 1972, pp. 18-22.
Describes a successful job enrichment project in the CRYOVAC Division of W.R. Grace Co.

PRELOVSKAIA, I.V.
Problemy ispol'zovaniia rabochei sily v usloviiakh nauchno-tekhnicheskoi revoliutsii. /Problems of technological change for the industrial workforce./ Moskva, Izdatel'stvo Ekonomika, 1973. 262 p.
A monograph outlining the implications of technological change for the industrial work force in the USSR. Covers job requirements and occuptional qualifications and retraining.

PRENTING, Theodore O.
"Job enrichment: how important is the work itself?" Michigan business review, 28(1), 1976, pp. 26-30.

PRESTAT, Claude.
"L'enrichissement des tâches et l'autogestion." /Job enrichment and self-management./ Entreprise, (1043), Sept. 1975, pp. 36-37.
The article defines the limits to Herzberg's theory. Despite the disputes and problems which may arise, the author notes the emergence of a new type of power, based on technical skills, management ability and the ability to arbitrate, which encourages initiative and discussion.

PRIDEAUX, Geoffrey.
"Job design using autonomous groups." Work and people, 1(2), Winter 1975, pp. 8-13.
The author suggests that semi-autonomous groups "offer a form of job design with a considerable contribution to employee satisfaction, industrial democracy and work performance". The groups are discussed in terms of their size, the characteristics of group members, the role of supervisors, group goals and adjustments to the wider system.

"Production: des groupes très autonomes." /Production: autonomous groups./ La technique, (10), Nov. 1976, pp. 16-19.

"Les projets danois de democratie économique." /Danish economic democracy projects./ Intersocial, 28, Fall 1975.

"Propositions d'aménagement du travail posté." /Proposals for shift work./ Bulletin d'informations sociales. (3), Sept. 1976, p. 274.

PROST, G.
Les équipes semi autonomes: une nouvelle organisation du travail. /Semi-autonomous groups: a new form of work organisation./ Paris, Ed. d'Organisation, 1976.

PROTT, Jürgen.
Industriearbeit bei betrieblichen Umstrukturierungen. /Industrial work under processes of plant restructuring./ Köln. n.d.
A survey of attitudes of workers regarding restructuring of industrial work processes, expecially rationalisation measures and the possibilities of co-determination works councils on such occasions.

PRUDKÝ, L.
"Některé sociologické souvislosti technologickych inovací." /Some sociological aspects of technological innovations./ Syntéza, 6(1), 1973, pp. 17-22.

Psycho-physiologische und ästhetische Grundlagen der Wissenschaftlichen Arbeitsorganisation. /Psycho-physiological and esthetic bases of the scientific work organisation./ Berlin, Die Wirtschaft, 1976.

PUTNEY, M.
"Work and enjoy it, Inc." The national observer, Mar. 17, 1973.
A broad, popular overview of a number of successful work redesign projects.

QUARTLY, C.I.
"Job rotation is more than musical chairs." Supervisory management, 18(2), 1973, pp. 21-26.

QUINAT, L.
"L'usine dernier cri." /The latest thing in factories./ La vie ouvrière, (1665), Jul. 1976, pp. 14-15. (L'usine VOLVO B.M.)

RACKEL, Klaus.
"Neue Arbeitsstrukturen in einem Werk für Gartengeräte." /New work structures in a factory for gardening tools./ In: INSTITUT FÜR ANGEWANDTE ARBEITSWISSENSCHAFT, Köln. Arbeitsstrukturierung in der deutschen Metallindustrie. Köln, 1975. pp.

RAMONDT, J.
Bedrijfsdemocratisering zonder arbeiders; een evaluatie van ervaringen met werkoverleg en werkstructurering. /Industrial democratization without workers; an evaluation of experiences with work consultation and work structuring./ Alphen aan de Rijn, Samsom, 1974. 230 p. (Thesis.)

RANDALL, Robert F.
"Job enrichment insures savings at Travelers." Management accounting, Jan. 1973, pp. 68-69.
Presents the results of a job enrichment programme undertaken by Travelers Insurance Companies (Hartford, Conn.). The organisation hoped to motivate employees by using simultaneously techniques of management by objectives from the top down and job enrichment from the bottom up. The author notes that annual savings based on productivity was $100,000 in a single unit.

"Rapport paritaire sur l'usine Volvo de Kalmar sans chaîne de montage." /Joint report on the Volvo Kalmar factory where the assembly line has been abolished./ U.I.M.M. documentation étrangère, (335), Nov. 1976, p. 4.

"Le rapport Wisner sur le travail posté propose de reduire au maximum le travail en équipe." /The Wisner report proposes reducing shift work to a minimum./ L'humanité, 17 Jul. 1976.

RASKO, A.
"Vynalezectvo a zlepsovatel'stvo v epoche vedeckotechnickej revolucie." /Invention and innovation in the epoch of the scientific-technical revolution./ Ekonomické rozhl'ady, 8(1-2), 1975, pp. 229-242.

RASMUS, J.
"Job control not job enrichment." Canadian dimension, Jul. 1974, pp. 23-30.

RATIONALISIERUNGS-KURATORIUM DER DEUTSCHEN WIRTSCHAFT (RKW).E.V.
Menchengerechte Arbeit - Erfahrungsaustausch zwichen Forchung und betrieblicher Praxis. /Humanised work - An exchange of experiences between researchers and practitioners in enterprises./ Frankfurt, 1976.
Conference report with a comprehensive section on cases of new forms of work organisation in various major enterprises in the Federal Republic of Germany.

RAUTAVAARA, A.
"Yritysdemokratia ja osittain itseohjautuvat työryhmät; företagsdemokrati och delvis självstyrande arbetsgrupper." /Industrial democracy and partly autonomous groups./ Puhelin, (6), 1972, pp. 15-17, 19.

"The redesign of jobs." Dialogue, 7(4), 1974, pp. 14-22.
Discusses the utility of autonomous work groups, professional education, attribution of responsibilities and participation in the enterprise management as means of eliminating, in the USA, workers' dissatisfaction due to the nature and the conditions of work.

"Réforme de l'entreprise: humaniser et responsabiliser." /Reforming the undertaking: more humanity and greater responsibility./ L'usine nouvelle, (17), Apr. 1976, p. 76.

REIF, William E.; LUTHANS, Fred.
"Does job enrichment really pay off?" California management review, 15(1), Fall 1972, pp. 30-38.

REIF, William E.; MONCZKA, Robert M.
"Job redesign: a contingency approach to implementation." Personnel, May-June 1974, pp. 18-28.

REIF, William E.; SCHODERBEK, Peter P.
"Job enlargement: antidote to apathy." Management personnel quarterly, Spring 1966, pp. 16-23.

REIF, William E.; TINNELL, Ronald C.
"A diagnostic approach to job enrichment." MSU business topics, Autumn 1973, pp. 29-37.

"Renewed interest in job enlargement." Administrative management, Apr. 1964, pp. 22-23.

"La restructuration des tâches." /Job restructuring./ Liaisons sociales, Oct. 1974.

"La restructuration des tâches dans le secteur tertiaire." /Job restructuring in the tertiary sector./ Liaisons sociales, (49), June 1975. 5 p.

"La restructuration des tâches dans le secteur tertiaire." /Job restructuring in the tertiary sector./ Panorama C.D.C., 1975, pp. 43-49.
An assessment of experiments with job enrichment in the tertiary sector.

"Revalorisation du travail manuel." /Improving the status of manual work./ L'ecole et la nation, May 1976.

RHYS, D.G.
"Employment, efficiency and labour relations in the motor industry." Industrial relations journal, 5(2), Summer 1974, pp. 4-24.
An examination of some factors that explain the poor labour-management relations record in the British motor industry including payment systems, conditions of work, degree of worker participation and general absence of job enrichment schemes of the Continental type. Suggests that there is room for improvement in all these areas and concludes that such improvement is a joint task for management and the unions.

RICE, A.K.
Productivity and social organization. The Ahmedabad experiment. London, Tavistock Publications, 1958. 298 p.
Describes experiments in social and technological change in an automatic weaving shed and in a group of non-automatic loom sheds in an Indian textile mill. Due to changes introduced in the weaving sheds, and in the environment itself, management had to face reorganization. The process and implications of organizational change is analysed and principles outlined.

RICKLEFS, Roger.
"Variety is the spice of work." Supervisory management, Dec. 1972, pp. 24-27. (Condensed from Wall street journal, Aug. 21, 1972.)

"Riprogettazione partecipativa presso le acciaierie di Piombino." /Workers' participation in redesigning the Piombino steelworks./ Sociologia dell organizzazione, 2(4), Jul.-Dec. 1974, pp. 283-320.
Considers a last check on a methodology under which workers are to participate in designing installations to meet their own requirements. Technology is seen as a dependent variable.

ROBERTS, C.; WEDDERBURN, D.
ICI and the unions. The place of job enrichment in the weekly staff agreement. London, 1974.

ROBINSON, John F.
"Job enrichment; the supervisor." Supervision, May 1973, p. 32.

ROEBER, J.
Social change at work: the I.C.I. weekly staff agreement, London, Duckworth, 1975.

ROUSSEL.
"Parcellisation et enrichissement des tâches." Management. /Job fragmentation and enrichment./ (Paris), July 1973.

*ROY, W. WALTERS AND ASSOCIATES, Glen Rock, N.J.
Job enrichment for results: strategies for successful implementation. Reading, Mass., Addison-Wesley Pub., 1975. xi. 307 p.
Monograph on the successful implementation of job enrichment programmes. Covers the problems of motivation, job design, the middle management orientation session and the role of the supervisor. Includes case histories and models of organisational change and development.

RUEHL, G.
"Work structuring." I-II. Industrial engineering, Jan. 1974, pp. 32-37; Feb. 1974, pp. 52-56.

*RUSH, Harold M.F.
Job design for motivation; experiments in job enlargement and job enrichment. New York, 1971. 83 p. (Conference Board. Report, No. 515.)
Review of the theory, strategy and tactics of job design, including case descriptions of seven successful job design projects.

SAINSAULIEU, R.
"L'élargissement des tâches et quelques problèmes de fonctionnement humain de l'organisation." /Job enrichment and some problems of human functioning of the undertaking./ Etude du travail, July 1966.

SALPUKAS, A.
"Plant is experimenting with changing work on line." New York times, Apr. 9, 1975, p. 24.
An early report of the experiment at Harmon International in Bolivar, Tenn. which emphasises the union-management collaboration in the project.

SALPUKAS, A.
"Series on work reform." New York times, Nov. 11-12 and 13, 1974.
Review and analysis of reform activities, with special reference to the Scandinavian experiments.

SANDERS, Rick.
"Job enrichment; one route to improved performance." Canadian training methods, Nov.-Dec. 1970, pp. 14-15.

SARAN, G.
"Work redesign approach for productivity services functions." Industrial engineering news, 4(11), Nov. 1975.
The paper touches upon the prevailing status of the human factors in India in general and the public sector in particular and presents a concept for re-organising the Industrial Engineering/ Productivity services function for obtaining better results. Subsequently it presents a case study on the reorganisation of the Industrial Engineering/Productivity Services activity of Bharat Heavy Electricals Ltd., Hardwar (public sector).

SAUSSOIS, J.M.
"Réalisations actuelles en matière d'enrichissement du travail." /Current achievements in job enrichment./ Hommes et techniques, 31(374), Dec. 1975, pp. 746-755.
Article on job enrichment experiences in France.

SAVALL, H.
Enrichir le travail humain dans les entreprises et organisations. /Enriching human work in undertakings and organisations./ Paris, Dunod, 1975. xxii, 213 p.
Monograph on the current trends in the humanisation of work in France. Includes a discussion of job enrichment experiments, continuing education, workers' participation and labour relations problems. Also considers the economic implications and sociological and psychological aspects of the organisation of work.

SAYLES, Leonard R.
"Job enrichment: little that's new, and right for the wrong reasons." *In*: INDUSTRIAL RELATIONS RESEARCH ASSOCIATION. *Proceedings of the 26th Annual Winter Meeting, New York, 1973*. Madison, Wis., 1974, pp. 201-209.

SCHAPPE, R.H.
"Twenty-two arguments against job enrichment." *Personnel journal*, 53(2), Feb. 1974, pp. 116-123.
Analyses the best known and most frequent arguments of managers and workers on the subject of job enrichment as a means of promoting a better understanding of the concept.

SCHARMANN, T.
Teammarbeit in der Unternehmung. Theorie und Praxis der Gruppenarbeit. /Team-work in the enterprise. Theory and practice of group work./ Bern, 1972.

SCHEIPS, Charles D.
"The humanisation of work." *Personnel*, Sept.-Oct. 1972, 49, pp. 38-44.
The author feels that industrial engineers, together with the management, have dehumanised jobs to the point of alienating the worker and making him a "combatant against management, rather than a willing contributor to organisational goals". He suggests possible ways of reversing this trend.

*SCHLAFFKE, W.; RUEHL, G.; WEIL, R.
Qualität des Lebens am Arbeitsplatz. /The quality of life at the workplace./ Köln, Deutschen Instituts-Verlag, 1974. 131 p.
Compilation of conference papers on the humanisation of work and the work environment with particular reference to the Federal Republic of Germany. The book covers such subjects as work organisation, job enrichment, working groups, motivation and satisfaction.

SCHODERBEK, Peter P.
"Use of job enlargement in industry." Personnel journal, Nov. 1968, pp. 796-801.

SCHODERBEK, Peter P.; REIF, William E.
Job enlargement: key to improved performance. Ann Arbor, Bureau of Industrial Relations, University of Michigan, 1969. 113 p.
"The purpose of job enlargement is to eliminate the undesirable characteristics of the highly repetitive, specialized job by enlarging it to include: (1) a greater variety of knowledge and skill, (2) a more complete utilization of the important cognitive and motor abilities possessed by the worker, and (3) more freedom and responsibility in the performance of the task at hand."

SCHRANK, Robert.
"Work in America: what do workers really want?" Industrial relations, 13(2), May 1974, pp. 124-129.
Discusses the present position of thinking on job enrichment in assembly line work and other aspects of the humanisation of work in the USA.

SCHREIBER, K.H.; ZIPPE, B.H.
Systematische Zusammenstellung von in- und ausländischen Beispielen zur Verbesserung industrieller Arbeits- und Organisationsformen. /A systematic survey of domestic and foreign examples of the improvement of industrial work and organisation approaches./ Stuttgart, Institut für Produktionstechnik und Automatisierung (IPA) der Fraunhofer-Gesellschaft. e.V., 1976 (Unveröffentlichte Studie.)

Schriftenreihe: Arbeitsstudium - Arbeitsgestaltung - Arbeitsnormung. /Series: Work study - Work design - Work norms./ Berlin, Kammer der Technik, 1965-1966.
Topics covered included: Investigations of work studies to acquire knowledge and data regarding the circumstances and factors influencing meaningful interaction between workers and means of production: implementation of scientific work organisation; work design as seen by the engineer including methods for the implementation of socialist rationalisation measures to achieve maximum usage of existing machines and installations; technological processes and production techniques; organisation of production and working methods; work norms, including content, object and tasks of qualitative work evaluation, work norms and their role etc.

SCHUSTER, K.
"Lebensqualität und Arbeitsplatzgestaltung im Büro." /Quality of life and work place design in the office./ Personal, 23(3), 1975, pp. 110-113.

"Searching for a better way to work." Saddleman's review, 19(2), Summer 1975, pp. 3-7.

SEASHORE, Stanley E.; MARROW, A.J.; BOWERS, D.G.
Management by participation. New York, Harper and Row, 1967.

SELVIK, Arne.
Bedriftsdemokrati som kriseadferd; case-studie. /Enterprise democracy a means for the avoidance of crisis; a case study./ Bergen, Universitetet i Bergen, Sosiologisk Institutt, 1973. 3, 31 p.

SHEPARD, J.M.
"Job enrichment: problems with contingency models." Personnel journal, Dec. 1974, pp. 886-889.

SHEPARD, J.M.
On loving the one you're with; an agenda for job enrichment research. Springfield, National Technical Information Service, 1971. 34 p.
Technical report giving suggestions for job enrichment research. Includes a literature survey and suggests extension of the motivational theory of job enrichment of all employees.

SHEPPARD, Harold L.
"Job redesign, new careers, and public service employment." General government, Fall, 1970, pp. 1-7.
The author feels that job redesign and new career programs benefit those who need the training and also offer public and private agencies new sources of manpower. He points out the benefits of job redesign of professionals and other employees and suggests ways to restructive jobs.

SHEPPARD, Harold L.
"Tasks enrichment and wage levels as elements in worker attitudes." Journal of management studies, 13(1), Feb. 1976, pp. 49-61.
Conference paper on a survey undertaken in the USA to analyse the importance of job enrichment and wage increases in determining job satisfaction levels of manual workers.

*SHIMMIN, Sylvia.
"After the assembly line." Personnel management, 6, Aug. 1974, pp. 35-37.
Final article in a series concerned with the quality of work life.

SIMMONDS, R.H.; ORIFE, J.N.
"Worker behavior versus enrichment theory." Administrative science quarterly, 20(4), Dec. 1975, pp. 606-612.
The results of a survey in the USA showing that workers feel that interesting work is less important than wages.

SINGER, Jack N.
"Participative decision-making about work: an overdue look at variables which mediate its effects." Sociology of work and occupations, 1, Nov. 1974, pp. 347-371.

SIROTA, David.
"L'enrichissement des tâches: une autre marotte des dirigeants?" /Job enrichment-another managerial whim?/ Journal des associations patronales, 70(1-2), Jan. 1975, pp. 15-19.
An article on the motivational aspects of, and the limitations to, job enrichment.

SIROTA, David.
"Job enrichment: is it for real?" S.A.M. advanced management journal, Apr. 1973, pp. 22-27.

SIROTA, David.
"Production and service personnel and job enrichment." Work study, 22(1), Jan. 1973, pp. 9-15.
Uses the successful introduction of a job enrichment programme in a specific company to illustrate the contention that job enrichment will have a lasting impact on mangement practices only if it is applied to correct the problem of the under-utilisation of workers' skills and abilities. Contends that the increased output, improved quality and more positive employee attitudes which resulted from that programme were due to this factor.

SIROTA, David; WOLFSON, Alan D.
"Job enrichment." Personnel, May-June. 1972, pp. 8-17; Jul.-Aug. 1972, pp. 8-19.
Two articles in which the author discusses, first the obstacles to the implementation of job enrichment programmes and then the ways in which these obstacles might be surmounted. Eleven basic categories of obstacles are listed and analysed, including managerial (resistance to change); educational (practical obstacles to the implementation of programmes), ideological technological etc. Overcoming obstacles involved the location of problems, training for managers in new methods, a larger number of people trained to introduce job enrichment, the awareness of limitations, flexibility etc. Four illustrative case studies are presented with their respective results.

SKARD, Øyvind.
"Industrial democrats in Norway." Journal of general management, Summer 1974, pp. 70-73.
A review of Norwegian experiments with autonomous work groups which discusses the difficulties involved in the operationalization of the concept. It considers also the function and possible influence on industrial relations of the recently introduced "corporate assemblies" which allow for worker participation through the election of one-third of their members by and from worker ranks.

SKARD, Øyvind.
Organisational change and job design. /Oslo?/ Cooperation Council of LO-N.A.F., 1976.

SMITH, Howard R.
"The half-loaf of job enrichment." Personnel, Mar.-Apr. 1976, pp. 24-31.

SMRČKA, J.
"Role vedoucích pracovníků při řízení inovací." /The role of management in the direction of innovations./ Moderní řízení, 10(12), 1972, pp. 14-18.

Social ownership and the socialist enterprise; the socialist enterprise I. Budapest, Academy Publishing House, 1975.
The volume is the first of a five-part series containing the papers presented on the general research topic "The socialist enterprise" at the anniversary session in the Karl Marx University of Economics. The papers in this volume are grouped around the following three main topics: (i) Social ownership and workplace democracy; (ii) The socialist enterprise in the system of social ownership relations; (iii) Socialist emulation and questions of enterprise structure.

SOCIETE D'ETUDES POUR LE DEVELOPPEMENT ECONOMIQUE ET SOCIAL, Paris.
La restructuration des tâches dans le secteur tertiere. /Job restructuring in the territory sector./ Paris, 1974. 158 p.

SOZIOLOGISCHES FORSCHUNGSINSTITUT, Göttingen.
Neue Formen betrieblicher Arbeitsgestaltung. /New forms of work organisation in the plant./ Göttingen, 1975. Forschungsbericht. /Research report./

Sozialistische Arbeitswissenschaft: Theoretische Zeitschrift für arbeitswissenschaftliche Disziplinen. /Socialist labour sciences: theoretical journal for labour science disciplines./ Berlin; Verl. Die Wirtschaft, 1969.
This journal deals with the following problems:
- Study of economic laws and their requirements regarding work for society and productive human potential in Socialism.
- Formation and emergence of the new character of societal work and relations resulting from the work process from the interaction between man and material-technical production factors and the whole societal development.
- Scientific generalisation of experiences of economic policies especially in the field of social work organisation.
- Labour economic research and practice.

SOTNIKOFF, C.
"Enrichissement des fonctions et formation." /Job enrichment and training./ Entreprises et formation continue, (5), May-June 1973.

SOUJANEN, W. William.
A case study of the longitudinal effects of a job enrichment program. Cambridge, Mass., Sloan School of Management, 1974. (Thesis)

SPINDLER, Gert P.
Neue unternehmensführung in der industriellen Gesellschaft, Problematik - Weg - Praxis. /New enterprise management in industrial society, problems - solutions - practice./ Hilden, 1958.

SPOONER, P.
"Job enrichment at Olivetti." Business administration, Apr. 1975, pp. 25-27.

*SRIVASTAVA, Bhupendra K.
Conditions and organisations of work; paper prep. for the National Seminar on Quality of Working Life. Bombay, Central Labour Institute, 1975.
This paper emphasises the need to redesign work systems in India based on reviews of numerous literatures in this field. The author considers the existing work organisations and the need for changing the socio-cultural conditions. The rationale for alternative work conditions is also presented. Finally he presents a brief description redesigning the work systems in a fabrication shop of a heavy industry plant.

SRIVASTAVA, Bhupendra K.
"Towards a participative system design: the case of National Labour Institute." National Labour Institute bulletin, 1(7), July 1975, pp. 21-27.
One of the basic objectives of this Institute has been to work towards creating a work culture by generating commitment to work among employees of the organised sectors through action research and through programmes of continuing education. This paper describes an attempt made at the Institute to evolve a participative system, with emphasis on semi-autonomous work groups, at the Institute. The rationale for the design, the emergence and an impressionistic assessment of the design are provided.

STAUDACHER, F.
Die Informationspolitik. Ein Instrument betrieblicher Personalpolitik. /Information policy. An instrument of personnel policy in enterprises./ (Diss.) München, 1967.

STEPHENS, Leslie.
"A case for job enlargement." Personnel management, Sept. 1963, pp. 102-106.

STEWART, Paul A.
Job enlargement: in the shop, in the management function. Iowa City, 1967. 64 p. (Iowa University, Center for Labor and Management. Monograph, No. 3.)

STIRN, Hans.
"Arbeiten in kleinen Gruppen." /Working in small groups./ Arbeit und Leistung, (3), 1973, p. 74.

STRASSBURGER, J.
"Wissenschaftliche Arbeitsorganisation in der DDR - II." /Scientific work organisation in the German Democratic Republic./ Deutschland Archiv, 8(6), June 1975, pp. 611-637.
Production and work in the enterprises of the DDR have to take into account scientific work organisation. This implies perfectioning of methods and working conditions, improvement of the task structuration etc.

STRAUSS, George.
Job satisfaction, motivation, and job redesign. Berkeley, Calif., Institute of Industrial Relations, University of California, 1974. (California University. Institute of Industrial Relations. Reprint No. 390.)

STRENDER, B.
"Neue Formen der Arbeitsorganisation." /New forms of work organisation./ REFA-Nachrichten, 29(5), Oct. 1976.
Review of experiments of new work organisation in about 1000 enterprises during the last 5 years. Analyses expectations and results of these experiments. Concludes that better collaboration cannot be imposed and that therefore work studies are absolutely necessary to create efficient new working structures.

SUESSMUTH, Patrick.
"Three case studies in the job enrichment area." Canadian training methods, 6(3), Oct. 1973, pp. 18-22.

SUSMAN, Gerald I.
Autonomy at work: a sociotechnical analysis of participative management. New York, Praeger, 1976.

SUSMAN, Gerald I.
"The concept of status congruence as a basis to predict task allocations in autonomous work groups." Administrative science quarterly, 15, 1970, pp. 164-175.
A study of the effects of the allocation of workers to two task levels within independent work groups by group members themselves. For the higher position there was a positive correlation between competence and the allocation of tasks on the basis of perceived competence but for the lower position the correlation was negative. The author suggests that differentiated formal positions within independent work groups may reduce motivation and performance, as well as opportunities for learning, thereby reducing potential group resources.

SUSMAN, Gerald I.
"The impact of automation on work group autonomy and task specialisation." Human relations, 23, 1970, pp. 567-577.
Results of a study of thirteen, three-man work groups in a continuous process oil refinery demonstrating that in a highly automated industrial setting work groups, that are not restrained by exact job descriptions, develop in an autonomous fashion with each member becoming multiskilled.

SUSMAN, Gerald I.
"Task and technological prerequisits for delegation of decision-making to work groups." In: DAVIS, Louis E.; CHERNS, Albert B. The quality of working life. New York, The Free Press, 1975, T. 2, pp. 242-255.

SWEDISH DELEGATION FOR THE STATE OWNED COMPANIES.
The Karlskrona Ship Yard. Stockholm, 1972. (In Swedish.)

SWEDISH DELEGATION FOR THE STATE OWNED COMPANIES.
The Restaurant Company VARA. Stockholm, 1971. (In Swedish.)

SWEDISH DELEGATION FOR THE STATE OWNED COMPANIES.
The Swedish Tobacco Company, Arvika Factory. Stockholm, 1970. (In Swedish.)

SWEDISH DELEGATION FOR THE STATE OWNED COMPANIES.
The Swedish Tobacco Company, Härnösand Factory. Stockholm, 1971. (In Swedish.)

SWEDISH DELEGATION FOR THE STATE OWNED COMPANIES.
Trials with industrial democracy in state-owned companies: development - experiences - suggestions. Stockholm, 1973. (In Swedish.)

SWEDISH DELEGATION FOR THE STATE OWNED COMPANIES.
The Uddevalla Ship Yard. Stockholm, 1971. (In Swedish.)

SWEDISH DEVELOPMENT COUNCIL.
Increased influence on the job, Atlas Copco MCT AB. Stockholm, /n.d./. (In Swedish.)

SWEDISH DEVELOPMENT COUNCIL.
People, groups and social partners working for change: experiences from the program. Stockholm, /n.d./. (In Swedish.)

SWEDISH DEVELOPMENT COUNCIL.
Reports, 1-21. Stockholm, /n.d./. (In Swedish.)
A series of reports on various changes in work organisation and production planning. The reports include:
Changes in work organisation, Perstorp AB. (Reports 1-4)
Changes in work organisation, Atlas Copco MCT AB. (Report 5)
Changes in work organisation, Skandia Insurance Co. (Reports 6&7)
Changes in production planning, Åkers Styckebruk. (Reports 8&9)
Changes in production planning, Husqvarna. (Report 10)
Representative participation, Eldon AB. (Reports 11&12)
To work with personnel policy, Trelleborg Rubber Factory. (Report 13)
Organisational changes for increased participation, Skandia Insurance Co. (Reports 14-17)
Changes in production planning, Husqvarna AB. (Reports 18&19)
Changes in production planning, Åkers Styckebruk. (Report 20)
Changes in the supervisory functions and roles. (Report 21)

SWEDISH DEVELOPMENT COUNCIL.
Supervision; experiences from the program. Stockholm, /n.d./. (In Swedish.)

SWEDISH EMPLOYERS' CONFEDERATION.
Autonomous groups and payment by results. Stockholm 1973.

SWEDISH EMPLOYERS' CONFEDERATION.
The Essem-Sinter report. Stockholm, 1974. (In Swedish.)

SWEDISH EMPLOYERS' CONFEDERATION.
The Hallstar report. Stockholm, 1975. (In Swedish.)

SWEDISH EMPLOYERS' CONFEDERATION.
The Holmsund report. Stockholm, 1973. (In Swedish.)

SWEDISH EMPLOYERS' CONFEDERATION.
Job reform in Sweden. Stockholm, 1975. 131 p.
Gives a broad overview of job reform in Sweden. Analyses the conditions, the causes and the methods of worker participation; considers experiments in new work organisation (eg. job redesign and shop-floor participation, new supervisory roles, wages systems, group production methods) and presents some

case studies. Concludes that the trend towards humanisation of work will continue more or less swiftly depending on the obstacles, (eg. inflexible production systems).

SWEDISH EMPLOYERS' CONFEDERATION.
The Matfors report. Stockholm, 1975.

SWEDISH EMPLOYERS' CONFEDERATION.
The Orrefors report. Stockholm, 1975.

SWEDISH EMPLOYERS' CONFEDERATION.
The Saab-Scania report. Stockholm, 1973.

SWEDISH EMPLOYERS' CONFEDERATION.
The Volvo report. Stockholm, 1975.

SWEDISH EMPLOYERS' CONFEDERATION.
With varying success: Gränges-Essem Foundry. Stockholm, 1974.

SWEET, W.; KENT, H.
"Which way industry...job enlargement or job specialization?" Factory, Dec. 1973, pp. 66-67.

"Tackling the turnover problem." American Telephone and Telegraph Co., 195 magazine, June 6, 1969, pp. 14-15.

TARCHDEAU, Jean-Claude.
"La restructuration des tâches, outil de politique générale." /Job restructuring as an instrument of general policy./ Direction et gestion, Jan.- Feb. 1974.

*TAYLOR, James C.
Concepts and problems in studies of the quality of working life. Los Angeles, Graduate School of Management, University of California, 1973. 56 p.

TAYLOR, James C.
Employee participation in socio-technical work system design: a white collar example. /N.p./, 1976. (UCLA Center for Quality of Working life. Working paper.)
Describes a recent socio-technical system design in a semi-professional white collar setting.

TAYLOR, James C.
Experiments in work system design: economic and human results. Los Angeles, University of California, 1975.
Analysis of recent instances of work design experiments in terms of the outcome sought or reported in each case. Concludes that the numbers of the experiments are increased rapidly for instance in Sweden, which has a programme for "Humanising the workplace" since 1970. The author deplores a certain carelessness in reporting and documentation which, he feels, makes it difficult to characterise all cases. The appendix contains case studies of the humanisation of work in several countries.

TAYLOR, James C.
"Some effects of technology in organisational change." Human relations, 24(2), 1971, pp. 105-123.
A study involving over 1000 persons in 140 non-supervisory work groups employed by a large petroleum refinery - designed to explore the relationship between sophisticated technology and a more autonomous and participative group process. On the basis of the findings, the author concludes that as technology advances, the idea of participative management will have more meaning and application.

*TAYLOR, James C.
Technology and planned organisational change. Ann Arbor, Mich., Institute for Social Research, University of Michigan, 1971. 151 p.
A survey of non-supervisory personnel of three hundred work groups in two large companies which looks at the effects of attempts at organisational change in the direction of more participative groups. In the case of the successful attempt at change, peer leadership and the group process increased, especially in the groups with a more sophisticated technology; while in the case of the unsuccessful attempt these group characteristics changed negatively or remained static, demonstrating that technology had the effect of constraining group effects counter to company actions which were perceived as being harmful.

TAYLOR, Lynda King.
Not for bread alone. An appreciation of job enrichment. 2nd ed. London, Business Books, 1973. xiv, 155 p.
A study of job enrichment, job satisfaction and employee motivation illustrated by case studies of experiments in nine firms in the UK, West Germany and Sweden. Covers the workers needs for recognition and responsibility. The relationship between improvements in the work environment and increased productivity and decreasing turnover is demonstrated.

TAYLOR, Lynda King.
"Worker participation in Sweden." Industrial and commercial training, 5(1), Jan. 1973, pp. 6-15.
An article which describes the impact of the group work and reassignment experiments carried out at Volvo and Saab-Scania on motivation and job satisfaction.

"Les tendances nouvelles de l'organisation industrielle et des relations du travail." /New trends in industrial organisation and labour relations./ Liaisons sociales, 14 Mar. 1974.

"Tendances nouvelles en organisation du travail." /New trends in work organisation./ Economie et humanisme, Jan.-Feb. 1976, 95 p. (Special issue.)

"Testing, training, and job rotation improve productivity." Modern manufacturing, Aug. 1968, pp. 68-69.

THIERRY, D.
"Une expérience d'élargissement des tâches en milieu employé." /An experiment in job enrichment among white-collar workers./ Pour, (47-48), Mar.-Apr. 1976, p. 24. (Dans une banque parisienne.) /In a Parisian bank./

THOMPSON, Donald B.
"Enrichment action convinces sceptics." Industry week, 14, Fall, 1972, pp. 36-39, 42-43.

THOMSEN, Sven F.; OLSEN, Erik Ekholm.
Summary of experiments in industrial cooperation within the Danish engineering industry, Federation of Mechanical Engineering and Metalworking Industries in Denmark. Copenhagen, Federation of Danish Mechanical Engineering and Metalworking Industries, 1974.

THORNELY, D.H.; VALANTINE, G.A.
"Job enlargement; some implications of longer cycle jobs on fan heater production." Philips personnel management review, (23), 1968, pp. 12-17.
Description of a case study in a Philips plant in Great Britain.

THORIN, H.
"Erfahrungen mit Gruppenarbeit im Rahmen von Dezentralisierungsbestrebungen bei der Firma Radiotechnique." /Experiences with group work in connection with decentralisation efforts at the company "Radiotechnique"./ Mitteilungen. Institut für Angewandte Arbeitswissenschaft (Köln), (44), Feb. 1974, pp. 35-46.

THORSRUD, Einar.
"Changes in work organization and management roles." In: ORGANISATION FOR ECONOMIC CO-OPERATION AND DEVELOPMENT. Work in a changing industrial society. Paris. 1974. pp. 65-82.

THORSRUD, Einar.
"Democracy at work; Norwegian experiences with non-bureaucratic forms of organization." To appear in Applied behaviour science, Summer 1977.

THORSRUD, Einar.
"Job design in the wider context." In: DAVIS, Louis E.; TAYLOR, James C., eds. Design of jobs. Harmondsworth, Penguin Books, 1972, pp. 451-459.

THORSRUD, Einar.
"Organisation du travail et évolution du rôle des syndicats." /Organisation of work and evolution of the unions' role./ Monde du travail libre, (289-290), Jul.-Aug. 1974, pp. 12-15. Experience with reorganising work in a Norwegian paper and cellulose factory under an industrial democracy project.

THORSRUD, Einar.
"Socio-technical approach to job design and organizational development." Management international review, 8(4-5), 1968, pp. 120-136.

*THORSRUD, Einar.
Mot en ny bedriftsorganisasjon. Eksperimenter i industrielt demokrati. /Towards a new organization of work. Experiments in industrial democracy./ Oslo, Tanum, 1970. 231 p. (Fra samarbeidsprosjektet LO/NAF.)
The author reports on four experiments with new forms of work organization in different Norwegian factories. These new forms were designed to enhance individual participation and involvement in work. They indicate the possibilities that exist for radically improving the industrial culture, however, they also highlight the difficulty of overcoming traditional attitudes and assumptions.

THORSRUD, Einar; SØRENSEN, B.A.; GUSTAVSEN, B.
"Socio-technical approach to industrial democracy." In: DUBIN, R., ed. Handbook of work, organisation and society. Chicago, Rand McNally, 1976.

TICHY, Noel M.; NISBERG, Jay N.
"When does work restructuring work? Organizational innovations at Volvo and GM." Organizational dynamics, Summer 1976, pp. 63-80.
This paper, by two O.D. consultants, contains a framework for "Evaluating Organizational Improvement Efforts". For this purpose they describe "twenty questions", dealing with the outcomes, as against the objectives, of the project or programme; and a much longer list of questions dealing with the environmental context and with the characteristics of the programme itself. They go on to use this approach to evaluate two programmes of this kind - one at General Motors in the States, and the other at Volvo in Sweden. Although the words are slightly misleading, within this particular approach, the General Motors programme was unsuccessful and that of Volvo successful. There are very great difficulties in making such comparisons; even so, there are important lessons in the paper.

TICHY, Noel M.
"Organisational innovations in Sweden". Columbia journal of world business, Summer 1974, pp. 18 - 28.

TICHY, Noel M.; SANDSTRÖM, T.
"Organisational innovations in Sweden." Columbia journal of world business, Summer 1974, pp. 18-28.
Outlines factors which have influenced experiments in workers' participation and work structuring and presents two detailed case histories (Volvo and Saab) of group work experiments pointing to benefits and to areas of resistance. Suggests that team work may become repetitive and boring and speculates about future innovation which might replace it.

"To relieve monotony on repetitive tasks try rotating workers to new assignment." Employee relations bulletin, Aug. 1962, pp. 6-8.

TOMESKI, E.A.
"Job enrichment and the computer." Computers and people, Nov. 1974, pp. 7-11.

"Transports publics: encouragements à l'initiative et prise de responsabilité du personnel." /Public transport: encouragements to initiative and taking of responsibility by the staff./ Qualité de la vie, lettre No. 6, Nov. 1976, p. 15.

TREGOE, B.B.
"Job enrichment: how to avoid the pitfalls." Personnel journal, 53(6), June 1974, pp. 445-453.
While many programmes for job enrichment failed, others - especially those which advocate "the use of the mind rather than the hands" - were very successful. One of these latter programmes (Analytical Trouble Shooting) advocates augmenting ones own capacity and communicating when necessary with persons in other fields and at different levels.

TRIPIER, P.
"Enrichissement des tâches: problèmes de théorie et de méthode." /Job enrichment: theoretical and methodological problems./ Perspectives, (1344), June 1974, 9 p.

TRIPIER, P.
"Les études de restructuration des tâches." /Studies on job restructuring./ L'année sociologique, 1972.

TRIST, E.L.
"Epilogue and summary: from the Tavistock perspective." In: HILL, P. Towards a new philosophy of management: the company development programme of Shell UK Limited. London, Gower Press, 1971, pp. 195-203.

TRIST, E.L.
"On socio-technical systems." In: BENNIS, W.G.; BENNE, K.D.; CHIN, R., eds. The planning of change. New York, Holt, Rinehart, and Winston, 1969, pp. 269-282.
The author feels that there is a shift away from viewing organisations as closed social system and towards seeing them as open-systems in which there is interaction between the social and technical systems. As a result of this new approach there is an idea that group autonomy should not be maximized in all productive settings but that there is an optimal level of autonomy that is determined by the requirements of the technological system.

TRIST, E.L.; HIGGIN, G.W.; MURRAY, H.; POLLOCK, A.B.
Organizational choice: capabilities of groups at the coal face under changing technologies. London, Tavistock Publications, 1963. 332 p.
Research which compared mining systems at different levels of technology are used to develop the socio-technical systems approach to the study of the working group
productive enterprises in general. Alternative forms of work organisation which tended to generate better relationships were discovered and the way in which technical change can be constructively handled from a socio-psychological point of view is developed.

TRIST, E.L.; SUSMAN, Gerald I.; BROWN.
An experiment in autonomous working in an American underground coal mine. Philadelphia, Pennsylvania State University, 1976. (Unpubl.)

TYNON, O.
"Problems of job enrichment." European industrial relations review, (2), Feb. 1974, pp. 15-17.
Discusses the problems inherent in job enrichment and considers various ways in which productivity can be increased and industrial relations improved.

"U.S. workers try Swedish approach." American machinists, Mar. 1, 1975.

ULICH, Eberhard.
"Arbeitswechsel und Aufgabenerweiterung." /Job rotation and job enlargement./ REFA-Nachrichten, (4), 1972, p. 257 et seq.

ULICH, Eberhard.
"Neue Formen der Arbeitsstrukturierung." /New forms of work structuring./ Fortschrittliche Betriebsführung, 23(3), 1974, pp. 187-196.

ULICH, Eberhard; GROSKURTH, Peter; BRUGGEMANN, Agnes.
Neue Formen der Arbeitsgestaltung. Möglichkeiten und Probleme einer Verbesserung der Qualität des Arbeitslebens. /New forms of work organisation. Possibilities and problems of an improvement of the quality of working life./ Frankfurt/M., 1973.

UMADIKAR, R.H.
"The CCCC story in Life Insurance Corporation of India." To be published in National Labour Institute bulletin.
The author reports his experience in utilising a newly installed Electronic Data Processing Department, to bring about a new work culture through work re-design using employee-participative methods in Centralised Cash Collection Centre (CCCC) of the Life Insurance Corporation of India in Bombay. The study (undertaken in 1969) is interesting in that, despite the expected anxiety of the employees about introduction of labour saving equipment in a labour intensive service industry and trade union reservations, the author was able to involve white collar employees in bringing about a successful change. Innovations included changes in the work system and the re-organisation on the lay-out of the department.

UNION DES INDUSTRIES METALLURGIQUES ET MINIERES, Paris.
"Canada: la satisfaction dans le travail: étude d'une expérience réalisée par Aluminium Co." /Canada: Job satisfaction: study of an experiment by the Aluminium Co./ UIMM-Documentation étrangère. (294), annexe 1, Mar. 1973, 16 p.

UNION DES INDUSTRIES METALLURGIQUES ET MINIERES, Paris.
Deux expériences de groupes semi-autonomes à la Télémécanique. /Two experiments with semi-autonomous groups at the Télémécanique works./ Paris, 1975. (Its: Cahiers techniques, 7.)
Job enrichment through expansion of the tasks performed and autonomy of organisation. Description of two experiments at Thiberville and Menilles, with their results in human and economic terms.

UNION DES INDUSTRIES METALLURGIQUES ET MINIERES, Paris.
L'enrichissement des tâches en tréfilage chez Chatillon-Gorcy. /Job enrichment in wire drawing at the Chatillon-Gorcy works./ Paris, 1976.

UNION DES INDUSTRIES METALLURGIQUES ET MINIERES, Paris.
"Etats-Unis: restructuration et enrichissement des tâches: exploration de leurs limites." /United States: restructuring and job enrichment: an exploration of their limits./ UIMM-Documentation étrangère, (304), Annexe 2, Jan. 1974, 13 p.

UNION DES INDUSTRIES METALLURGIQUES ET MINIERES, Paris.
Evolutions dans l'organisation du travail. /Developments in work organisation./ Paris, 1974. 72 p.
Work organisation as illustrated by French experience with reference to working conditions, nature of work, shift work and new production structures.
Proposes that efforts should be made to improve working conditions, reduce constraints and increase autonomy at work.

UNION DES INDUSTRIES METALLURGIQUES ET MINIERES, Paris.
L'expérience FACOM. / The FACOM experiment./ Paris, 1974.
A description giving detailed information on material conditions. The experiment was based on participation. Appendices in the form of tables and analytical diagrams.

UNION DES INDUSTRIES METALLURGIQUES ET MINIERES, Paris.
L'expérience Guilliet. /The Guilliet experiment./ Paris, 1974. 30 p.
The study reports on an experiment by the Guilliet undertaking in France in progressively setting up a system of participation covering all members of the staff known as "participatory management by objectives, from the Chairman and Managing Director to the unskilled manual worker". The new structure, which is of the vertical type, consists of autonomous "job enrichment groups".

UNION DES INDUSTRIES METALLURGIQUES ET MINIERES, Paris.
L'expérience Leroy-Somer. /The Leroy-Somer experiment./ Paris, 1974. 21 p.
A case study of a workers' participation experiment developed in an industrial enterprise of the electrical machinery industry in France.

UNION DES INDUSTRIES METALLURGIQUES ET MINIERES, Paris.
Expériences d'enrichissement des tâches chez Klocker-Moeller, Dausenau. /Experiments in job enrichment at Klocker-Moeller's Dausenau plant./ Paris, 1974. (Cahiers techniques, 5.)
An analysis of experiments in work organisation from the point of view of management and the workers, with comments on the results obtained from different angles.

UNION DES INDUSTRIES METALLURGIQUES ET MINIERES, Paris.
Expériences de restructuration du travail chez Philips, Eindhoven, Pays Bas. /Experiments in work restructuring at the Philips Eindhoven plant in the Netherlands./ Paris, 1973. (Its: Cahiers techniques, 2.)
Deals with job satisfaction and describes the evolution of the Philips line management over the years with the aid of diagrams. Description of the Eindhoven experiment using an analysis of the technical and economic results achieved through assembly-line production.

UNION DES INDUSTRIES METALLURGIQUES ET MINIERES, Paris.
Quatre expériences étrangeres sur une nouvelle organisation de tâches. /Four foreign experiments with new forms of work organisation./ Paris 1973. (Its: Cahiers techniques, 6.)
Nobo Fabrikken A/S (Norway): shift from assembly-line work to autonomous working groups: firm chosen by the Norwegian Joint Research committee as an example of this type of experiment.
Götaverken (Sweden): Arendal shipyards - description of preliminary steps in an experiment in reforming the remuneration system and improving working conditions, with an analysis of the difficulties encountered.
Atlas-Copco (Sweden): an experiment designed to increase autonomy and job satisfaction.
Philips (Netherlands): Eindhoven - simultaneous comparison of the conventional system and the autonomous working group system by setting up two groups for the purpose.

UNION DES INDUSTRIES METALLURGIQUES ET MINIERES, Paris.
Restructuration du travail chez Bosch, Stuttgart, et chez Olivetti, Ivrea. /Work restructuring in the factories of Bosch, Stuttgart, and Olivetti, Ivrea./ Paris, 1975. 39 p. (Its: Cahiers techniques, 3.)
A technical report on the job enrichment programmes introduced in assembly-line work in metalworking industries in Italy (Olivetti) and West Germany (Bosch) based on the expansion of group work.

UNION DES INDUSTRIES METALLURGIQUES ET MINIERES, Paris.
Le travail en groupes à la CIAPEM à Lyon. /Group work at CIAPEM, Lyon./ Paris, 1975. (Its: Cahiers Techniques, 15.)
Description of change from the assembly-line production of washing machines to production by assembly groups, from the point of view of work organisation. Positive and negative results from the work and production angles at each stage. Final experience found positive. The undertaking is now allowing workers to choose between the traditional assembly-line and the group.

VAN BEEK,
"Veränderung der Fliessbandarbeit bei Philips." /Changes in assembly-line work at Philips./ Mitteilungen. Institut für Angewandte Arbeitswissenschaft. (Köln), (41), /n.d./.

VAN BEINUM, H.J.J.; VAN GILS, M.R.; VERHAGEN, E.J.
Taakontwerp en werkorganisatie: een sociotechnisch veld-experiment. /Job design and work organization: a socio-technical experiment./ The Netherlands, Commissie Opvoering Produktiviteit van de Sociaal-Economische Rand, 1967.

VAN DER GRAAF, M.H.K.; GIPSEN, J.H.
"Work structuring." Progress, (4), 1970, pp. 116-121.

VAN OOSTEROM, C.
The concept of teamwork. Canberra, Department of Police and Customs, 1975. 9 p.
Provides a brief comparison between traditional organisation and the concept of "teamwork" (semi-autonomous groups).

VAN VLIET, A.A.
A work structuring experiment in television assembly. Eindhoven, Philips, 1970.

VAROQUAUX, J.
"La participation du personnel à la gestion des entreprises en Europe occidentale." /Staff participation in the management of undertakings in Western Europe./ ACADI, (309), Feb. 1976.

VENNIN, B.
De la transformation du procès de production au changement social; le cas de la sous-traitance pour l'automobile dans la région stéphanoise. /From transformation of the production process to social change: The case of subcontracting in the automobile industry in the St. Etienne area./ Recherche pour le CRESAL, Jan. 1974-Mar. 1975. (Study under way)

"Les vertus de l'enrichissement des fonctions. /The virtues of job enrichment./ Entreprise, (870), May 1972, pp. 51-65.

VERVOOT, J.
"Humaniser la chaîne." /Making the assembly-line more human/ L'entreprise et l'homme, 46(1), Jan. 1974.

VIGNET, V.
"Groupes autonomes et enrichissement des tâches. /Autonomous groups and job enrichment./ Economie et humanisme, (227), 1976.

VILMAR, Fritz.
"Arbeitsgruppenbesprechungen in Betriebsverfassungsgesetz verankern." /Work group discussions need to be incorporated into the Works Constitution Act./ Gewerkschaftliche Monatshefte, 21(3), 1970.

VILMAR, Fritz.
"Humanisierung und Demokratisierung der Arbeitswelt; Betriebsdemokratische Modelle und Kämpfe in Europa." /Humanisation and democratisation of work. Enterprise democracy models and struggles in Europe./ Vorgänge, Zeitschrift für Gesellschaftspolitik, 12(4), 1973, p. 112.

VILMAR, Fritz.
Industrielle Arbeitswelt, Herrschaftsstrukturen und Demokratisierungspotentiale. /Industrial world of work, hierarchical structures and democratisation potentials./ Nürnberg, 1973.

"VOLVO KALMAR: bilan nuancé d'une expérience pilote." /Volvo Kalmar: mixed results of a pilot experiment./ Intersocial, (22), Dec. 1976, pp. 1-13.

VOUGH, C.F.; ASBELL, B.
Tapping the human resources; a strategy for productivity. New York, Amacon, 1975. xii, 212 p.
A monograph on operational management and management policies and techniques for the improvement of productivity and job satisfaction based on the author's own experience with efforts at motivation through job enrichment at IBM.

WAHI, S.P., et al.
"Innovative strategy at Central Foundry Forge Plant of Bharat Heavy Electricals Limited at Hardwar." To be published in National Labour Institute bulletin.
A new plant for meanufacturing heavy castings and forgings was to be commissioned with the Steel Melting Shop in July, 1976. With the participative design of the organisation structure, functions and multi-skilled training, the Plant was commissioned in April, 1976 - four months ahead of schedule. The study highlights the importance of an integrated approach involving all personnel from managers to unskilled workers in creating a converging work culture with appropriate training system as an input. Participative design was followed all through with the result that skilled workmen, and even the managers, started with the norm that even routine unskilled work,(normally to be carried out by the lowest level of blue collar worker)could be shared by the senior colleagues. On this basis the Scheme was successfully implemented in the plant.

WAISGLASS, Harry Jacob.
Job enrichment, decision sharing and industrial democracy. L'enrichissement des fonctions, la co-décision et la démocratic industrielle. /Ottawa, 1973./ (Reprinted from the December 1973 issue of the Civil Service Review.) Text in English and French.

WALKER, K.
"The diffusion of new work structures: explaining why success didn't take." Organizational dynamics, Winter 1975, pp. 3-22.

*WALKER, K.
"Innovative restructuring of work." In: ROSOW, Jerome M., The worker and the job. Englewood Cliffs, Prentice-Hall, 1974.

WALLICK, Franklin.
"Humanizing work is not a sexy issue." Condensed from a speech presented at the Industrial Relations Centre's 22nd Annual Conference. McGill University industrial relations review, Spring 1973, p. 3.

WALSH, W.
"Job enrichment in the office." Work study, 22(6), 1973, pp. 28-31.

WALTER, H.
"Vom Fliessband zum Einzelarbeitsplatz." /From the assembly-line to the industrial workplace./ Mitteilungen. Institut für Angewandte Arbeitswissenschaft (Köln), (43), Jan. 1974, pp. 13-37.

WALTERS, Roy W.
"Job enrichment for results; strategies for successful implementation." Personnel psychology, 29(1), 1976, pp. 127-130.

WALTERS, Roy W.
"The need for job enrichment is urgent." Industrial engineering, July 1972, pp. 14-16.

WALTERS, Roy W.
"The rewards of job enrichment." Supervisory management, 18(1), 1973, pp. 39-41.

WALTON, Richard Eugene.
"The diffusion of new work structures: explaining why success didn't work." Organizational dynamics, Winter 1975, pp. 2-22. The author evaluates and discusses difficulties which can arise in the middle period of successful projects on work reorganisation. He feels that "There is an advantage in (1) introducing a number of projects at the same time in the same firm; (2) avoiding over-exposure and glorification of particular change efforts; and (3) having the innovative programme identified with top management at the initial project stage."

WALTON, Richard Eugene.
"From Hawthorne to Topeka and Kalmar." In: Man and work in society. New York, Van Nostrand Reinhold. (In press.) The article compares the changes made, at the new Topeka plant of General Foods with Volvo's Kalmar plant, summarising the major alterations in work design made in the course of both these projects.

WALTON, Richard Eugene.
"How to counter alienation in the plant." Harvard business review, 50(6), Nov.-Dec. 1972, pp. 70-81.
The author uses the example of comprehensive organizational redesign effort in a large pet-food manufacturing enterprise to support the contention that the total restructuring of the workplace and the organization of work is necessary to counter alienation, to meet the changing expectations of employees and to increase productivity. He also examines briefly the efforts of other companies such as Proctor and Gamble (US) and Saab Scania (Sweden) to improve productivity and enhance the quality of working life.

WALTON, Richard Eugene.
"Innovative restructuring of work." In: ROSOW, Jerome M., ed. The worker and the job; coping with changc. Englewood Cliffs, N.J., Prentice-Hall, 1974, pp. 145-176.
According to the author worker alienation affects workers, as well as management. He feels therefore that organisational redesign must be comprehensive and must include: the elimination of fragmented tasks, greater flexibility, more delegation of authority, more information and the setting up of adequate reward systems. Workers must also be given more control over the arrangement of their schedules, possibly through the elimination of time clocks. Noting the existence of potential threats to such systems, the author suggests, however, that these can be minimised through careful foreplanning.

WANOUS, John P.
"Who wants job enrichment." Advanced management journal, 41(3), Summer 1976.
The article notes that the present confusion which surrounds the applications of job enrichment schemes and the diverse opinions as to the probable achievements of this new form of work organisation, has its origin in the fact that particular conditions and certain kinds of employees are necessary to ensure success. The author puts forward some suggestions about the conditions under which job enrichment efforts will have the best possible chances of success.

WEED, E.D. Jr.
"Job enrichment 'cleans up' at Texas Instruments." In: MAHER, J.R., ed. New perspectives in job enrichment. New York, Van Nostrand Reinhold, 1971. pp. 55-78.

WEIL, Reinhold.
"Auf der Suche nach einer besseren Arbeitsorganisation." /Search for a better work organisation./ Mitteilungen. Institut für Angewandte Arbeitswissenschaft (Köln), (45), Mar. 1974, pp. 1-7.

WEIL, Reinhold.
"Die Bedeutung des Falles Klöckner-Moeller." /The significance of the case Klöckner-Moeller./ "Einführung." /Introduction./ Mitteilungen. Institut für Angewandte Arbeitswissenschaft (Köln), (43), Jan. 1974, pp. 8-12. "Anmerkungen." /Conclusions./ (44), Feb. 1974, pp. 14-34.

WEIL, Reinhold.
"Der geistige Hintergrund; wissenschaftliche Theorien." /The mental background; scientific theories./ Mitteilungen. Institut für Angewandte Arbeitswissenschaft (Köln), (42), Sept. 1973, pp. 1-12.

WEIL, Reinhold.
"Mehr Arbeitszufriedenheit durch Bereicherung des Arbeitsinhaltes: Künftiger Schwerpunkt der Wünsche der Arbeitnehmer?" /More job satisfaction through enrichment of job content. Main future request of workers?/ Mitteilungen. Institut für Angewandte Arbeitswissenschaft (Köln), (41), Sept. 1973, pp. 1-7.

WEIL, Reinhold.
"Neue Arbeitsstrukturen bei Volvo." /New work structures at Volvo./ Mitteilungen. Institut für Angewandte Arbeitswissenschaft (Köln), (47), May 1974, pp.7-58.

WEIL, Reinhold.
"Neue Formen der Arbeitsorganisation bei Saab-Scania." /New forms of work organisation at Saab-Scania./ Mitteilungen. Institut für Angewandte Arbeitswissenschaft (Köln), (46), Apr. 1974, pp. 16-57.

WEIL, Reinhold.
"Veränderte Arbeitsformen bei Danfoss." /Changed work organisation at Danfoss./ Mitteilungen. Institut für Angewandte Arbeitswissenschaft (Köln), (45), Mar. 1974, pp. 32-57.

WEIL, Reinhold.
"Überblick über Ansatz und Entwicklung von Untersuchungen und Experimenten bei Philips." /Overview of approaches and development of studies and experiments at Philips./ Mitteilungen. Institut für Angewandte Arbeitswissenschaft (Köln), (41), Sept. 1973, pp. 8-14.

WEIL, Reinhold.
"Die Veränderung der Arbeitswelt bei Fiat." /Changes in the work environment at Fiat./ Mitteilungen. Institut für Angewandte Arbeitswissenschaft (Köln), (56), May 1975, pp. 18-51.

WEIL, Reinhold.
"Veränderungen der Arbeitswelt durch neue Führungs-, Organisations- und Arbeitsstrukturen." 1. /Work enrichment changes through new management organisation and work structures./ REFA-Nachrichten, (3), 1976, pp. 131-144.
Provisional conclusions on new forms of work organisation in industrialised countries. Deals with humanisation of work, job satisfaction, delegation of responsibility and the results of experiments of more human work organisation.

WEIL, Reinhold.
"Veränderung der Arbeitsformen in der Metallindustrie." /Changes of work organisation in the metal industry./ In: Qualität des Lebens am Arbeitsplatz. Köln, 1974, pp. 100-126. (dev-Sachbuchreihe.)

WEIL, Reinhold.
"Verbesserung der Arbeitsbedingungen und der Arbeitsorganisation bei Renault." /Improvement of working conditions and work organisation at Renault./ Mitteilungen. Institut für Angewandte Arbeitswissenschaft (Köln), (48), June 1974, pp. 1-56.

WEIL, Reinhold.
"Versuche mit neuen Formen der Zusammenarbeit in der dänishen Metallindustrie." /Experiments with new forms of cooperation in the Danish metal industry./ Mitteilungen. Institut für Angewandte Arbeitswissenschaft (Köln), (45), Mar. 1974, pp. 8-31.

WEIL, Reinhold.
"Vorzüge und Grenzen der Arbeitsteilung." /Advantages and limits of the division of work./ Mitteilungen. Institut für Angewandte Arbeitswissenschaft (Köln), (43), Jan. 1974, pp. 1-7, (44), Feb. 1974, pp. 1-13.

WEIL, Reinhold.
"Die wichtigsten Experimente." /The most important experiments./ Mitteilungen. Institut für Angewandte Arbeitswissenshaft (Köln), (46), Apr. 1974, pp. 1-3.

WEIL, Reinhold.
"Neue Arbeitsstrukturen in der europäischen Metallindustrie; Gedanken aus der Sicht des Instituts." /New work structures in the European metal industry; reflexions from the point of view of the Institute./ Mitteilungen. Institut für Angewandte Arbeitswissenschaft (Köln), (41-47, 56), 1973-1975. (Series of articles. Noted separately.)

WEINBERG, Arthur S.
"Een experiment in witwisseling van arbeiders bij Saab-Scania." /An experiment in job rotation at Saab-Scania./ Mens en onderneming, 29(6), Nov.-Dec. 1975, pp. 334-346.
Considers the objectives of different experiments of work reorganisation carried out by Saab-Scania. The author refers to the large scale attempts at economic democratisation and to the invitation issued to a group of American automobile workers to enable them to compare working conditions in the USA and Sweden.

WEINBERG, Arthur S.
"Six American workers assess job redesign at Saab-Scania." Monthly labour review, 98(9), Sept. 1975, pp. 52-53.
Discussion of the reactions of American automobile workers who participated in a month-long experiment at the Saab-Scania plant in Södertälje where several job redesign and worker participation experiments are being carried out. While the workers were favourably impressed by physical working conditions in the plant and by some job redesign experiments, they were indifferent to the worker participation schemes.

WEINBERG, Nat.
"Job enrichment." In: NEW YORK UNIVERSITY INSTITUTE OF LABOR RELATIONS. Proceedings of the 27th Annual Conference on Labor, 1974. New York, M. Bender, 1975, pp.275-287.

WERTHER, William B.
"Beyond job enrichment to employment enrichment." Personnel journal. 54(8), Aug. 1975, 6 p.
The author criticises job enrichment schemes on the ground that by concentrating on the employee-job sub-system they do not concern themselves with larger employee-organisation sub-system. Consequently, the broader, more demanding problems of this level remains unaffected.

WESOLOWSKI, Zdzislaw P.
"Organizational structure and morale." Advanced management journal, Jul. 1970, pp. 50-54.
The author argues that flat organisation with decentralisation of control are the most conducive to the development of the individual and to high morale.

WHITSETT, David A.
"The enriched job." Personnel administrator, Sept.-Oct. 1972, pp.53-54.

WHITSETT, David A.
"Job enrichment, human resources and profitability." In: MAHER, J.R., ed. New perspectives in job enrichment. New York, Van Nostrand Reinhold, 1971, pp.21-34.

WHITSETT, David A.
"Where are your enriched jobs?" Harvard business review, 53(1), Jan.-Feb. 1975, pp. 74-80.
A discussion of eleven structural clues for recognising opportunities to improve jobs and also the productivity and satisfaction of those filling them. The author warns, however, that job enrichment is not an overall problem-solving technique that can be used indiscriminately and should, therefore, be undertaken only when organisational conditions call for, and favour its implementation.

WILD, Ray.
"Job restructuring and work organization." Management decision, (3), 1974, pp. 117-126.

WILD, Ray.
"The nature and context of job restructuring in the engineering industries of Europe." In: WEIR, Mary, ed. Job satisfaction: challenge and response in Modern Britain. Fontana, 1976, pp. 275-279.
The author lists several factors (eg. availability of labour, nature and demands of the market, emphasis on industrial democracy, government policies and possible EEC legislation) which might influence future developments in industrial engineering in the UK. His own conclusion is that increased attention will be paid to the formation of formal functional work groups within flowline systems following the examples of Volvo and Saab Scania and that this organisational form will offer greater benefits than single job changes which increase cycle time or formal job rotation.

WILD, Ray.
"Stages and dimensions in job design." Personnel management, Dec. 1974.

WILD, Ray; BIRCHALL, D.W.
"Job structuring and work organization." Journal of occupational psychology, 48(3), 1975, pp.169-177.

WILKINSON, A.
A survey of some Western European experiments in motivation. Enfield, England, The Institute of Work Study Practitioners, 1970.

WILLENBACHER, K.
"Praktische Arbeitsstrukturierung." /Practical work structuring./ In: INSTITUT FÜR ANGEWANDTE ARBEITSWISSENSCHAFT, Köln. Arbeitsstrukturierung in der deutschen Metallindustrie. Köln, 1975.

WILLIAMSON, D.T.N.
"The anachronistic factory." Personnel review, 3(3), Autumn 1974.
Contending that trends of management organisation in flowline and batch manufacturing and the work patterns they have created have been coming increasingly into conflict with the values, aspirations and expectations of workers. The author suggests that industry should stop trying to mould man to meet its needs and should instead be reshaped to meet the needs of man. He describes the present position of these types of manufacturing and considers possible directions of change which would provide both improved efficiency and a better match with society.

WILLIAN, J.P.; ROBERTSON, K.B.
"Qu'est-ce que l'enrichissement des emplois? Comment l'appliquer? Quels résultats en attendre?" /What is job enrichment? How can it be applied? With what results?/ Documents de la CECOS (Puteaux, France), Jul. 1969.

WINPISINGER, William W.
"Job enrichment; a union view." Monthly labor review, Apr. 1973.
The author contends that jobs can only be enriched by enriching paychecks and that this is the best cure for the "blue-collar blues."

Wirtschaftspolitik u. Vermenschlichung des Arbeitsplatzes. /Economic policies and humanisation of the work place./ 7. Bundeskongress des OeGB, Arbeitskreis 1. Wien, Oesterr. Gewerkschaftsbund, /n.d./

WISEMAN, A.
"Job redesign; two more examples." Work and people, 1(3), Spring 1975, pp.16-19.
Describes two job redesign and job enrichment schemes in Australia.

Wissenschaftliche Arbeitsorganisation - Grundsätze, Aufgaben, Erfahrungen. /Scientific work organisation - principles, tasks, experiences./ Berlin, Verl. Tribüne 1975, 270p.
Describes the implementation of Scientific Work Organisation (SWO) and gives several practical examples in enterprises. Stresses certain aspects of SWO such as the planning of SWO measures and improvements of work content through the utilisation of such procedures and methods.

"Work experiments and improving the quality of work life in the United States." European industrial relations review, (10), Oct. 1974, pp. 2-5.
In the light of experiments of job enrichment in the USA the author reviews changes in opinion about work organisation in general and some experiments in particular, in some of the more important American enterprises.

"Work itself; STAR programs aimed at providing truly satisfying jobs." American Telephone and Telegraph Co. 195 News, Sept. 27, 1968, pp. 1-2.

*WRÓBLEWSKI, S., ed.
Programy humanizacji pracy w przedsiebiorstwach. /The programs of work humanisation in enterprises./ Warszawa, 1975.

WUNDERLICH, D.
"Bessere Arbeitsgestaltung durch Tätigkeitswechsel - Job Rotation, Job Enlargement, Job Enrichment." /Improved job design through changes in activity - job rotation, job enlargement, job enrichment./ Personal, 25, 1973, pp. 5-7.

YORKS, Lyle.
"Determining job enrichment feasibility." Personnel, 51(6), Nov.-Dec. 1974, pp. 18-25.

YORKS, Lyle.
A radical approach to job enrichment. New York, AMACOM, 1976. 209 p.

ZEITLIN, L.R.
"A little larceny can do a lot for employee morale." Psychology today, 5(1), 1971, pp. 22, 24, 26, 64.
The author advocates controlled stealing as a form of job enrichment.

ZIEGLER, B.
"Moderne Arbeitsgestaltung in der Motoren-Montage bei Klöckner-Humbolt-Deutz." /Modern work design in motor-assembly at Klöckner-Humbolt-Deutz./ Mitteilungen. Institut für Angewandte Arbeitswissenschaft (Köln), (51), June 1974, pp. 39-43.

ZIMBALIST, A.
"The limits of work humanisation." The review of radical political economics, 7(2), Summer 1975, pp. 50-59.
In American enterprises scientific work organisation has been replaced by the humanisation of work. This implies extensive changes in the control of production processes.

IV. ECONOMIC COSTS AND BENEFITS OF NEW FORMS OF WORK ORGANISATION

"Accord de participation et résultats financiers: un bilan statistique au 31 décembre 1974. /Participation agreements and financial results: a statistical balancesheet at 31 December 1974./ Liaisons sociales - législation sociale , (4336), Nov. 1975.

ANSARI, K.A.
"Industrial relations and productivity." Andhra Pradesh labour bulletin, 2(5), Aug. 1971. pp. 5-9.

BAUM, S.J.; YOUNG, W.M.
Practical guide to flexible working hours. London, Kogan Page, 1973. 186 p.
A textbook on flexible working hours in the UK which includes an outline of a model to be used for cost benefit analysis purposes.

BENCZE, L.
A technikai eszközök szerepe a munkaszervezésben. /The role of technical tools in the work organisation./ Budapest, Ministry of Labour, Research Institute for Labour, 1976. (Target study)
Work place activity, whether directly or indirectly a productive activity, constitutes an economic and social process of basic importance. Efficiency should be interpreted not only in respect to the means of production and funds but also in respect to the labour force. Each production process requires both human activity and the use of various technical tools and these two aspects should be optimally concerted in any well organised, up-to-date production process.

BORNEMANN, E., et al.
Gruppenarbeit und Produktivität; Bericht über eine Studienreise in die USA. /Group work and productivity; report on a study trip in the USA./ München, 1958.

BRIZAY, B.
"La participation: une nécessité économique." /Participation: an economic necessity./ Entreprise, (960), Feb. 1974, pp. 50-57, 63-65.

BORZEIX, A.; CHAVE, D.
Réorganisation du travail et dynamique des conflits. /Restructuring of work and dynamics of conflict./ Paris, Conservatoire National des Arts et Métiers, 1975. 492 p.

BRAUN, A.
Arbeitsproduktivität und Effektivität. Zur volkswirtschaftlichen Effektivität der Substitution lebendiger Arbeit durch Fonds. [Labour productivity and efficiency. The economic efficiency of the substitution of life work.] Berlin, Akademie-Verlag, 1976.

BUND KATHOLISCHER UNTERNEHMER e.V.
"Arbeitswelt menchlicher gestalten. Humanität und Rentabilität: ein Widerspruch?" [The creation of a more human work environment. Humanitarianism and profitability, a contradiction?] Beiträge zur Gesellschaftspolitik, (Köln), (13), Dec. 1974.

BUTERA, F.
I frantumi riscomposti. [Rebuilding the wreckage.] Padova, Marsilio, 1972.
In this book the analysis of recent developments in USA gives an account of the managerial reasons for humanising work.

CAULKINS, David.
"Job redesign: pay implications." Personnel, May-June 1974, pp. 29-34.

CONANT, E.H.; KILBRIDGE, M.D.
"An interdisciplinary analysis of job enlargement: technology, costs and behavioural implications." Industrial and labour relations review, 18, 1965, pp.377-395.

CONANT, E.H.; KILBRIDGE, M.D.
"De l'élargissement des tâches: ergonomie, technologie, coûts et réactions des travailleurs." [On the enlargement of jobs: ergonomic and technological aspects; cost and reactions of workers.] Personnel, (117), Aug. 1968.

"Conference assesses quality of working life and relationship to productivity." Daily labor report, Oct. 1, 1975, pp. A.17-A.18.

CUMMINGS, T.G.; MOLLOY, Edmond S.; GLEN, Roy H.
"Intervention strategies for improving productivity and the quality of work life." Organizational dynamics, Summer 1975, pp. 52-68.

DONNELLY, John F.
"Increasing productivity by involving people in their total job." Personnel administration, 34, Sept.-Oct. 1971, pp.8-13.

DUNAJEWSKI, H.
Décisions d'amélioration des conditions de travail sans influence sur la productivité. Etude d'un cas particulier aux garages en France. [Decisions to improve conditions of work without influencing productivity. A French case study.]
Aix-en-Provence, Laboratoire d'Economie et de Sociologie du CNRS, 1973. 157,281 p. (Roenogr.)

*DYONIZIAK, R.
Społeczne uwarunkowanie wydajności pracy. Próba analizy na tle funkcjonowania przedsiębiorstwa jako systemu społecznego. /Social factors which determine labour productivity./ Warszawa, Książka i Wiedza, 1967. 241 p.

ELLIOTT, J. Douglas.
"Increasing office productivity through job enlargement." In: The human side of the office manager's job. New York, American Management Association, 1953, pp. 3-15. (Office Management series No. 134.)

EMERY, Fred E.
The assembly line: its logic and our future. An address to the Institution of Engineers, Sydney, Australia. Canberra, 1975. (Australian National University. Centre for Continuing Education. Occasional paper, No. 7.)
Discussion of the economic costs and advantages of segmented work tasks such as those which comprise the paced assembly-line. Notes that such production systems are characterised by organisational instability. Considers analytically the new plant design at Volvo's Kalmar plant and stresses that the change here involves a move from a one-man-one-shift-one-work-station principle to a socio-technical unit which is able simultaneously to control all the basic parameters of gain and cost in the total production system.

FEIST, Rudolf.
"Verbesserungen der Arbeitsbedingungen. Erhöhung der Arbeitsproduktivität und Effektivität: Aufgabe und Verpflichtung aller Arbeitswissenschaftler." /Improving conditions of work, increasing labour productivity and efficiency: tasks and obligations of all labour scientists./ Sozialistische Arbeitswissenschaft, 5, 1976.

FELLOW, N.U.H.
The quality of work and its outcomes: estimating potential increases in labor productivity. Columbus, Academy for Contemporary Problem, 1975.
This study provides a conceptual framework for estimating potential increases in labour productivity which might occur in a manufacturing establishment through improvements of the quality of work. Types of data are proposed for evaluating work according to both economic/technical and human/social criteria. The concept of quality of work rests on the belief that the actions to increase labour productivity are the same actions which should be taken to increase human fulfilment through work.

FUSKO, Z.; ČAPKOVIČ, J.
Metódy merania efektívnosti organizácie výroby a prace. /Methods of measuring the effectiveness of production and work organisation./ Bratislava, Czechoslovak Research Institute of Labour and Social Affairs, 1975. 206 p.
A study dealing with the measuring of the effectiveness of production and work organisation by determining the extent to which the organisation of production makes use of production

factors, i.e. to establish the effectiveness of the structural, spatial and temporal arrangement of the production process in the enterprise. The results of the measurement obtained experimentally determine some possibilities of their application in the contemporary managerial, decision-making a rationalisation practice in the sphere of enterprise economy and the level superior to the organisation.

GAITANIDES.
"Kostentheorie und Job Enrichment." /Cost theory and job enrichment./ Management international revue, 16(2), 1976, pp. 23-35.
The question of costs involved in improving working conditions, especially through job enrichment, still remains largely unanswered. The article analyses relevant cost factors. It concludes that the cost of fixed capital is the dominant factor, therefore knowledge of the production function before and after changes in production organisation is essential. Variations in the production function also affect productivity and personnel cost. In addition, cost effects of changes in work motivation ought to be considered.

GAUGLER, E.; KOLB,M.; LING,B.
Humanisierung der Arbeitswelt und Produktivität. /Humanisation of work and productivity./ Mannheim, 1976.

Gebrauchswert-Kosten-Analyse als Leitungsinstrument. /Current value-cost analyses as a management instrument./ Berlin, Dietz Verl., 1974. 148 p.
Deals with current value-cost analysis as management instrument to develop socialist community work on the basis of scientific work organisation.

GLASER, Edward M.
Improving the quality of worklife...and in the process, improving productivity. A summary of concepts, procedures and problems, with case histories. Los Angeles, Human Interaction Research Institute, 1975. 356 p.

GLASER, Edward M.
Productivity gains through worklife improvement. New York, The Psychological Corporation, /n.d./. 352 p.
Using case studies and other relevant research, the author explores the ways in which improvements in the quality of working life can affect worker productivity, industrial relations and organisational effectiveness. The book includes some guidelines for the design and introduction of successful QWL programmes.

GONZALEZ, Arturo F.
"How to increase productivity through flexible working hours." Association management, 25, Aug. 1973, pp. 93-94. (Reprinted from TWA ambassador magazine, Sept. 1972.)
Based on experience in Germany and other European countries.

HAMERMESH, Daniel S.
The economics of job satisfaction. East Lansing , Michigan State University, 1974. 67, 24, 4 l.

HARRISON, Gordon F.
"Flexible hours system produces impressive results." Canadian personnel and industrial relations journal, 20, Sept. 1973, pp. 27-31.
A discussion of flexible working hours which covers the introduction of such systems and their impact on motivation and cost of production.

HENGSTLER, Heinz.
"The impact of flexible working hours on staff productivity." Association management, 27, Sept. 1974, pp. 60-63.

HERZBERG, Frederick; PAUL, William A.; ROBERTSON, Keith B.
"Job enrichment pays off." Harvard business review, Mar.-Apr. 1969.
A summary of five job enrichment studies. The authors conclude that while job enrichment programmes often do enhance job performance they do not necessarily affect job satisfaction. As satisfaction is a result of performance, it is slower to change.

HÉTHY, Lajos; MAKÓ, Csaba.
A teljesitményelv érvényesitése és az üzemi érdek- es hatalmi viszonyok. /The implementation of the productivity principle and relationships based on interest and power in the undertaking./ /N.p./, Institut de Sociologie, 1970.
On the basis of a sample survey the book describes the formation, within the undertaking, of relationships based on interest and stresses the importance of more democratic decisionmaking.

HOPWOOD, Anthony G.
"Towards assessing the economic costs and benefits of new forms of work organisation." Paper prepared for the International Institute for Labour Studies, Geneva, 1976. (To be published shortly.)

"Humanisierungs-Kosten." /Cost of humanisation of work./ Monatsblätter für freiheitliche Wirtschaftspolitik, 2, 1974, p.100.

JUNGBLUT, Michael.
Nicht vom Lohn allein. /Not for wage alone./ Hamburg, Hoffmann und Campe, 1973, 275 p.
Enlarged participation and workers' profit sharing are not followed by negative effects. The case studies discussed demonstrate that enterprises in which these are carried out often are the most successful ones in their branch of activity.

KADLEC, Z.
"Kvalifikace důsledků inovačních změn na výrobní program." /The evaluation of the consequences of innovative changes on production programmes./ Ekonomika stavebníctva, 11(2), 1976, pp. 51-58.

*KALINIA, N.P.; MAKUSTIN, V.G.
The influence of conditions of work on productivity. Moscow, Economica, 1970. (In Russian.)
A description of the influence of various aspects of conditions of work on productive capacity of individual worker, demand of work done in accordance with its level on the effectiveness of the utilisation of working time. It gives a consensus of the description of enterprise activities aimed at improving conditions of work.

KAPP, B.; PROUST, O.
Les horaires libres. Paris, Chotard, 1973. 316 p.
The book considers the trend towards the introduction of flexible working hours in France covering such aspects as the economic and social implications of the experiments, the cost implications for the enterprise and worker motivation. Contains a list of enterprises (in various countries) which apply flexible working hours.

KÁPOLNAI, György; VÁRKONYI, László.
Anyagi és erkölcsi ösztönzés a munkaszervezés szolgálatában /Material and non-material incentives and the organisation of work./ Budapest, Közgazdasági és Jogi Kiadó, 1976.
The book describes ways and means of activating workers in undertakings and the conditions under which this should be done, analyses relations between heads of undertaking and their workers and employees (motivation, satisfaction, etc.), and outlines the role of social policy in activating workers.

KATZELL, M.E.
Productivity; the measure and the myth. New York, American Management Association, 1975. 38 p.
Survey report on management attitudes in the USA with regard to employee motivation, job enrichment and productivity improvement - includes references and statistical data.

KEMPNER, T.; WILD, Ray.
"Job design and productivity." *Journal of management studies*, Fall 1973, pp. 62-81.

KERPPOLA, Klaus.
"Liikkeenjohto ja me-henki, työntekijän etu - yrityksen etu." /Business management and the 'We' spirit: company's benefit - - worker's benefit./ *Liiketaloudellinen aikakauskirja*, 1, 1972, pp. 54-67.

KILBRIDGE, M.D.
"Reduced costs through job enrichment: a case." *The journal of business of the University of Chicago*, 33, 1960, pp. 357-362.
Description of an early job enrichment experiment involving the assembly of small pumps and includes analysis of the costs of different assembly methods.

KRAFT, W.P.; WILLIAMS, K.L.
"Job redesign improves productivity." *Personnel journal*. 54(7), 1975, pp. 393-397.

LAWLER, Edward E. III; HACKMAN, J. Richard.
"Corporate profits and employee satisfaction: must they be in conflict?" California management review, Fall 1971, pp. 46-55.

LIKERT, Rensis.
"Improving cost performance with cross-functional teams." Conference Board record, 12, Sept. 1975, pp.51-59.

MACY, Barry A.; MIRVIS, Philip H.
"A methodology for assessment of quality of worklife and organizational effectiveness in behavioural-economic terms." Administrative science quarterly, June 1976, pp. 212-226.
Description of the development and utilisation of a standardized set of definitions, measures and costing methods for behavioural outcomes. Based on industrial engineering, accounting-work measurement and behavioural concepts. The conceptual framework and methodology are designed for use in assessing organisational effectiveness and QWL experiments and allow for the identification and quantifying of cost components of various behaviours and for estimating total cost of such behaviour over three-year periods.

MALTESEN, I.
Omkostninger, prioritering og planlaegning i arbejdsmiljøet. /The costs, setting of priorities and planning of the work environment./ Forthcoming.

*MATTHES, Harry.
"Aufgaben der Arbeitswissenschaften bei der Steigerung der Arbeitsproduktivität." /Tasks of labour sciences for increasing the productivity of work./ Sozialistische Arbeitswissenschaft, (GDR), 6, 1976, pp. 406-411.
Labour sciences are increasingly channelled to assist in the promotion of labour productivity through new relations including factor analysis and continuous collaboration between theory and practice.

MATTILA, John Peter.
On the economics of worker alienation. Ames, Industrial Relations Center, 1974.

MILLER, F.G., et al.
"Job rotation raises productivity." Industrial engineering, 5(6), 1973, pp. 24-26.

MOSKI, Bruno A.
"Productivity and the quality of life." S.A.M. advanced management journal, Jul. 1973, pp. 15-22.

PENZER, William N.
Productivity and motivation through job engineering. New York, AMACOM, 1973. 31 p.

PFEIFFER, W. von; STANDT, E.
"Ökonomische Konzequenzen der Humanisierung durch neue Formen der Arbeitsorganisation." /Economic consequences of humanisation of work and new forms of work organisation./ Fortschrittliche Betriebsführung und Industrial Engineering, 3, June 1976.

PRENDERGAST, C., ed.
Productivity: the link to economic and social progress. /N.p./ Work in America Institute, 1976.
Contains the proceedings of a conference co-sponsored by the Federation of Swedish Industries and Work in America Institute (1976). The United States and Sweden are compared on employment, economic growth, role of Government policy, management and participation. Discussions on participation and productivity conclude that participation can improve joint problemsolving, understanding and information and therefore increase productivity.

"Productivity, job enrichment, and worker participation." Atlantic economic review, May-June 1974, 62 p. (Special issue.)

RANSOM, G.M.
The economics of group technology. Proceedings of the Fourteenth International Machine Tool Design and Research Conference. London, Macmillan, 1974.

REYNAUD, Jean-Daniel, et al.
Les aspects techniques, économiques et financiers de la valorisation des tâches d'exécution. /Technical, economic and financial aspects of the upgrading of executive tasks./ Paris, Ministère du Travail, 1974. 55p.

ROBERTSON, Keith B.
"Job enrichment pays off." Industrial Canada, Jul. 1969, pp. 73-74.

ROSE, Irwin.
"Manufacturing and the challenge of change; increasing productivity through job enlargement." Management bulletin, (18), pp. 43-47.

ROSS, D.P.
The economics of privately negotiated technological change provisions. A paper prepared for the Twentieth Annual Winter Meeting of the Industrial Relations Research Association, Washington, D.C., December 28, 29, 1967. Ottawa, Canada Department of Labour, 1967.

SCHLITZBERGER, H. H.
"Produktivitätssteigerung durch Zufriedenheit am Arbeitsplatz." /Productivity increase through job satisfaction./ In: Institut für Angewandte Arbeitswissenschaft. (1975 b), pp. 38-54.

SCHONBERGER, Richard J.
"Private lives versus job demands." Human resources management, Summer 1975, pp. 27-32.
A general discussion and analysis of the costs and benefits of more flexible management policies in the areas of working hours, part-time employment, job change options, sabbaticals, day-care facilities etc.

SLOCUM, John W. Jr.; MISSHAUK, Michael J.
"Job satisfaction and productivity." Personnel administration, 33, Mar.-Apr. 1970, pp. 52-58.

SRIVASTA, Suresh, et al.
Job satisfaction and productivity; an evaluation of policy-related research on productivity, industrial organisation and job satisfaction: policy development and implementation. Cleveland, School of Management, 1975.

SUOJANEN, Waino W.; MILLER, James R.
"Productivity, job enrichment, and quality of worklife." Atlanta economic review, May-June 1974, pp. 4-5.

SUOJANEN, Waino, et al., ed.
Perspectives on job enrichment and productivity. Atlanta, Ga., School of Business Administration, 1975. 279 p. (20 articles.)

TAYLOR, James C.
"Experiments in work system design: economic and human results." UCLA, Sept. 1976.

TCHOBANIAN, R.
Reflexions sur l'analyse économique des conditions de travail. /Reflexions on the economic analysis of conditions of work./ Aix-en-Provence, 1972, 135 p. (Roneogr.) (Mémoire. Aix-en--Provence.)

Tecnologia, organizzazione del lavaro, qualificazione. /Technology, work organisation, qualification./ Roma, Ed. Arpes, 1973.

TRABALSKI, K.
Arbeitsorganisation und Arbeitsleistung - Auswirkungen auf das Arbeitsstudium. /Work organisation and work performance - consequences on the work study./ Köln, 1964. (Arbeits- und betriebskundliche Reihe. Bd. 2: Arbeitsorganisation und Arbeitsleistung.)

TRADE UNIONS THEORETICAL RESEARCH INSTITUTE, Budapest.
The effect of the new work structure on the workers, with particular reference to the socialist brigade movement in the Zalaegerszeg Clothing Factory. Budapest, 1976.
A social psychology study carried out in the Zalaegerszeg Clothing Factory in early 1975. On the basis of experience in other countries, new work organisation procedures were introduced into the factory in recent years, resulting in an increase in productivity without major material investment. The study sought to define the influence of the new work organisation on manpower, (i.e. the human aspect.) It demonstrated that there was no reduction in the degree of humanisation of the jobs concerned as a result of the new work organisation and the change did not cause any negative distortion in the personalities of the participants.

TRIVEDI, H.R.
"Impact of social factors on productivity." Labour bulletin, 30(12), Dec. 1970, pp. 33-37.

UNITED STATES CIVIL SERVICE COMMISSION.
Human factors in organizational productivity. /N.p./, 1973. (Its: Measuring and enhancing productivity in the Federal Government. Special report, No. 5.)
Report of investigations conducted by CSC/GAO/OMB on identification of managerial incentives and disincentives to more effective use of human resources and an assessment of the usefulness of new behavioural science techniques in the improvement of employee motivation and organisational productivity. The research team concluded that there is little opportunity to exchange experiences about these developments. Includes a brief annotated bibliography on the behavioural aspects of productivity improvement.

VAN BROEKHOVEN, R.
Experiment work structuring television receiver factory Eindhoven, Part 1: Evaluation of business economic effects of autonomous task-oriented production groups. Eindhoven, Philips, 1973.

WALTERS, Roy W.
"The rewards of job enrichment." Supervisory management, Jan. 1973, pp. 39-41.

WEIL, Reinhold.
"Alternative forms of work organisation in Western Europe: implications for conditions of work and economic efficiency." Paper prepared for an International symposium on social aspects of work organisation: implications for social policy and labour relations. (Moscow, 15-18 February 1977.)

WEIL, Reinhold.
Alternative work organization: improvements of labour conditions and productivity in Western Europe. International Institute for Labour Studies, Research Series (4), 1976, 26 p.

WHEELER, Kenneth E.
"Putting the flexible workweek to work; a tool for increasing productivity in the daily newspaper business." Editor and publisher, 108, June 14, 1975, p. 24.
Article describing the use of a flexible, rearranged workweek at the Toronto Star newspaper.

YORKS, Lyle.
"Job enrichment boosts performance." Journal of systems management. 26(1), Jan. 1975, pp. 16-21.

ZIPPE, H.
Wirtschaftsvergleich alternativer Arbeitssysteme. /Comparison of the economic effects of alternative work organisation systems./ Fachtagung Arbeitsgestaltung in der Produktion '76 des Instituts für Produktionstechnik und Automatisierung. /N.p./, IPA, 1976. (Vortrag No. 17.)

V. OTHER ASPECTS OF THE HUMANISATION OF WORK AND THE QUALITY OF WORKING LIFE

1. Problems of traditional work organisation

"Absentéisme élevé dans une usine de construction automobile." /High rate of absenteeism in an automobile factory./ U.I.M.M. documentation étrangère, (331), p.6.

"Accroissement de l'absentéisme ouvrier dans les industries des métaux." /Higher absenteeism among workers in the metal trades./ U.I.M.M. documentation étrangère, (335), Nov. 1976, p. 5.

ALDERFER, Clayton P.
Existence, relatedness, and growth; human needs in organizational settings. New York, Free Press, 1972. x, 198 p.
A literature survey of research in the areas of human relations and industrial psychology in the work environment. With particular reference to its theoretical implications. Topics covered includes attitudes, behaviour, mental stress, and satisfaction.

ALTMANN, N.; BECHTLE, G.
Betriebliche Herrschaftsstruktur und industrielle Gesellschaft. /Hierarchical structures of enterprises and industrial society./ München, 1971.

Arbetsorganisation. /Work organisation./ Diskussionsinlägg från en arbetsgrupp inom LO. Utg. av Landsorganisationen till LO-kongressen 1976. Stockholm, 1976. 111 p.

ARGYLE, M.; GARDENER, G.; GIOFFI, F.
"Supervisory methods related to productivity, absenteeism and labour turnover." Human relations, 11, 1958, pp. 23-40.

ARYA, V.P.
Principles and practice relating to punishment and disciplinary actions in private industries. 5th ed. Calcutta, 1968.

BALSARA, Fali H.
Discipline and disciplinary action in modern industries; a thesis on human relations in industries. Bombay, Personnel Training Institute, 1962.

BEACH, Dale S.
Managing people at work: readings in personnel. London, Macmillan 1969.

BJÖRK, L.
"Work organization and the improvement of the work environment." Ambio, 4(1), 1975, pp. 55-59.

BROCK, Adolf, et al.
Industriearbeit und Herrschaft. /Industrial work and authority/ Stuttgart, Europäische Verlagsanstalt, 1969.

BROWN, W.
Piecework abandoned. The effect of wage incentive systems on managerial authority. London, 1963.

BUSCHARDT, Dieter.
Zur rationellen Organisation von Arbeitsabläufen. /The rational organisation of work processes./ Berlin, Verl. Die Wirtschaft, 1973. 175 p.
Explains rational methods of organisational analysis and organisational principles and procedures in general use. The effective application of such methods can assist in the rational organisation of a company's work in all fields.

CENTRE D'ETUDES ET DE FORMATION SUR LA PLANIFICATION ET L'ECONOMIE SOCIALES.
Absentéisme, conditions de travail, condition de vie: vers une nouvelle interprétation de l'absentéisme. /Absenteeism, working conditions and living conditions: towards a new interpretation of absenteeism./ /N.p./, 1975.

CENTRE D'ETUDES ET DE FORMATION SUR LA PLANIFICATION ET L'ECONOMIE SOCIALES.
Les déterminations de l'absentéisme: approche préliminaire. /The determinants of absenteeism: a preliminary approach./ /N.p./, 1975.

CHAKRAPANI, T.K.
"A study of the factors influencing the incidence of absenteeism in a textile mill. A preliminary report." Journal of the Indian Academy of Applied Psychology. 1, 1964, pp. 93-97.

CHAKRABORTY, Parul.
Strikes and morale industry in India and her principal states. Calcutta, 1969.

CHAND, Prem; PARKASH, Ram.
"Absenteeism in Indian industry." Productivity, 9(182), Apr.-June, Jul.-Sept. 1970, pp. 178-186.

CHATTERJEE, Amitava; JAMES, E.V.
"An investigation into the problem of effective supervision." Journal of Indian Academy of Applied Psychology, 2, 1965, pp. 8-12.

CONFEDERATION OF TRADE UNIONS OF YUGOSLAVIA.
Abstenteeism; an analysis by Council of CTUY. Belgrade, 1976.

CONFERENCE ON WORK ORGANISATION, TECHNICAL DEVELOPMENT AND MOTIVATION OF THE INDIVIDUAL, Brussels, 1974.
Background papers. Brussels, Commission of the European Communities, 1974.

CULBERT, Samuel A.
The organization trap and how to get out of it. New York, Basic Books, 1974. 161 p.

DAVIS, Louis E.
"The coming crisis for production management; technology and organization." International journal of production research, 9(1), 1971, pp. 65-82.
Considers the conceptual framework of behavioural response to technological and social change in developed countries. Deals in particular with the socio-technical relationships in job satisfaction, motivation and job requirements. Looks at the implication for management and personnel management practices in post-industrial societies.

DELAMOTTE, Yves.
The social partners face the problems of productivity and employment. Paris, Organisation for Economic Co-operation and Development, 1971.

"Division du travail et technique de pouvoir." /Division of labour and the technique of power./ Temps moderne, Apr. 1970.

"Dossier conditions de travail:
- Ce travail qui nous enchaîne
- des réalités très dures
- des chiffres parlants
- des luttes efficaces avec la CFDT."
/Conditions of work:
- The bondage of work
- Harsh realities
- Telling figures
- Effective action with the CFDT./
CFDT Syndicalisme Magazine, (15), May 1976, pp. 1-13.

ECONOMICIAN (PSEUD.).
"Strained industrial relations inhibit production at Hindusthan Cables." Industrial times (Bombay), 14(12), June 1972, pp. 13-15.

EMERY, Fred E.
The assembly line, its logic and our future. Canberra, 1975, 16 p. (Australian National University. Centre for Continuing Education. Occasional papers in continuing education, No. 7.)
Based on an address to the Institution of Engineers, Australia, held in Sydney, February 1975. Discusses the assumptions on which assembly lines have been designed and examines the relevance of these assumptions for design of future mass flow production systems.

EMPLOYERS' FEDERATION OF INDIA.
Absenteeism in industries in Bombay: a survey. Bombay, 1969.

ENDLER, Kurt; NOWIKOW, Alexej.
Arbeitszeitverluste - Erkennen, Erfassen, Vermeiden. /Working-time losses - perceptions, comprehension, avoidance./ /N.p., n.d./
After stating the need to reduce losses of working time, this book explains their causes and the methods for dealing with them.

Enterprise organization and guidance; The socialist enterprise 2.
Budapest, Akadémia publishing House, 1975.
Gives a general picture of the present situation of Hungarian organisation and management science and deals in detail with the question of the direction in which research must be further developed in order to give further consideration to the problem raised by Hungarian enterprise practice and production relations.

Les équipes de recherche d'amélioration des conditions de travail. /Research teams on the improvement of work organisation./ Paris, ERACT APACT, 1974. 47 p.

EULER, H.P.
Arbeitskonflikt und Leistungsrestriktion im Industriebetrieb. /Work conflicts and performance restriction in industrial enterprises./ Düsseldorf, Bertelsmann Universitätsverlag, 1973.

FITZROY, Felix R.; NUTZINGER, Hans G.
Entfremdung, Selbstbestimmung und Wirtschaftsdemokratie. Eine kritische Übersicht. /Alienation, work autonomy and industrial democracy: a critical overview./ Dortmund, Universität Dortmund, 1974. (Arbeitspapier Nr. 3, 8. März 1974, Korrigierte Fassung 9. April 1974.

FRANCE. MINISTERE DU TRAVAIL. SERVICE DES ETUDES ET DE LA STATISTIQUE.
Premiers résultats d'une enquête sur l'absentéisme en octobre 1974. /Preliminary findings of a survey on absenteeism carried out in October 1974./ Paris, 1975.

FRIEDMANN, Georges.
Grenzen der Arbeitsteilung. /Limits of work division./ Frankfurt/M., 1959.

FRIEDMANN, Georges.
Le travail en miettes. /Fragmented work./ Paris, Gallimard, 1964. 374p.

FULCHER, James.
"Discontent in a Swedish ship-yard: the Kockums report." British journal of industrial relations, Jul. 1973, pp. 242-258.

GAUTRAT, Jacques.
"Les problèmes du diagnostic et de la décision dans le domaine des conditions de travail." /Problems of diagnosis and decision-making in the field of working conditions./ Pour, (47-48), Mar.-Apr. 1976, pp. 125-131.

GORZ, et al.
Critique de la division du travail. /A critical examination of the division of labour./ Paris, Le Seuil, 1973.

GRUJIC, Milenko.
"Uslovi rada i zadaci radnih organizacija." /Working conditions and tasks of work organisations./ In: Zaštita na radu br. 2. Belgrade, 1972.

HAATANEN. P.; HIKIPÄÄ, S.
Tehtaan johto ja tietojenvälitys. /Factory management and internal information./ Helsinki, University of Helsinki, 1970. (Helsingin Yliopisto. Sociaalipolitiikanalitos. Tutkimusksia, No. 9.)

HENDERSON, Richard I.
"Meeting changing aspirations and expectations." Atlanta economic review, 25(2), Mar.-Apr. 1975, pp. 24-28.

HERON, A.
"Le taylorisme hier et demain." /Taylorism, past and future./ Les temps modernes, (349-350), Aug.-Sept. 1975, pp. 220-278.

HONE, Angus.
"High absenteeism and high commitment." Economic and political weekly, 3(21), May 1968, M-31-M-32.

"Incitation à la productivité chez Westwood Engineering Lit." /Productivity incentives at Westwood Engineering Ltd./ Qualité de la vie, lettre n° 6, Nov. 1976, p. 16.

"Insuffisance de la qualité et de l'organisation du travail en U.R.S.S. dans l'automobile." /Defects in the quality and organisation of work in the automobile industry in the USSR./ U.I.M.M. documentation étrangère, (334), Oct. 1976.

ISTITUTO PER LO SVILUPPO DELLA FORMAZIONE PROFESSIONALE DEI LAVORATORI, Rome.
"Organizzazione del lavoro operaio in fabbrica." /Organisation production work in factories/ Quaderni di formazione, (9), Nov. 1974, pp. 1-130.
A field study on assembly line work and factory organisation in Italy describing recent trends, experience and obstacles to the humanisation of work.

JACQUELIN, P.; ALINAAC, M.
"Le travail manuel en question." /Revising the concept of manual work./ Options, (101), Nov. 1974, pp. 15-24.
Article covering the historical evolution of the division of labour between nonmanual and manual work, the need for humanisation of work in factory organisation and the possible role of the manual worker in the introduction of automation.

JUNGBLUT, M.
"Taylor schleicht sich ins Büro." /Taylor creeps into the office./ Die Zeit, (38), 13 Sept. 1974, p. 36.

KARCHER, Manfred A.
"Arbeitsstrukturierung, auch für Gastarbeiter?" /Work restructuring, also for foreign workers?/ Refa-Nachrichten, 27(3), 1974, p. 195 et seg.

KERN, B.; KERN, H.
"Krise des Taylorismus? Bemerkungen zur Humanisierung der Arbeit." /A crisis for Taylorism? Notes on the humanisation of work./ In: OSTERLAND, M., ed. Arbeitssituation, Lebenslage und Konfliktpotential. Frankfurt/M., 1975.

KINGSTON, ONT. QUEEN'S UNIVERSITY. INDUSTRIAL RELATIONS CENTRE.
Absenteeism: a bibliography. Kingston, Ont., 1975. 60 p. (Its: Bibliography series, No. 6.)

KNOX, J.B.
"Absenteeism and turnover in an Argentine factory." American sociological review, 26, June 1961, pp. 424-428.

*KOYOTO UNIVERSITY. RESEARCH INSTITUTE FOR HUMANISTIC STUDIES.
Report of the second symposium on the upheaval of industrial structure. /N.p., n.d./ (In Japanese.)
Three volumes of papers from the second symposium on the upheaval of industrial structure dealing with its relation to labour structures and problems.

LEMINSKY, G.
"Arbeitstruktur und Arbeitsorganisation." /Work structures and work organisation./ Afa-Informationen, (5), 1975, p. 143 et seg.

LEMINSKY, G.; HELFERT, M.
Der Wandel der Arbeitsanforderungen bei technologischen und organisatorischen Änderungen. /The changes in work requirements because of technological and organisational changes./ Köln, 1970. (WWI-Studie, No. 19.)

LÖSSL, E.
"Die betriebliche Personalorganisation und ihre psychologischen Probleme." /Industrial staff organisation and its psychological problems./ In: MAYER,A.; HERWIG, B., eds. Handbuch der Psychologie. 2. Aufl. Göttingen, 1970. (Betriebspsychologie, Bd. 9.)

MAIGNIEN, Y.
La division du travail manuel et intellectuel. /The division of labour, manual and intellectual./ Paris, Maspero, 1975.

MANGIONE, T.W.
Turnover: a model and a review of the literature. /N.p./, ISR, 1972.

MANGIONE, T.W.
Turnover: some psychological and demographic correlates. /N.p., n.d./

Mensch und Arbeit im sozialistischen Betrieb; Lehrbuch für Ingenieur- und Fachschulen. /Man and work in socialist enterprises; a handbook for engineering and technical schools./ Leipzig, Fachbuchverl., 1967. 359 p.
Introduction to the principles and main problems of work design and personality developments in socialist enterprises.

MIANI, G.
"Organizzazione del lavoro e decentramento produttivo." /The organisation of work and the decentralisation of production./ Fabbrica aperta, 2(1), Jul. 1975, pp. 34-53.
This article, which draws largely on the findings of research into organisation of work and labour disputes in general, deals with the following subjects: technology and the organisation of work; the response of capital to the breakdown of traditional models; documents, proposals and points of view of the unions.

MINĎAŠ, A.
Postavenie a úloha manstra v procese riadenia. /Position and role of the foreman in the management process./ Bratislava, Práca, 1975. 117 p.

Munkaszervezés. /Work organisation./ Budapest, Ministry of Labour, Research Institute for Labour, 1976. (Course notes.)

NAIR, V.N.S.
"Absenteeism in industry; a case study." Indian manager, 1(3), Jul.-Sept. 1970, pp. 56-72.

NEMESHÁZI, Pál; SEBESTYÉN, Gy. Tamás.
A munkaidő és az üzemidő felhasználása. /Utilisation of working time./ Budapest, Közgazdasági és Jogi Könyvkiadó, 1975.
The book analyses the problems of effective utilisation of working time and the relationship between hours of work and recreation periods; it outlines a relationship between working hours and worker fatigue.

NEUMANN, Jochen; TIMPE, Klaus-Peter.
Arbeitsgestaltung - Psychophysiologische Probleme bei Überwachungs- und Steuerungstätigkeiten. /Job design - psychological and physiological problems of supervisory and steering activities./ Berlin, Dt. Verl. der Wissenschaften, 1971. 142 p.
Gives a general picture of the knowledge gained in industrial and engineering psychology and discusses psychological and ergonomic conditions for job design and the methodology of its psychological aspects.

OHLSTRÖM, Bo.
Kockumsrapporten. Om orsaker till missnöje bland varvsarbetare. /The Kockum report. Reasons for discontent among shipyard workers./ Stockholm, Prisma i samarbete med LO, 1970. 418 p.
A report on the effect of a reorganisation of work at Kockum. The reorganisation resulted in discontent among the workers. This report was prepared by the LO as a first step towards analysing and improving the work situation at Kockum.

PARÁNYI, György.
Modern work organization. Budapest, Economics and Law Publishing House, 1965.
Covers the most important questions of work organisation, giving the theoretical background and serving as a guide for practical work. Places special emphasis on mechanical and manual jobs for blue-collar workers, since these are the most important jobs from the point of view of manual effort. Considers the characteristics of jobs in offices, warehouses, conveyor belt operators, etc. Gives examples of complex work organisation analyses illustrating work organisation aspirations based on the interests of the workers.

PRENTING, Theodore O.; THOMPOULOS, Nicholas T.
Humanism and technology in assembly line systems. Rochelle Park, N.J., Hayden Book Company, 1974. 404 p.

PREWITT, Lena B.
"Discontent in the ranks: is the operative worker really trapped?" Personnel journal, Oct. 1973, 6 p.
Argues in favour of a human resources programme to resolve "discontent in the ranks", pinpointing the quality of first line supervision and lack of promotion as the reasons behind employee discontent.

QUINN, R.P.; LEVITIN, T.; EDEN, D.
"The multi-million dollar misunderstanding: an attempt to reduce turnover among disadvantaged workers." In: DAVIS, Louis E.; CHERNS, Albert B. The quality of working life New York, The Free Press, 1975, T.2, pp. 83-93.

RAJPUT, Kuldip Singh.
"Problem of labour turnover: a case study." Industrial management, 10(7), Jul. 1971 pp. 7-13.

RECK, Ross.
"Can the production line be humanized?" MSU business topics, Autumn 1974, pp. 27-36.

RYANT, J,C.
Work organization behaviour and attitudes. Study conducted for the Pilot Projects Branch, Program Development Service, Department of Manpower and Immigration, by the Industrial Relations Centre, McGill University, Montreal, 1968.

SARAPATA, Adam.
Plynnosc zalog. /Labour turnover in industrial crews./ Warsaw, Lanstwowe Wydawnictwo Ekonomiczne, 1968.

SCHARMANN, Th.
"Betriebsorganisation und Gruppenpflege." /Enterprise organisation and group care./ In: PAUL,H., ed. Probleme der Gruppenarbeit im Betrieb. Göttingen, 1954. (Schriftenreihe für Gruppenwissenschaften, Heft 1.)

SCHOUTEN, J.
Vrijheid in het werk; over organisatiestruktuur en het welzijn van produktiewerkers. /Freedom in work; aspects of organisation structure and well-being of production workers./ Meppel, Boom, 1974. 208 p.

"Une semaine perdue par an dans la métallurgie." /One week lost every year in the metal industry./ Le nouvel économiste, (52), Oct. 1976, p. 72.

SHIVDASANI, H.K.
"Dependence proneness in work organisation." Indian journal of industrial relations, 7(1), Jul. 1971, pp. 53-58.

SINCLAIR, Peter.
Authority and technology. 2nd ed. Ottawa, Information Canada, 1971.

Sociálno-ekonomické otázky práce vo vtr. Zborník referátov a koreferátov prednesených na pracynom seminári v Zdáni v roku 1975. /Socioeconomic questions of labour in the scientific and technological revolution. The collection of reports and co-reports delivered on the working seminar in Zdan in 1975./ Bratislava, Czechoslovak Research Institute of Labour and Social Affairs, 1976. 223 p.
The volume contains the evaluation of the common, complex empirical research carried out in two machinery plants.

SOCIETY FOR HUMANISTIC MANAGEMENT. ANNUAL CONFERENCE, 2nd, Annapolis, 1973.
Worker alienation and job motivation in a democratic society, a look at organization today and tomorrow; proceedings. Washingston, Society for Humanistic Management, 1974. 94 p.

SVENSKA ARBETSGIVAREFÖRENINGEN.
The condemned piecework. A study of 73 plants in Swedish industry. Stockholm, 1973.

ULICH, E.
Über Fehlzeiten im Betrieb. Eine Sammlung von Untersuchungsergebnissen und Erfahrungen. /About absenteeism in enterprises; a collection of studies and experiences./ Köln, 1965.

UNION DES INDUSTRIES METALLURGIQUES ET MINIERES, Paris.
L'absentéisme en 1971; résultats d'ensemble - répartition suivant les causes - effets de la mensualisation. /Absenteeism in 1971. Over-all results - classification by cause - effects of calculating monthly rates./ Paris, 1971. 58 p.

UNITED STATES CONGRESS. SENATE. COMMITTEE ON LABOR AND PUBLIC WELFARE.
Worker alienation, 1972; hearings, 92d Cong., 2d sess., S.3916, July 25 and 26, 1972. Washington, U.S. Govt. Print. Off., 1972. 354 p.

VERBAND DER AUTOMOBILINDUSTRIE e. V.
Probleme der Fliessbandarbeit - steht eine Abkehr von der Fliessbandarbeit bevor? /Problems of assembly line work - will assembly line work be suppressed?/ Frankfurt/M., 1973.

WEISS, Dimitri; SARTIN, Pierette.
Absentéisme et rotation du personnel. /Absenteeism and personnel turnover./ Paris, 1976. 28 p. (Dossier BTE formation promotion.)

2. Attitudes and policies towards work organisation and the quality of working life.

BASS, Bernard M.; ELDRIDGE, Larry D.
"Accelerated managers' objectives in twelve countries." Industrial relations, 12(2), 1973, pp. 158-171.

BIRKWALD, Reimar.
"Gestaltung der Arbeit durch Tarifvertrag." /Work design by wage agreement./ Das Mitbestimmungsgespräch, (5-6), 1974.

BIRKWALD, Reimar.
"Über die gewerkschaftlichen Ideen zur Humanisierung." /On the ideas of unions regarding humanisation./ Kursbuch, (43), Mar. 1976.

*BLUESTONE, Irving.
"Decision making by workers." The personnel administrator, 19(5), Jul.-Aug. 1974, pp. 26-30.
An article by a top union leader examining the trends towards the humanisation of the working environment. The author emphasises that the unions have a continuing responsibility for the improvement of the quality of working life through collective bargaining, experiments and demonstration projects and suggests that the 1973 negotiation between General Motors and the United Automobile Workers reflected this increased concern with job-enrichment. He predicts an intensification of this trend in worker/management and union/management relations and sees the union as playing a vital role in this area and sharing with management the task of developing and implementing programmes which will achieve a better quality of working life.

BLUESTONE, Irving.
"The union and improving the quality of worklife." Atlanta economic review, 24(3), 1974, pp. 32-37.

BOPP, William J.
Police personnel administration: the management of human resources. Boston, Holbrook Press, 1974. 425 p.

BOWERS, D.G.; SEASHORE, S.E.
"Changing the structure and functioning of an organization." In: EVAN, W.M., ed. Organizational experiments: laboratory and field research. New York, Harper and Row, 1971, pp. 185-201.
A description of a multi-faceted change effort in a large packaging materials firm, which focused on the proposition that "...an organisation is likely to achieve its purposes better: (a) if there is an emphasis on the work group, rather than exclusively on the individual, as the unit supervised, (b) if there is a high rate of interaction and mutual influence among work group members, (c) if there is a high degree of participation in decision-making and control activities in the lower echelons of the organisation, and (d) if supervisors provide to subordinates a high degree of supportiveness." Concluded

that while there was evidence to support the proposition it was neither so strong or so well-controlled from external factors as to be conclusive.

CAMERON, Sheila.
Organisation change: a description of alternative strategies. London, Department of Employment, Work Research Unit, 1973 Paper directed towards academics which discusses organisational change in general and various different approaches to change programmes. Covers leading change strategies: human relations and organisation development strategies are described in some detail and compared. Outlines typical stages in development process. Also includes an appraisal of job enrichment.

CLIFF, T.
The employers' offensive: productivity deals and how to fight them. London, 1970.

"La codécision: les employeurs révèlent leurs pensées secrètes sur la codécision et sur le mouvement syndical et le gouvernement qui les forcent à accepter la codécision." /Codecision: employers reveal their secret thoughts on codecision and on the trade union and government move to make them accept it./ U.I.M.M., (333), Aug.-Sept. 1976, annexe 3.

CONFEDERATION GENERALE DU TRAVAIL. COMMISSION EXECUTIVE.
"Position et propositions CGT pour des conditions de travail plus humaines en rapport avec notre temps." /Standpoint and proposals of CGT on more human working conditions relevant to our time./ La peuple, (Paris), (887), Feb. 1972.

COOPER, Robert.
"Task characteristics and intrinsic motivation." Human relations, 26(3), 1973, pp. 387-413.

DELAMOTTE, Yves.
"The attitudes of French and Italian trade unions to the 'humanisation' of work." Labour and society, Jan. 1976, pp. 49-62.

DELAMOTTE, Yves.
Union attitudes to the quality of working life. Paper prepared for the International Conference on the Quality of Working Life, Arden House, New York, Aug. 1972.

DIENA, Vittorio.
"Rassegna delle posizioni politico sindacali sull'organizzazione del lavoro." /Review of the political stand of the trade unions on the question of work organisation./ In: SERVIZIO RICERCHE SOCIOLOGICHE E STUDI SULL'ORGANIZZAZIONE OLIVETTI. Le trasformazioni del lavoro esecutivo. Ivrea, 1972. (Roneogr.) An account of the evolving interest of labour unions in this issue between 1968-1972.

DUCKER, John P.
Worker participation and productivity: a trade union point of view. Address by Mr. John P. Ducker /to the/ 16th General Management Conference, Canberra, July 1974. 19 l. (Unpublished.)
Tenders the view that worker participation can best be achieved by developing a three-pronged approach: job redesign for workers "who have inherited monotonous, repetitive, uncreative jobs"; participative management at the production level; and effective representation of workers at the board-level. Cautions against "gimmicky schemes", points to the need for unions and workers to be fully consulted and supports the need for trade union training.

EUROPEAN COMMUNITIES.
"La Commission publie un livre vert sur la participation des travailleurs et la structure des sociétés." /The Commission publishes a green paper on the participation./ Bulletin d'information sociales, (1), 1976, p. 30.

*GERMANY (Federal Republic). BUNDESMINISTER FÜR FORSCHUNG UND TECHNOLOGIE.
Humanisierung des Arbeitslebens. /Humanisation of working life./ Bonn, 1976.
Description of a detailed research programme on humanisation of work, the main objective of which is to adapt working conditions to workers' needs. The report considers the conditions and problems of new work structures, the volume of research in the field and the possibilities of achieving the objectives of the programme itself.

HAWKINS, Kevin.
"Productivity bargaining: a reassessment." Industrial relations journal, 2, Spring 1971, pp. 10-34.

HELFERT, M.
"Humanisierung der Arbeit und gewerkschaftliche Aktivierung der Arbeitnehmenr." /Humanisation of work and trade union activation of workers./ WSI-Mitteilungen, (10), 1972, p. 320.

HERRICK, Neal Q.
"Government approaches to the humanisation of work." Monthly labour review, 96(4), Apr. 1973, pp. 59-61.

HERZBERG, Frederick.
The managerial choice: to be efficient and to be human. Homewood, Ill., Dow Jones-Irwin, 1976.

HÉTHY, Lajos; MAKÓ, Csaba.
Workers' attitudes and the economic organization. Budapest, Akadémia Publishing House, 1972.
Drawing on the sociological study of a Hungarian factory, on the basis of workers' attitudes and a search for their motivations, the work analyses the internal life of the workers' groups, the workshops and the plant and the whole internal operation of the economic organisation and the enterprise. Also attempts to outline methods which could lead to the easing or solution of present problems.

HUGHES, J.; GREGORY, D.
"Richer jobs for workers?" In: WEIR, Mury, ed, Job satisfaction: challenge and response in modern Britain. London, Fontana, 1976, p. 288 et seg.
An article on job enrichment, covering the trade unionists' view of the phenomenon, which is much wider than the "narrow abstractions emanating from government and management".

ISEO; UDDA.
"Atti del convegno Organizzazione del lavoro, iniziativa imprenditoriale e potere sindacale." /Documents from the conference on the Organisation of work , enterprise initiatives and trade union power./ Direzione aziendale, (1-2), Jan.-Feb. 1974.
For the first time managers, union leaders and specialists come together to discuss on work organisation.

INDIA. MINISTRY OF LABOUR AND EMPLOYMENT. INDUSTRIAL PSYCHOLOGY DIVISION.
Study on the attitudes of officers towards changes in management practices in a textile factory. Delhi, 1964.

JEDRZYCKI, W., ed.
Planowanie społeczne w zakładzie pracy. Aspekty humanizacyjne. /Social planning in enterprise. Human aspects./ Warszawa, 1974.

KAUFHOLD, B.
"Bürgerliche Konzeptionen zur 'Humanisierung der Arbeitswelt'." /Bourgeois conceptions of "humanisation of work"./ IPW Berichte, 4(3), Mar. 1975, pp. 50-54.
Discusses the bourgeois conception of humanisation of work and considers the way in which socialist countries face this problem from the point of view of the interests of workers.

KRAJCEVIĆ, F.
"Organisationsentwicklungen Jugoslawischer Betriebe." /Organisation evolution in the Yugoslav enterprise./ Verantwortliche Betriebsführung. Stuttgart, 1969.

LANDORGANISATIONEN I SVERIGE.
LOs handlingsprogram för företagsdemokrati och data. /LO programme of action for democracy in the undertaking./ Stockholm, 1976. 94 p. + annex.

LANDORGANISATIONEN I SVERIGE.
Solidariskt medbestämmande. Rapport till LO-kongressen 1976. /Decision-making in solidarity. Report to the LO Congress 1976./ Stockholm, Prisma i samarbete med LO, 1976. 110 p.

LEMINSKY, Gerhard.
"Arbeitsgestaltung als Lernprozess." /Job design as a learning process./ Gewerkschaftliche Monatshefte, (1), 1973, p. 28 et seg.

LEMINSKY, Gerhard.
"Gewerkschaftliche Ansatzmöglichkeiten zur Humanisierung der Arbeit." /Possible trade union approaches towards the humanisation of work./ Das Mitbestimmungsgespräch, (5-6), 1974.

LEMINSKY, Gerhard.
Trade union strategies for humanisation of work in a developed economy. Referat auf dem IFAC Workshop on Productivity and Man in Bad Boll vom 21. - 25. Januar 1974.

LESIEUR, Fred G., ed.
The Scanlon Plan: a frontier in labour management co-operation. Cambridge, Mass., Massachusetts Institute of Technology Press, 1962.

LESIEUR, Fred G.; PUCKETT, Elbridge S.
"The Scanlon Plan has proved itself." Harvard Business review, 47(5), Sept.-Oct. 1969, pp. 109-118.
Outlines the basic philosophy and structure generally employed in a Scanlon-type participation and incentive system plan, analysing the experiences of three companies that have used it and drawing conclusions from their experiences, pointing out benefits in the areas of acceptance of change, measurement of performance, and impact on efficiency. The plan's message would seem to be that management, union, and employees can collaborate without strife to improve operations.

LOOS, W.
"Humanisierung der Arbeit aus der Sicht der Gewerkschaft." /Humanisation of work from trade union point of view./ AFA-Informationen, (2), 1974.

McINTOSH, J.
"Employer's attitudes." In: Seminar on Worker Participation in Australia. University of Melbourne, 1975, proceedings. Parkville, Vic., Department of Legal Studies and Industrial Relations Programme, Universtiy of Melbourne and Melbourne Chamber of Commerce, 1975, pp. 36-41.
Describes steps taken by I.C.I. Australia Limited to become more adaptable to changing conditions, particularly in the management of people, by increasing participation at all levels in the organisation.

MATTHÖFER, Hans.
"Die Bedeutung der Mitbestimmung am Arbeitsplatz und im Betrieb für die politische Bildungsarbeit der Gewerkschaften." /The significance of participation at the levels of the shop-floor and the undertaking for the political education activities of trade unions./ Die Neue Gesellschaft, 16, 1969.

MAURICE, M.
"Politiques syndicales pour l'amélioration des conditions de travail et de l'organisation de l'entreprise." /Trade union policies for the improvement of conditions of work and the organisation of the undertaking./ Revue française des affaires sociales, 28(1), Jan.-Mar., 1974, pp. 53-99.
The problem of working conditions has recently been posed in new terms in a number of industrialised countries. A preliminary analysis of the position taken by the trade unions on conditions of work, and of various kinds of experience; convergent and divergent positions and policies of the trade unions, and future prospects.

MEHER, M.R.
"Achieving industrial democracy through collective bargaining." Capital, 172(4314), May 1974, pp. 710-712.

MENDNER, J.
"Humanisierung der Arbeit als gewerkschaftspolitiches Problem." /Humanisation of work as a problem for the unions./ Mehrwert, 9, 1975.

Metodika plánováni sociálního rezvoje podnikových kolektivů v průmyslových podnicích. /Methodology of planning of enterprise collectives social development in industiral enterprises./ Bratislava, Czechoslovak Research Institute of Labour and Social Affairs, 1975. 257 p.
A research study adapted for publication. It serves as a handbook for uniform management activity of enterprises in the field of planning of social development of organisational collectives.

*MIRE, Joseph.
"Improving working life: the role of European unions." Monthly labour review, 97(9), Sept. 1974, pp. 3-11.
Describes efforts to restructure and reorganise work in several Western European countries. Lists some of the programmes and approaches developed to combat worker dissatisfaction and considers briefly specific efforts being made in Sweden, Great Britain, France, Italy and West Germany. Focusses on union attitudes towards these programmes and their role in inplementing them. Suggests that unions will be compelled to participate as a result of management initiatives and their own long-term interests. Concludes that without union cooperation and support the goals of job improvement could not be achieved.

MYERS, M. Scott.
"Overcoming union opposition to job enrichment." Harvard business review, 49, May-June 1971, pp. 37-49.
Contending that union, as well as management involvement is essential to ensure the success of efforts at organisational change, the author describes four company approaches to making job enrichment and other aspects of organisational development feasible in a unionised workforce.

"Le nouveau système de cogestion des grandes entreprises en R.F.A.: un point de vue syndical." /The new system of co-management of large undertakings in the Federal Republic of Germany: a trade union point of view./ Problèmes économiques, (1476), June 1976, pp. 18-20.

NORTH, D.T.B.; BUCKINGHAM, G.D.B.
Productivity agreements and wage systems. London, 1969.

PAILHOUS, Jean.
"Le travail à la chaîne et ses répercussions sur les conditions de travail." /Assembly-line work and its repercussions on working conditions./ Economie et politique, (224), Mar. 1973.

PÁNEK, Z.; ŠALKOVÁ, H.
Podniková sociální politika. /Social policy in the undertaking./ Praha, ČSKVR, 1974. 180 p.

PAUL-CAVALLIER, Marcel.
Strategies patronales d'organisation du travail. /Employers' strategies for work organisation./ Paris, 1975. 93 p. (Mémoire Science Politique.)

PETITGUYOT, Bernard.
Les conditions de travail dans la practique des négociations collectives. /Working conditions in collective bargaining practice./ Montrouge(France), Agence Nationale pour l'Amélioration des Conditions du Travail, 1975.
Deals with the treatment of problems of working conditions in collective bargaining. Analyses its results from the view points of national and other level collective agreements. Four fields are considered: safety and health, payment by results, hours of work and the organisation of work. The author notes that the number of agreements on conditions of work remains limited; as regards job enrichment, employers' federations in France advise their members against entering into written commitments.

*Planning and social development of the personnel of enterprises: methodological recommendations. 2nd ed., Moscow, Publishing House of Trade Unions, Provisdad, 1975.
The book describes the following aspects of social planning: improving social structure of the personnel, improving conditions of work and health of working people, improving systems of remuneration, improving housing conditions and cultural and welfare facilities of the working people. Educational activities in the Communist way, and the development of public activities of the working people. Organisation of elaboration and execution of the plan of social develoment of the personnel or enterprises. The State Committee of the USSR, the All Union Council of Trade Unions of the USSR, and the State Committee of Labour of the USSR have recommended this work as a practical guide for elaborating planning of social development of the personnel of enterprises and industrial associations.

PRŮŠA, J.
Vedení lidí v socialistickém podniku. /Managing people in a socialist undertaking./ Praha, Svoboda, 1974. 218 p.

"Un rapport officiel: 33 propositions pour améliorer le travail posté." /An official report: 33 proposals for improving shift work./ Le figaro, 17-18 Jul. 1976, p. 3.

"Revaloriser le travail manuel." /Improving the status of manual work./ Objectif formation, (10), Dec. 1975, pp. 8-24.
The points of view of the Government, employers and the principal trade union organisations, and the findings of a recent study on worker motivation.

REIF, William E.; FERRAZZI, D.N.; EVANS, R.J.
"Job enrichment: who uses it and why." Business horizons, 17(1), Feb. 1974, pp. 73-78.
An article based on a questionnaire survey of a random sample in the USA. Aimed at revealing management attitudes to and experiences with job enrichment. The authors conclude that while some benefits have been achieved in terms of productivity and job satisfaction, the majority of the firms practicing job enrichment still have a limited understanding of the concept.

"Ristrutturazione e organizzazione del lavore nelle fabbriche metalmeccaniche bolognesi." /Work restructuring and organisation in metal works in Bologna./ Inchiesta, 5(19), Jul.-Sept. 1975, pp. 6-29.
Discusses the commitment of the Bologna Metalworkers' Federation to restructuring and decentralisation of production (surveys, conferences, etc.).

ROETHLISBERGER, F.J.
"Von Hawthorne bis heute." /From the Hawthorne experiments up to now./ Fortschrittliche Betriebsführung, 21(2), 1972.

ROSOW, Jerome M.
"Now is the time for productivity bargaining." Harvard business review, Jan-Feb. 1972, pp. 79-89.
Examines the mechanics and argues the merits of productivity bargaining in which management and labour agree to establish a set of quid pro quos whereby labour agrees to scrap old work habits for the new and more effective ones desired by management in return for some of the gains of modernisation and increased efficiency in the form of new and better work incentives.

ROY, S.K.; MENON, A. Sreekumar, eds.
Motivation and organizational effectiveness. /N.p./, 1974.
A book of readings which focusses on motivation and organisational effectiveness and their implications for managerial practices.

SCHMUNK, Günter; WINKLER, Gunter.
"Probleme der weiteren Verbesserung der Leitung und Planung der Arbeits- und Lebensbedingungen." /Problems of a further improvement of the direction and planning of working and living conditions./ Sozialistische Arbeitswissenschaft, 19(1), 1975, p. 36.
The relationship between the planning of working and and living conditions and the enterprise collective contract (BKV) is described here and special attention is paid to its significance. The study makes some suggestions for the direction and planning of working and living conditions.

SCHUMANN, Michael.
"Gewerkschaften, Humanisierung und menschengerechte Arbeitsgestaltung." /Trade unions, humanisation and human work organisation./ Gewerkschaftliche Monatshefte, Aug. 1974, p. 520.

SCHUMANN, Michael.
"Humanisierung der Arbeit als gesellschaftspolitische und gewerkschaftliche Aufgabe; ein Konferenzbericht." /Humanisation of work as a social, political and trade union task; a conference report./ Das Mitbestimmungsgespräch, (7-8), 1974.

SMITH, Ian G.
"Productivity agreements and productivity: an appraisal and a possible approach to productivity measurement at the plan/firm level." Industrial relations joutnal, 2, Winter 1971, pp. 63-80.

STEINKÜHLER, Franz.
"Humanisierung der Arbeit durch Tarifvertrag." /Humanisation of work through collective agreements./ AFA-Informationen, (1), 1975.

TANNENBAUM, Robert; SCHMIDT, Warren H.
"How to choose a leadership pattern." Harvard business review, 1958. Revised in May-June 1973 issue. 8 p.
Discusses several patterns or styles of leadership and the factors to be considered in choosing that which is appropriate to an organisation or an organisational unit. Identifies such factors as, "forces in the situation". Stresses the fact that a manager must take these factors into account in any attempt to encourage participative management.

TCHOBANIAN, R.
"Trade unions and the humanisation of work." International labour review, 111(3), Mar. 1975, pp. 199-217.
After examining the consequences of job restructuring for the occupational and economic interests of workers and for the structures and activities of the trade union movement, the author analyses the different strategies adopted by unions according to the countries and their ideological tendencies.

TENGELMANN, C.
Antiautoritäre Unternehmensführung. /Non-authoritarian enterprise management./ Heidelberg, 1972.

THORSRUD, Einar.
"Work organisation and the changing role of trade unions." Free labour world, Jul.-Aug. 1974, pp. 12-15.

UNION DES INDUSTRIES METALLURGIQUES ET MINIERES, Paris.
"Réactions négatives d'ouvriers américains de l'automobile en stage chez Saab-Scania." /Negative reactions of American automobile workers working at Saab-Scania./ Documentation étrangère, annexe 2, Mar. 1975.

UNION DES INDUSTRIES METALLURGIQUES ET MINIERES, Paris.
L'étude d'opinion chez Bergerat Monnoyeur. /Opinion poll at Bergerat Monnoyeur./ Paris, 1975. (Its: Cahiers techniques, 9.)
An opinion poll on job satisfaction among workers at Bergerat Monnoyeur on work, the undertaking and personal aims. Extracts from questionnaires; results shown partly in the form of graphs.

VASZKÓ, Mihály.
Psychological analysis of the workplace and the work process. Budapest, Textbook Publishing House, 1975.
Analysis of the workplace and the work process, as a constant source of stimuli or lack of stimuli, on the basis of their influence on the worker. The working environment can exercise favourable or unfavourable influences on work activity and a knowledge of the direction and nature of these influences is indispensable in order to create the optimum working environment. The study and measurement procedures described have two objectives: on the one hand to raise productivity and, on the other hand, the aspect which has been given greater emphasis in this book, to protect the workers' mental and physical well-being.

VIGNET, V.
Enquête exploratoire sur les attitudes ouvrières face à un projet de réorganisation. /Exploration survey of workers' attitudes to a reorganisation project./ Caluire, Economie et Humanisme, 1974. (Roneogr.)

3. Shop-floor participation

ACHUTAN, R.
"Worker's participation in the public sector." Socialist India, 1(1), May 1970, pp. 33-34.

AEGERSNAP, Flemming; JUNGE-JENSEN, Finn.
Rapport om samarbejdsforsøg i jernindustrien. /Report on experiments in industrial co-operation within the metalworking industries./ Copenhagen, 1974. 318 p. (Nyt fra samfundsvidenskaberne, 36.) - English summary issued separately: Experiments in industrial co-operation. Summary. 2. edition. Publ. by the Federation of Danish Mechanical Engineering and Metalworking Industries. Copenhagen, 1974. 37 p. + 2 appendices.

AHRENSBURG; HOLSTEIN; BAHVENS, J.F.; MAIER, Kurt.
Interdependenzen zwischen Mitbestimmung und betrieblicher Partnerschaft. /Interdependencies between participation and enterprise partnership./ Berlin, Duncker und Humblot, 1969.

ANDREATTA, Helen; RUNBOLD, Bronwen.
"Worker participation in decision making." In: Organisation development in action. Melbourne, Productivity Promotion Council of Australia, 1974, pp. 57-63.
Chapter 6, "Worker Participation in Decision Making", discusses various interpretations of this term including formal schemes, e.g. worker control in Yugoslavia, codetermination through worker directors as in West Germany, joint consultation and works councils; as well as other forms of participation, eg. job redesign and team building. A short summary of Australian experience is given, pointing out that "there have been few experiments in which worker representatives exercise significant control or influence over organisational objectives and policy".

ANKER-ORDING, Aake.
Betriebsdemokratie, Wege zur sozialistischen Gesellschaft in Norwegen. /Democracy in the plant: paths to a socialist society in Norway./ Frankfurt/M., Europäische Verlagsanstalt, 1966.

ARYA, R.C.
"BSP's experience in workers' participation." Indian worker, 24(20), Mar. 1976, p. 4.

AUSTRALIAN LABOR PARTY. NEW SOUTH WALES BRANCH.
"Worker participation in management." In its: Special report of the Industrial Relations Committee to State Congress. Sydney, 1975, pp. 27-33.
Provides introductory information on European and Scandinavian systems of worker participation. Examines concepts such as joint consultation, job enrichment, worker participation and worker control in relation to Australian experience, and puts forward recommendations for adoption by future Labor Governments in NSW. These include the setting up of Joint Industrial Committees in companies and governmant bodies employing more than 100 persons; a two-tier system of control of publicly listed companies

including a Supervisory Board consisting of 50 % employee representation; and the establishment of a "Job Enrichment Bureau" within the State Department of Labour to give advice to companies on latest developments.

AYRES, M.
"Worker's participation: good industrial relations vital." Economic times, 4 Oct. 1963, 7 p.

BANKS, J.A.
Industrial participation theory and practice; a case study. Liverpool, Liverpool University, 1963. 150 p.

Bedriftsdemokrati. /Enterprise democracy./ Oslo, Arbeidernes Opplysningsforbund, 1973. 5 pts.

"Betriebsrat und Personalplanung." /The works council and personnel planning./ Das Mitbestimmungsgespräch, (8-9), 1972.

BILANDZIC, Dusan.
"Difference between neighbours: two different examples in workers' self-management." Yugoslav trade unions, Jul.-Sept. 1961, pp. 28-32.
The author argues that at the present state of development the central point in the system of workers' self-management is the problem of distribution of income within the economic organisation, and between the organisation and society. As the work collective is neither constrained or restricted by any legal requirements as to the distribution of its income to individual funds, the work collective which manages better, shows better results, because it has a larger income and consequently more funds for the promotion of enterprise. This paper analyses the case of two Yugoslav collectives which, although they operate under similar conditions, are very different one from the other.

BIRKWALD-PORNSCHLEGEL, ed.
Mitbestimmen im Betrieb. /Co-determination at the plant level./ Köln, 1973.

BOLGER, M.; CLARK, A.W.; FOSTER, P.M.
"A large organization consults its staff." In: CLARK, A.W.,ed. Experiences in action research. New York, Plenum Press, 1975.

BOWES, L.B.
"Worker participation in management: the South Australian developments." The journal of industrial relations, 17(2), June 1975, pp. 119-134.
An article on the recent evolution of workers' participation in Australia including experiments with mixed committees in hospital sector and the introduction of job enrichment in the construction sector. The cases of the Royal Adelaide Hospital and the Fricker Carrington Group are cited as examples of each type of innovation.

BRACCIALARGHE, P.
"Evoluzione partecipativa dell'organizzazione nell'industria." /The development of participation in industrial organisation./ Sociologia dell'organizzazione, (2), Jul.-Dec. 1973, pp.324-335.

BROWN, Julius S.
"How many workers enjoy discretion on the job?" Industrial relations, May 1975, pp. 196-202.

*BUNCH, J.D.
"How Danish workers participate." Journal of general management, Summer 1974, pp. 59-69.
Traces the history of the workers' participation movement in Denmark, describing the provisions of the national co-operation agreement between unions and employers. Looks critically at the experimental schemes now being introduced in the field of workers' participation.

*BUZA, Márton.
Questions of the development of workplace democracy. Budapest, Kossuth Publishing House, 1976.
As a continuation of his earlier work the author (director of the Trades Unions Theoretical Research Institute) defines the concept of socialist, workplace democracy and analyses the application of its mechanisms. His analysis is supported by examples taken from practice and by results of surveys. Two politically and economically effective cases of workplace democracy are presented in support of his arguments. Finally, the author sums up the situation in other socialist countries and also the struggle being waged in capitalistic countries for workers participation in management.

*CAINE, J.A.J.
Workers' participation in decisions within undertakings in Australia. A paper presented at the Symposium on Workers' Participation in Decisions Within Undertakings, Oslo, August 1974. Geneva, International Labour Office, 1974. 6 p.
Examines the special constitutional and legal aspects of industrial relations in Australia vis-a-vis worker participation. Reports on a survey of advanced organisational practices conducted by the Department of Labor and Immigration, emphasising the development of joint consultative practices and shop-floor democracy initiatives involving job redesign.

CHANANA, K.M.
"Workers' participation in management." Modern review, 118(1), Jul. 1965, pp. 42-46.

CHANEY, Frederick B.; TEEL, Kenneth S.
"Participative management; a practical experience." Personnel, Nov.-Dec. 1972, pp. 8-19.
The authors discuss results of pilot studies designed to introduce participative management in a large company. While they offer no single solution to all organisational problems,

the authors feel that managers who are willing to work hard at participative management will yield a high payoff in both increased production and improved employee attitudes.

DAHLSTRÖM, E.
Fördjupad företagsdemokrati. /Intensified democracy in the undertaking./ Stockholm, Prisma, 1972.

DAVIES, B.
"Some thoughts on organisational democracy." Journal of management studies, 4, 1967, pp. 270-282.

Demokrati på arbetsplatsen. /Democracy at the workplace./ Stockholm, Allmänna Förlaget AB, 1974. (Summary in English.)

DONALDSON, William V.
Participatory management: employees are creative. Washington, Labor-Management Relations Service, 1973. 8 p. (Strengthening local government through better labour relations series, No. 16.)

DUA, B.D.
"Worker's participation in Hindustan Insecticide LTD.: a case study." AICC economic review, 17(6), Apr. 1966, pp. 27-32.

EMERY, Fred E.
"Democratization of the work place." Manpower and applied psychology, 1(2), 1967, pp. 118-129.

EMERY, F.E.; THORSRUD, E.
Democracy at work. Leiden, Martinus Nijhoff Social Sciences Division, 1976. 178 p. (International series on the quality of working life.)

EMERY, F.E.; THORSRUD, E.
"Industrial democracy in Norway." Industrial relations, 9, 1970, pp. 187-196.

ESTIVILL, Jordi, et al.
La participación de los trabajadores en la gestion de la empresa. /Participation of workers in the management of the enterprise./ Barcelona, Editorial Nova Terra, 1971.

FEDERATION OF DANISH MECHANICAL ENGINEERING AND METALWORKING INDUSTRIES.
Experiments in industrial cooperation. Copenhagen, 1974. 37 p.

FREIER, Peter.
"Betriebsdemokratie und emanzipatorische Arbeitswissenschaft? Ein Diskussionsbeitrag." /Industrial democracy and emancipatory labour sciences? A contribution to the debate./ Arbeit und Leistung, (5), 1973, p. 123.

FRENCH, J.R.P., et al.
"An experiment in participation in a Norwegian factory." Human relations, 13, 1960, pp. 3-10.

FROIDEVAUX, P.; GRAVEJAT, A.
Recherche sur la participation du personnel aux décision dans l'entreprise. /Research on the participation of personnel in enterprise level decisions./ Lyon, Institut de Recherches Appliquées en Sociologie, 1970. 159 p.
The authors hypothesise that the formal processes of participation do not improve the job satisfaction of the rank and file worker if he cannot influence the decisions which affect his own job. The study deals largely with the participation of workers at the workshop level which is the basis of workers' demands for the humanisation of working conditions.

GITTER, Hans.
Möglichkeiten und Grenzen einer Mitbestimmung am Arbeitsplatz. /Possibilities and limitations of shopfloor participation./ Hamburg, Hochschule für Wirtschaft und Politik, 1971. (Hausarbeit.)

GLASER, W.
"Employer's attitudes." In: Seminar on Worker Participation in Australia, University of Melbourne, 1975: proceedings. Parkville, Vic. Department of Legal Studies and Industrial Relations Programme, University of Melbourne and Melbourne Chamber of Commerce, 1975, pp. 42-46.
Presents a case study of the development of worker participation in a small Australian company.

*GUEST, D.; FATCHETT, D.
Worker participation: individual control and performance. London, Institute of Personnel Management, 1974. 252 p.
Discusses worker participation in the UK, providing a theoretical framework for its analysis and explores employee attitudes towards the various types of participation. The part played by wage incentive schemes, human relations programmes and strategies such as job enrichment are also examined.

GULOWSEN, J.
Mitbestimmung in der Norwegischen Industrie. /Participation in Norwegian industry./ Wien, Herrnstein Institut für Unternehmensführung, 1972.

HAATANEN, P.; HIKIPÄÄ, S.; VÄHÄTALLO.
Valmetlaiset ja yristysdemokratia, ennakkotietoja. /The workers at Valmet and industrial democracy, advance information./ Helsinki, 1970. (Helsinki University. Sosiaalipolitiikanlaitos, tutkimuksia No. 1.)

HINCE, K.W.
"The meaning of worker participation." In: Seminar on Worker Participation in Australia, University of Melbourne, 1975: proceedings. Parkville, Vic., Department of Legal Studies and Industrial Relations Programme, Universtiy of Melbourne and Melbourne Chamber of Commerce, 1975, pp. 9-15.
The author points out that there is no simple meaning of the

term worker participation in management, and discusses terms such as joint consultation, job enrichment, job enlargement, job redesign, worker director, joint industrial committee, organisation development, co-ownership, profit sharing and works councils.

HOLLEY, Bill.
"Participative management and innovation." Rydge's, 44(10), Oct. 1971, pp. 147, 149, 151, 153.
Stating that the traditional style of management does not permit full employment contribution to organisation, the author suggests that management could get better results by allowing employees to help run the business. However, it must be remembered that introducing a substantially different management system is a complex undertaking and involves many time-consuming problems.

HOPPMANN, K.
"Mitbestimmung am Arbeitsplatz durch die Einrichtung von Arbeitsgruppen - Erfahrungsbericht." [Co-determination of the work place through work groups - a report on recent experience.] AGP 1975, pp. 272-281.

"How worker participation could function here." Rydge's, 48(6), June 1975, pp. 59-61.
The first article in a 2 part series. It distinguishes the variety of approaches to worker participation, viz informal consultation, joint consultation, collective bargaining, co-partnership, profit-sharing and co-ownership, worker-directors, job enrichment and worker control. A number of Australian examples including ICI Australia, James Hardy, Fletcher Jones, Shell and Hoover (Australia) are described.

ISHWAR, Dayal.
"Experiment in participation." Industrial relations (Calcutta), 12(4), Jul.-Aug. 1960, pp. 153-156.

IYER, K.V.
"Role of workers' participation in management in improving productivity." Labour gazette (Maharashtra), 47(12), Aug. 1968, pp. 1714-1719.

"Ja, ja, ja, - nein, non, no: worker participation." The Economist, 27 Mar. 1976, pp. 87-88.

JENKINS, David.
Beyond job enrichment: workplace democracy in Europe. Working papers for a New Society. Cambridge, Cambridge Policy Studies Institute, [n.d.]
European workers are gaining both a voice in company affairs and a say about how their work is organised. While this does not amount to a revolution, it is more than mere window-dressing.

JENKINS, David.
"Democracy in the factory." Atlantic, Apr. 1973, pp. 78-83.

JENKINS, David.
Industrial democracy in Europe. - The challenge and management responses. Geneva, Business International, 1974. 170 p.
A three part report which explores the dimensions of industrial democracy, survey developments in ten European countries and presents a portfolio of case studies analysing management's response towards the phenomenon. It focuses on the various means which have been devised to increase employee influence in companies and presents the view that, while managers still tend to think of industrial democracy in terms of worker representatives, employees show more interest in acquiring control over their own day-to-day work. The author feels that it is this area which will present the most serious challenge to management in the future.

JENKINS, David.
Job power: blue and white collar democracy. London, Heinemann, 1974. viii, 375 p.
An overview of developments in the field of industrial democracy in several countries including the United States, Israel, Yugoslavia, the Scandinavian countries and France.

KARLSSON, L.E.
Demokrati på arbetsplatsen. /Democracy at the workplace./ Stockholm, Prisma, 1969.

KITTNER, M.
"Mitbestimmung der Arbeitnehmer über die Arbeitorganisation und über die Ausgestaltung und Umgebung des Arbeitsplatzes." /Participation of the employees in work organisation and work design and environment./ WSI Mitteilungen, 28(5), May 1975, pp. 256-258.
The workers' participation in solutions of problems of work organisation and environment in the Federal Republic of Germany.

KOLJONEN, Niilo.
"Yritysdemokratiakokeilut meillä ja muualla." /Experiments of hospital democracy in Finland and in other countries./ Sairaanhoitaja, 10, 1972, pp. 515-517.

LENK, Erhard.
"Mitbestimmung am Arbeitsplatz durch gewerkschaftliche Vertrauensleute." /Shopfloor participation by union "men of confidence."/ Gewerkschaftliche Monatshefte, 21(3), 1970.

LIDBOM, T.
"Industrial democracy in Sweden." Free labour world, (257), Nov. 1971, pp. 14-17.

LISCHERON, J.A.; WALL, Toby D.
"Attitudes towards participation among local authority employees." *Human relations*, 28(6), Aug. 1975, pp. 499-517.
A questionnaire study of the attitudes of one hundred and twenty seven blue collar employees towards participation in management decision-making. The findings demonstrate that while the employees who experienced little participation wished to be involved in decision-making, the preferred form of participation depended on the nature of the decision in question. Additionally, attitudes towards participation were positively correlated with job satisfaction.

LISCHERON, J.A.; WALL, Toby D.
"Employee participation: an experimental field study." *Human relations*, Dec. 1975, pp. 863-884.
A field study over 300 blue-collar male employees and their superiors which investigated the hypothesis that participation in management decision-making is a determinant of job satisfaction. Action Planning Groups based on regular meetings between shop-floor employees and management effectively influenced organisational decision-making and was seen as worthwile by both parties, but this increased participation did not result in greater satisfaction.

LUND, Reinhard.
De ansattes indflydelse på ledelsens beslutninger inden for Københavns kommunale institutioner. /Employees' influence on management's decisions within municipal institutions of the city of Copenhagen./ Copenhagen, 1972. 139 p. (With a summary in English.)

MARY, J.A.
"Direction participative par objectifs et enrichissement des tâches." /Participatory management by objectives and job enrichment./ *Personnel*, (177), Mar.-Apr. 1975, pp. 28-42.
An experiment in participatory management by objective at the Guilliet factory in Auxerre, France. Contains a description of the transition from the authoritarian to the participatory style of management with details of the conditions under which the operational teams were introduced and worked, their composition, their problems and the results achieved. The management concludes that the objectives of a society can be reconciled with the interests of those working in it.

MATEJKO, Alexander.
"Industrial democracy: a sociotechnical approach." *Our generation*, 9(1), 1973.

MÓD, A.; KOZÁK, Gyula.
The stratification, work and knowledge of workers and workplace democracy in two sections of the Danube Steel Mills. Budapest, Akadémia Publishing House, 1974.
A study of workplace democracy - from the workers' point of view - at the Danube Steel Mills. Attempts were made to estimate the strength of the employees demands for active participation in worklife, their capability in this direction and the ways in which these demands were satisfied. Aspects considered included

the nature and circumstances of the work, working conditions, earnings and their evaluation, production conferences and the extent of the workers' knowledge and its source (e.g. factory meetings).

MÓD, A.; KOZÁK, Gyula.
"Workers in the Ozd Foundry Works and workplace democracy." Valóság, (2), 1975, pp. 55-70.
A study which aims at illustrating the most characteristic forms of direct workplace democracy, its institutions and its legal and social guarantees in the Ozd Foundry Works. Based on interviews with workers, the study also considers the workers' objective situation and their subjective evaluation of it. Comparisons are made between the findings of this study and a similar one carried out at the Danube Steel Mills where production tasks are similar.

"Mode de participation des travailleurs dans la firme automobile Leyland." /Worker participation system at Leyland automobile factory./ Bulletin d'informations sociales, (1), 1976, pp. 28-29.

MORTON, D.
"Theory Y is not participative management." Human resources management, 14(4), 1975, pp. 25-28.

NATZE, Benno.
"Zur Mitbestimmung bei der menschengerechten Gestaltung der Arbeit." /About participation in humanised work design./ Recht der Arbeit, (5), 1974, pp. 280-284.

* NEAL, Leonard.
"Making shop-floor participation work." Journal of general management, Autumn 1974, pp. 44-50.
Relates the demand for greater worker participation in decision-making to the devolution of union power to the shop-floor and to the higher expectations of the labour force. Advocates already-defined management policy objectives for jointly agreed procedures and working relationships at plant level, enlargement of the scope of joint regulation and job enrichment and suggests that an independent third party can play an important part in improving employer/employee relations.

* ORGANISATION FOR ECONOMIC CO-OPERATION AND DEVELOPMENT.
Workers' participation in management; final report of an international management seminar, Versailles, 1975. Paris, 1976.

PAHLOW, E.M.
Employee consultation and participation: a decision for disaster or development? Recent experiences in I.C.I. Australia Ltd. Prep. for the Conference on Human Management. Sydney, Institution of Engineers, 1975, pp. 49-54.
Discusses I.C.I.'s basic attitude to "consultation and participation", and describes recent activities pursued in a number of the company's establishments.

" Participation: future trends." Industrial participation, Winter 1974-1975, pp. 14-20.

PATCHEN, Martin.
Participation, achievement, and involvement on the job. Englewood Cliffs, N.J., Prentice-Hall, 1970. 285 p. Reports the results of a study conducted by Survey Research Center of the University of Michigan in the Tennessee Valley Authority.

PEACH, David A.
"Participation in action: how it was applied at Alcan, Kingston, Ontario, Canada." Industrial and commercial training, 7(3), Mar. 1975, pp. 109-116.
Describes new organisational approaches in Alcan's Kingston plant. Based on the belief that conscientious employees, properly informed and carrying out their duties in a responsible manner are the best assurance of effective operation, the experiments include the elimination of time clocks, and of the inspection department and the discontinuation of the traditional hourly pay system. Unions and management have collaborated in introducing the changes and it has been claimed that the workers are more productive and have a more responsible attitude towards and interest in their work and that, consequently, job satisfaction has increased.

PETERSON, R.B.
"The Swedish experience with industrial democracy." British journal of industrial relations, 6, 1968, pp. 185-203.

PHILLIPS A.G. PERSONNEL AND INDUSTRIAL RELATIONS DEPARTMENT. COMMITTEE ON PARTICIPATION.
Participation. Eindhoven, 1975.

PINTHER, Helmuth.
"Mitbestimmung am Arbeitsplatz." /Shopfloor participation./ Gewerkschaftliche Monatshefte, 21(4), 1970.

POSTEL, Guy.
Gestion par objectifs et participation. /Management by objectives and participation./ Paris, Editions d'Organisation, 1971. 152 p.

"Les projets et expériences de participation en France et en Suède." /Participation projets and experiments in France and Sweden./ Economies et sociétés, (11-12), Nov.-Dec. 1975, pp. 1845-1884.

QUALE, T.U.
The industrial democracy project in Norway. Paper read at the Second World Congress of the International Industrial Relations Association, Geneva, Sept. 1970.

QUALE, T.U.
"A Norwegian strategy for democratization of industry." Human relations, 29(5), 1976.

RAMSAY, Harvie,
"Participation: the shop floor view." British journal of industrial relations, 14(2), Jul. 1976.

"Un rapport suédois: la démocratie sur le lieu de travail." /Democracy at the workplace: a Swedish report./ Intersocial, Feb. 1975, pp. 26-27.

RHENMAN, Eric.
Industrial democracy and industry management. London, Tavistock Publications, 1968.
A "critical essay on the possible meanings and implications of industrial democracy" based on experience in Sweden and the other Scandinavian countries.

SCHAIRER, Ursula.
Mitbestimmung am Arbeitsplatz bei wachsender Automatisierung. /Shopfloor participation with increasing automatisation./ Mannheim, Universität Mannheim, 1974. (Diplom-Arbeit.)

SCHEFLEN, K.C.; LAWLER, E.E.; HACKMAN, J.R.
"Long-term impact of employee participation in the development of pay incentive plans: field experiment revisited." Journal of applied psychology, 55(3), 1971, pp. 182-186.
Follow-up to an earlier study by Lawler and Hackman on the effects of worker participation in the development of pay incentive plans. Discontinuation of participation in this area in two of the three groups during the year between the 2 studies, resulted in a drop in attendance. It was also found that the attendance level had risen in those groups where incentive plans were always imposed by management.

SCHUMANN, Michael.
"Möglichkeiten der Mitbestimmung am Arbeitsplatz." /Possibilities of shopfloor participation./ Gewerkschaftliche Monatshefte, 20(4). 1969.

"Shop-floor version of industrial democracy proves productive." Business international, Dec. 19, 1975.

SOUTH AUSTRALIA. COMMITTEE ON WORKER PARTICIPATION IN MANAGEMENT PRIVATE SECTOR.
Worker participation in management; report. Adelaide, Govt. Printer, 1973. 109 l.
A major survey of worker participation in Australia and overseas commissioned by the South Australian Government. Concluded "that real advantages would result, both to South Australian managers and workers, from the introduction of worker participation in management, especially those forms of worker involvement known as joint consultation and job enrichment". (p. 41.) Precipitated the establishment of a "Unit for Quality of Work Life" (later Unit for Industrial Democracy).

SYMANOWSKI, Horst.
Demokratie am Arbeitsplatz. Sozialethische Erwägungen zur Mitbestimmung in der Wirtschaft der Bundesrepublik Deutschland. /Democracy of the workplace. Social and ethical reflexions on participation in the economy of the Federal Republic of Germany./ Eine Studie der Kammer für soziale Ordnung der EKD. Sonderdruck aus ad hoc 3 - Kirche progressiv. Dokumente neuen Denkens, herausgeben von Karl Wilheln Barwitz, Burkhardthaus-Verlag, Gelnhausen/Berlin, 1971.

TANNENBAUM, Arnold S.
"Systems of formal participation." In: STRAUSS, George, et al. Organizational behaviour, Madison, Industrial Relations Research Association, 1974.

TEWARI, R.L.
"Workers' participation in management: a case study of diesel locomotive works, Varanasi." Indian journal of commerce, 21(75), June 1968, pp. 17-23.

*THOMASON, George F.
Experiments in participation. London, Institute of Personnel Management, 1971. 55 p.
Conference report on British experiments in workers' participation covering the demand for participation and its motivation in terms of job satisfaction and job enrichment.

THORSRUD, Einar.
"La démocratisation du travail et le processus de transformation de l'organisation." /Democratisation of work and the process of organisational change./ Sociologie du travail, 17(3), Jul.-Sept. 1975, pp. 243-265.
The Norwegian experience with the democratisation of work organisation in the merchant marine sector.

THORSRUD, Einar.
"Demokratisierung der Arbeitsorganisation. Einige konkrete Methoden zur Neustrukturierung des Arbeitsplatzes." /Democratisation of work organisation has concrete methods for restructuring workplaces./ In: VILMAR, F. Menchenwürde im Betrieb. Reinbek, Rowohlt, 1973, pp. 117-142.

THORSRUD, Einar.
Democracy at work and perspectives on the quality of working life in Scandinavia. Geneva, 1976. 15 p. (International Institute for Labour Studies. Research Series No. 8.)

THORSRUD, Einar; EMERY, Fred E.
Democracy at work: the report on the Norwegian industrial democracy programme. Canberra, Center of Continuing Education, 1975.

THORSRUD, Einar; EMERY, Fred E.
"Industrial democracy in Norway: employees representation and personal participation." In: ADIZES, I.; BORGESE, E.M., eds. Self-management, pp. 101-115.

TIEFENTHAL, Rolf.
"Avoiding the pitfalls of participation." International management, Mar. 1975, pp. 27-28, 30.

VAN GORKUM, P.H.
Industrial democracy at the level of enterprise. Brussels, The European Association of National Productivity Centres, /n.d./

VAN OTTER, C.
Försök med förvaltningsdemokrati: en utvärdering. /Experiment with democracy in administration; an evaluation./ Stockholm, 1975. 179 p. (Delegationen för Förvaltningsdemokrati. Rapport 7.)

VILMAR, Fritz.
Mitbestimmung an Arbeitsplatz. Basis demokratischer Betriebspolitik. /Shopfloor participation. Basis of democratic enterprise policy./ 3. Aufl. Neuwied, 1973.

VILMAR, Fritz.
"Die Mitbestimmung muss am Arbeitsplatz beginnen." /Participation must start at the workplace (shopfloor)./ Gewerkschaftliche Monatshefte, 19(8), 1968.

VISWANATHAN, R.; SRIDHARAN, S.
"Participative management and management by objectives; an overview." Integrated management, Oct. 1975, pp. 5-12, 25.

WALKER, K.F.
"Workers' participation in management; conceptual framework and scope of national studies." Bulletin. International Institute for Labour Studies, (5), 1968, pp. 138-152.

WANG, K.K.
"A worker participation matrix." Personnel practice bulletin, 30(3), Sept. 1974, pp. 264-277.
Suggests that worker participation consists progressively of information, consultation, joint decision-making and self-management at shopfloor, departmental, organisational and corporate levels and that a matrix can therefore be constructed to demonstrate the degree of participation achieved. It can also be used to illustrate the implications of future change in the technological, social, economic and political elements of participation.

WIIO, O.A.
Yristysdemokratia ja muuttuva organisaatio. /Industrial democracy and the changing organisation./ Weilin, Tapiola, 1970.

WILLOT, D.
"Une expérience de participation." /An experiment in participation./ Le dirigeant, (73), Sept.-Oct. 1976, p. 10.

"Worker participation: good, but now?" The Economist, May 1976, p. 100.

4. Flexible working hours and other time arrangements

ALLENSPACH, Heinz.
Flexible working hours. Geneva, International Labour Office, 1975. 64 p.
A report on flexible working hours based on experiments in Switzerland. Discusses its effects on job satisfaction and management attitudes.

ALLENSPACH, Heinz.
L'horaire mobile de travail. /Flexible hours of work./ Paris, Jeune Association Patronale, Nov. 1972.

"Aménagement du temps de travail: horaire à la carte, travail à temps partiel; loi n° 73 - 1195 du 27 déc. 1973." /Arranging hours of work: hours in line with preference; part-time work; law n° 73 - 1195 of Dec.27, 1973./ Liaisons sociales, législations sociales, (4105), Jan. 1974, 8 p.

"L'aménagement du temps de travail: temps et vie de travail: l'étalement des vacances, vers la semaine de 4 jours, l'horaire variable." /Arranging hours of work: hours of working life; spread of holiday periods, towards a four-day week, flexible hours./ Problèmes économiques et sociaux, (214 - 215), Feb. 1974, 60 p.

ASSEMAT, B.
"Des expériences tous azimuts pour un travail à la carte." /Experiments for working in line with preferences./ La technique, (5), June 1976, pp 11 - 13.

AUSTRALIAN DEPARTMENT OF LABOUR
"Flexitime in Australia." Personnel practice bulletin, 29(4). Dec, 1973, pp 337 - 352.
The results of a survey on the development of flexitime in twenty public and private organisations in Australia. Details are given of the introduction and operation of each scheme and of managements assessement of its effectiveness. In general it was found that the introduction of flexitime met with staff approval and resulted in a more responsible attitude towards work, improved staff morale, reduced unpunctuality, absence and turnover rate, easier recruitment, increased productivity and improved customer services. Despite some problems the managements and staffs concerned expressed reluctance to revert to a standard 9 a.m. to 5 p.m. type arrangement.

"Automobile U.S.: vers la semaine de quatre jours? /U.S. Automobile: towards a four day week?/ Intersocial, (21), Nov. 1976, pp. 11 - 13.

BACON, F.
"Principe de mise en oeuvre de l'horaire variable." /Principles for the implementation of flexible working hours./ Travail et méthodes, (326 - 327), June - Jul. 1976, pp 7-11.

BAUDRAZ, Jean-François.
L'horaire variable de travail. /Flexible working hours./ Paris, Editions d'Organisation, 1973. 135 p.
Discusses the technical problems of introducing flexible hours of work, and the advantages and disadvantages of the system of flexible working hours for both the individual and the enterprise. Includes two case studies.
Originally issued as thesis, Université de Lausanne, 1971.

BAUM, Stephen J: YOUNG, W. McEWANS.
A practical guide to flexible working hours.
Park Ridge, N.J., Noyes Deta Corp., 1974. 190 p.

BELL, R.L.
"New arrangements for the working week." Personnel practice bulletin. 30 (1), May 1974, pp 30 -37
The results of a survey of Australian organisations which have introduced new systems of working hours ranging from a four-day week or nine-day fortnight to a nineteen-day month. Gives details of individual schemes and discusses the advantages and problems reported and the reactions of the employees involved.

BOIVIN, J.; SEXTON, J.; BELANGER, L.; BOUCHER, M.C.
L'aménagement des temps de travail; l'horaire variable et la semaine comprimée. /Arranging working hours; flexible hours and the compressed work week./ Québec, Presse de l'Université Laval, 1974. 337 p.
A conference report covering various aspects of the introduction of flexible working hours and compressed work weeks in Canada. The attitudes of unions and management and governments reactions are discussed.

BOLTON, J. Harvey.
Flexible working hours. Wembley, Anbar, 1971. 51 p.

BORNEY, J.
"Gervais-Danone : les horaires personnalisés." /Gervais-Danone personalized working hours./ Personnel revue de l'ANDCP Mar. 1973, 9 p.

BOUCHER, M.C.
"Horaire variable de travail: progrès ou anachronisme?" /Flexible working hours: progress or anachronism?/ In: SEXTON, H.; BOIVIN, J. Aménagement des temps de travail. Québec, Université Laval, 1974, pp. 45-82.
Discusses the advantages and disadvantages of flexible hours of work in the Canadian context.

"Horaires libres." /Flexible working hours./ Cahier d'information du Chef de personnel, (69). 1975. pp. 43-58.

CANADA. LABOUR CANADA. WAGES RESEARCH DIVISION. ECONOMICS AND RESEARCH BRANCH.
Trends in working time. Ottawa, 1974. 36 p.
Report on trends in hours of work in Canada, covering compressed work weeks, flexible working hours, dual job holding and overtime.

CAULKIN, S.
"Flexible working age." Management today, Mar. 1976, pp. 81 - 84.
Considers the pros and cons of flexible working hours in the U.K. from a management point of view.

CENTRALE DES METALLURGISTES DE BELGIQUE. CENTRALE CULTURELLE DES METALLURGISTES.
"Les horaires libres." /Flexible working hours./ C.M.B.inform. Sept. 1974, pp. 11 - 16.
Assesses trends in flexible working hours in developed countries.

CHALENDAR, Jacques de.
L'aménagement du temps. /Arranging working hours./ Paris, Desclée de Brouwer, 1971, 171 p.
Considers the national organisation of hours of work - both flexible and variable - and the staggering of holidays. Examines the rationalisation of time utilisation and its importance for working conditions.

CLUFF, M.M.
4 days, 40 hours for streamlined government. El Monte, Calif., M.M.H.C. Public Relations Agency, 1972. 73 p.
Recommends changes in hours of work and rest in the USA on the basis of the experience of some civil servants. Includes a list of government agencies with a four-day work week.

CRAWFORD, I.
"Varied working hours in Australia." Personnel practice bulletin, 30 (4), Dec. 1974, pp. 311 - 320.
Covers various new time arrangements - including flexible working hours - in Australia and presents the results of a survey of 90 enterprises using new working hours.

DANECKI, J.
Jedność podzielonego czasu. Czas wolny i czas pracy w społeczeństwach uprzemysłowionych. /The unity of divided time. Working time and free time in industrialised societies./ Warszawa, 1970.

DELFOSSE, M.N.
"L'horaire variable en pratique." /The practice of flexible working hours./ Production et gestion. (281), Mar. 1976. pp 47 - 51.
Covers the application of flexible working hours in France.

"2000 salariés de production en horaires libres." /2000 production workers with flexible working hours./ La technique, (10), Nov. 1976, pp. 13 - 16.

DONAHUE, Robert J.
"Flexitime systems in New York." Public personnel management, 4, Jul. - Aug. 1975, pp. 212 - 215.
Examines the advantages and disadvantages of systems of flexible working hours introduced in some New York establishments in response to demands by employees.

ELBING, Alvar O.; GADON, H.; GORDON, J.R.M.
"Flexible working hours; the missing link." California management review, 17 (3), Spring 1975, pp. 2, 50-57.
Discusses the advantages and disadvantages of flexible working hours for both employees and employers.

ELBING, Alvar O, et al.
"Flexible working hours: it's about time." Harvard business review, (52) Jan. - Feb. 1974, pp. 18-20.

ELBING, A.O.; GADON, H.; GORDON, J.R.M.
"Time for a human timetable." European business, (39), Autumn, 1973. pp. 46-54.
Description of the implementation and the results of flexible working hours schemes for European non-manual workers.

EVANS, A.A.
Flexibility in working life; opportunities for individual choice. Paris, Organisation for Economic Co-operation and Development. 1973. 110 p.
Suggests measures which will increase flexibility in working life. Covers recent trends and experiences with flexible working hours in OECD countries.

EVANS, M.G.
"Longitudinal analysis of the impact of flexible working hours." Studies in personnel psychology, 6(2), Spring 1975, pp. 1-10.
Illustrates the impact of flexible working hours on the job satisfaction of British workers by comparing two survey samples of workers on flexible and standard hours respectively.

EVANS, M.G.
"Système d'horaires flexibles." /Systems of flexible working hours./ Studies/Etudes, 6(2), Spring 1975. pp. 1-11.

FIELDS, Cynthia J.
"Variable work hours: the MONY experience." Personnel journal, 53, Sept. 1974, pp. 675-678.
Considers the diffusion of an experiment in flexible working hours in a large New York company, discussing in particular its results which were mainly positive insofar as production, morale, lateness and absenteeism were concerned.

FLEUTER, D.L.
Workweek revolution; a guide to the changing workweek. Reading, Mass., Addison-Wesley, 1975. viii, 167 p.
Guide to alternative strategies for flexible hours of work and changing patterns of weekly rest in the U.S. Contains suggestions for management.

"Flexible hours." Labour and employment gazette (Wellington, New Zealand), Aug. 1973, pp. 7-10.
Discusses flexible hours in New Zealand in terms of its benefits for management and employees, possible problems, legislative provisions. Concludes that a carefully planned system has numerous benefits for all concerned.

"Flexible working hours in Austria." European industrial and labour review, (28), Apr. 1976, p. 18.

"Flexible working hours in Italy: early results of experiments are favourable." European industrial relations review, 6, June 1974, pp. 5-6.

"Flexible working hours in Luxembourg: a company scheme." European industrial review, (32), Aug. 1976, pp. 15-17.

"Flexible working hours in West Germany: a company scheme; details of one of the more sophisticated schemes covering both manual and non-manual workers." European industrial relations review, (22), Oct. 1975. pp. 19-21.
Discusses the program of a large chemical firm (Henkel GmbH) and the results of its first four years in operation.

"Flexihours in Belgium: a company scheme." European industrial relations review, 18, June 1975, pp. 15-17.
"Looks at the first flexible working hours scheme introduced in Belgium (in the Royale Belge insurance firm) and considers the various reactions to it.

"Flexitime in Denmark: a company scheme." European industrial relations review, (15), Mar. 1975, pp. 10-11.
Describes the experience at Danfoss giving both favourable and unfavourable reactions and presenting the firm's own guidelines.

FRANCE. DIRECTION DE LA DOCUMENTATION.
L'horaire libre en 74. Synthèse des travaux du groupe d'études réuni à la demande de M. Gorse, Ministre du travail. /Flexible hours in 1974. Synthesis report of study group appointed by the Labour Minister./ Paris, Documentation Française, 1974. 89 p.

FRANCE. DIRECTION DE LA DOCUMENTATION.
L'horaire variable ou libre: l'aménagement des temps de travail au niveau de la journée. /Flexible hours: arranging working time during the work day./ Paris, Documentation Française, 1971. 82 p.

"France: horaire variable pour 700.000 personnes." /France: flexible hours for 700.000 persons./ Production et gestion, (282), Apr. 1976, p. 31.
An article based on the experiences of various firms such as Findus, Honeywell-Bull, IBM, Ciba-Geigy - France, Bergerat-Monnoyeur, Linvosges.

GJESDAHL, Torun; SMUKKESTAD, Oddvar.
Fleksibel arbeidstid. Teori og empiri; Bedriftsøkonomisk seminar. /Flexible working time. Theory and practice./ Utg. av Norges handelshøyskole. Bergen, 1972. 5, 105, 11 p.

GLICKMAN, A.S.; BROWN, Z.H.
Changing schedules of work: patterns and implications; final report. Washington, American Institute for Research 1973. ix, 116 p.
Considers issues and alternatives for the reorganisation of hours of work and leisure in the US and reviews some experiments with working hours.

"Gliding working time drastically cuts turnover and one day absences." Employee relations bulletin, Feb 21 1972, pp. 4-5.
Describes the use of flexible hours system at the Lufthansa office in New York.

HEDGES, Janice N.
"New patterns for working time". Monthly labor review, Feb.1973.
Covers changes in working patterns over the workweek, year and lifetime of workers. Indicates that in both the four-day and flexible work schedules, management can effectively achieve its objectives with productivity rising.

HILL, J.M.
Flexible working hours. London, 1972. 65 p. (Institute of Personnel Management. Information report, new series, No. 12)
Summarizes the results of experiments in the application of flexible hours of work in various firms in Western Europe.

"L'horaire libre pour un meilleur temps de vivre?" /Flexible hours for a better life?/ L'office des comités d'entreprise, (187), Oct. 1976, pp. 37-42.

"Horaires flexibles à la norvégienne." /The Norwegian way of flexible hours./ L'usine nouvelle, (11), Mar. 1973, p. 85.

"Les horaires libres." /Flexible hours./ Cahiers d'information du chef de personnel, (69), June 1975, pp. 43-58.
Comments on legislation authorising flexible hours of work in France and considers the role of trade unions and repercussions on living and working conditions etc.

JANNEY, Mary D.
"Designing jobs for people: flexible hours for women and men." Good government, 91, Summer 1974, pp. 8-11.

JARDINE, Paul R.
Flexible working hours; a study of their impact and consequences. Ottawa, Department of Labour, 1972. 32 p.

KAPP, Bernard.; PROUST, Odile.
Les horaires libres. /Flexible hours./ Paris, Chotard, 1973 316 p.
Considers flexible working hours, analysing their history, the rationale behind them and various opinions on them. Gives examples of their application in France, analyses the stages of implementation, the problems encountered and the different results. Concludes that flexible hours are advantageous for both employers and workers.

KLEMP, A.; KLEMP, J.
Arbeitszeitverteilung und Freizeitgestaltung; Möglichkeiten der Arbeitszeitvertteilung und ihre Auswirkungen auf die Freizeitgestaltung der Bevölkerung. /Distribution of work and the use of leisure time./ Göttingen, O. Schwartz, 1976. 187 p. (Germany (FR). Kommission für Wirtschaftlichen und Sozialen Wandel. Schriften, Bd. 39.)
Discusses research on the impact of innovations in working hours on leisure activities in the Federal Republic of Germany. Contains models of the different patterns of working hours. Examines their social implications.

LAMOUR, P ; CHALENDAR, Jacques de.
Prendre le temps de vivre: travail, vacances et retraite à la carte. /Time for a better living: work, holidays and retirement according to preferences./ Paris, Seuil, 1974. 118 p.
Paper on trends in the allocation of work and leisure time in France examining especially economic implications, aspects of personnel management productivity, social implications and social policy.

LANDIER, H.; PROUST, O.
"Faisons le point sur l'horaire libre en France." /Assessing flexible hours management in France." Hommes et techniques, (366), Apr. 1975, pp. 236-245.

LANDORGANISATIONEN, I SVERIGE.
Rapport om arbetstiden. /Report on working hours./ Stockholm, 1973. 116 p.

LANGHOLZ, Bernd.
"Variable working hours in Germany." Journal of systems management, Aug. 1972, pp. 30-33.
Discusses the effect of variable working hours on German business communities. Personnel problems which forced the companies to take a look at the efficiency of established business hours resulted in new work week schedules.

LE VERT, P.
L'étalement des activités: travail, transport, loisirs. /Distribution of activities: work, transport, leisure./ Paris, Fayard-Mame, 1972, 206 p.
Study of the functions of time budgeting with respect to working and living conditions in France.

LEWIS, Normande.
"L"horaire variable: principales coordonnées." /Flexible hours: the principal elements./ Travail Québec. (1), Jan. 1976, pp. 25-34.

LIENARD, G.
"La gestion de l'horaire variable." /Managing flexible hours/ Travail et méthodes, June-Jul. 1976, pp. 13-14.
Describes the implementation of flexible working hours in Delle-Alsthom.

LUDOWICI, J.W.
"Gleitende 5-Tage-Woche." /Gliding five day week/ Arbeitswissenschaft, 3(6), 1964, pp. 173-176.

MACHOL, L.; SWIERCZEWSKI, W.
Ruchomy czas pracy. Doświadczenia krajowe i zagraniczne. /Flexible working time and foreign and domestic experiences./ Warszawa, 1975.

MANTE, W.H.R.
Variabele werktijden /Flexible working hours./ Alphen ann den Rijn, S. Uitgeverij, 1975, x, 141 p.
Paper on flexible working hours in the Netherlands.

MANTE, W.H.R., et. al.
"Variabele werktijden-dossier." /Report on flexible working hours./ Ondernemen, (2), Feb. 1976, pp. 77-95.

MARTIN, G.P.

"Horaire mobile: le dossier technique préparant la mise en oeuvre." /Flexible hours: the technical problems of their implementation./ Travail et méthodes, (330), Oct. 1976, pp. 23-27.

MATHIEU, J.; FRENZ, W.

Untersuchungen zur Arbeitszeiteinteilung in kontinuierlich arbeitenden Betrieben. /Studies on the arrangement of working hours in enterprises working round the clock./ Köln, Westdeutscher Verlag, 1963. 65 p. Forschungsberichte des Landes Nordrhein-Westfalen, Nr. 1227.

MEERS, A.

"Variabele werktijden hebben voor - en nadelen." /The advantages and disadvantages of flexible working hours./ Alumni Leuven, (1), Mar. 1975, pp. 26-27.

MELANGE, D.

"Le travail de la femme et l'horaire dynamique; enquête auprès du personnel féminin d'une compagnie d'assurance, La Winterthur." /Women's work and flexible hours. An enquiry in the Winterthur Insurance Company./ Annales de sciences économiques appliquées, (2), 1974-1975, pp. 65-90.
Discusses the advantages of flexible hours of work for the women worker in the light of results of a questionnaire survey of female personnel of the Winterthur Insurance Company.

MELANGE, Monique.

"L'horaire variable." /Flexible hours./ Fabrimetal, (5), May 1975, pp. 22-25.

MUSZALSKI, W.

Metody skracania czasu pracy. Studium prawnoporównawcze. /The methods of shortening working time. Comparative study./ Warszawa, 1967.

MUSZALSKI, W.

Skracanie czasu pracy. /The shortening of working time./ Warszawa, 1973.

"NN Corp. employees have flexible working hours." National underwriter - Life ed. 77, Sept. 1973, p. 7.
Gliding time which was introduced on an experimental basis at NN earlier this year proved so popular that it was extended and modified to permit even more flexible hours for the summer.

ORGANISATION FOR ECONOMIC CO-OPERATION AND DEVELOPMENT.

New patterns for work time; international conference, Paris, 28th - 29th Sept. 1972 : final report. Paris, 1973. 86 p. (Its: International seminars 1972-1.)
Report on flexible working hours as a way of improving the

daily, weekly, yearly and lifetime distribution of time between employment and leisure activities. Examines the current trend towards reducing hours of work and discusses social and economic implications and the future prospects of shift work, staggered working hours, the four-day week, holidays, educational leave, early retirement, etc.

PELAPRAT, A.
"L'horaire mobile et la Société Mutuelle d'Assurances du Bâtiment et des Travaux Publiques." /Flexible hours and the Mutual Insurance Company for the Construction Industry and Public Works./ Travail et méthodes, (326-327), June-Jul. 1976.

PROULX, P.P.; LAGANA, A.
"Analyse des effets écomoniques de la semaine comprimée et des horaires flexibles sur l'entreprise." /Analysis of the economic effects on the entreprises of the compressed work week and of flexible working hours./ Actualité économique (Montréal), 51(1), Jan.-Mar. 1975, pp. 128-147, 157-158. Article on the economic implications and effects of flexible working hours and other innovations in hours of work. Draws up a theoretical and empirical model of the effect on productivity profitability.

ROBINSON, David.
"Conference examines the growth of alternative work patterns." World of work report, (5), Jul. 1976, pp. 7-9.
Report of a series of experiments with flexible working hours presented at a conference in New York in June 1976.

ROUSHAM, S.
Flexible working hours today; practices and experiences of over fifty British organisations. London, 1973, ix, 58 p. (British Institute of Management. Management survey report No. 17.)
Report on a questionnare survey, the experience of approximately 50 enterprises in the UK with flexible working hours. Considers administrative features, trade union attitudes etc.

SALVATORE, P.
Flexible working hours; the experiment and its evaluation. Ottawa. Communications Canada. Staff Relations Division, Personnel Branch. 1974, iv.
Evaluation of a pilot project on flexible working hours for civil servants, undertaken by the Federal Department of Communications in Canada in 1973. Covers the experiences of management and employees, and includes recommendations.

SARTIN, P.
"Horaires flexibles." [Flexible hours.] Relations industrielles - Industrial relations, 29(2), 1974, pp. 343-365.
Presents an overview of the European experience with flexible working hours, discussing the advantages, management and employees' attitudes, trade union reticence, etc., and setting out the ground rules for introduction of any such system.

SLOANE, P.J.
Changing patterns of working hours. London, H.M.S.O., 1975. v, 45 p. (Great Britain. Department of Employment. Manpower paper, No. 13.)
Report on various experiments with working hours including flexible working hours, the compressed work week, and staggered working hours.

STRZEMIŃSKA, H.
Czas pracy i jego skracanie. [Working time and its shortening] Warszawa, 1976.

STRZEMINSKA, H.
Konsekwencje ekonomiczno-społeczne skracania czasu pracy. [Socio-economic consequences of the shortening of working time] Warszawa, 1969.

"Succès des horaires à la carte." [Success of the systems of hours in line with preferences.] Production et gestion, (286). Sept. 1976.

SUMMERS, Derek.
Flexible working hours : a case study. London, Institute of Personnel Management, 1974. 77 p.

SWART, J.C.
"What time shall I go to work today?" Business horizons, 17(5), Oct. 1974, pp. 19-26.
Discusses the merits and drawbacks of flexible working hours illustrating the arguments with the experience of several enterprises.

TERRIET; DORMITZ.
Möglichkeiten, Voraussetzungen und Konsequenzen neuer Strukturen der Arbeitszeitverteilung. [Possibilities, conditions and consequences of new patterns in the distribution of working hours.] Wirtschaftlichen und Socialen Wandel, [n.d.] (Project, No. 97.)

THORNTON, L.V.
Report on flexible hours experiment in the personnel branch. Ottawa, Department of Consumer and Corporate Affairs, 1973, 1 v.

TJÄNSTEMANNENS CENTRALORGANISATION.
Arbetstid : förslag till reformer. Report to the TCO Congress. /Working hours, a proposal for reform./ Stockholm, 1976.

UNION DES INDUSTRIES METALLURGIQUES ET MINIERES, Paris.
Note technique sur les horaires flexibles /A technical note on flexible working hours./ Paris 1972, 11 p.

UNITED STATES. GENERAL ACCOUNTING OFFICE; U.S. CIVIL SERVICE COMMISSION.
Legal limitations on flexible and compressed work schedules for federal employees, report to the Congress by the Comptroller General of the United States. Washington, 1974. ii, 21 p.
Recommendations on the possible application of flexible hours of work and compressed work schedules to federal civil servants in the USA.

WADE, M.
Flexible working hours in practice. New York, J. Wiley, 1974. 112 p.
Paper on the application of flexible hours of work in the UK and Western Europe comprising case studies of practices in a number of organisations and describes employees and management attitudes, varieties of flexible working time and effects on non-manual worker social status. Also considers overtime and absenteeism and trade union views.

WALKER, James et. al.
"Flexible working hours in two British government offices." Public personnel management, 4, Jul.-Aug. 1975, pp. 216-222.
Article on a detailed evaluation of pilot programmes regarding flexible working hours in two offices of the British Civil Service. It is particularly concerned with the employees own assessment of the situation.

WARD, C.D.E.
"Flexible working hours in operation; the Cheshire County Council experiment." Administrative management, 27 (2), Summer 1973, pp. 38-43.
Describes the methods and the effect of introducing flexible hours of work for civil servants in the Cheshire County Council.

WAYLAND D.G.
"Horaire mobile? Une question de temps." /Flexible hours? A question of time./ Optimum (Ottawa), 6(3), 1975, pp. 15-32.
Article on the merits and problems of flexible working hours discussing several schemes which have been implemented in Western Europe and North America.

WILLATT, N.
"Flexitime at Sandoz". European business review, 39, Autumn 1973, pp. 56-61.
Describes introduction of flexible hours at Sandoz, a pharmaceutical industry in Switzerland, including an analysis of management and employees' attitudes.

WILSON, James A.
"Some philosophic and social implications of the flexible workweek." In : PITTSBURGH. UNIVERSITY. GRADUATE SCHOOL OF BUSINESS. The four-day workweek : fad or future? Proceedings of a conference. Pittsburgh, 1973, pp. 2-20.
Emphasis on the 4/40 schedule and increased leisure.

WNUK-LIPIŃSKI, E.
Praca i wypoczynek w budżecie czasu. /Work and leisure in time - budget./ Wrocław, 1972.

ZUMSTEG, Bernard.
L'horaire libre dans l'entreprise : ses causes, ses problèmes, ses conséquences. /Flexible hours in the enterprise : causes, problems and consequences./ Paris, Delachaux et Nestlé, 1971. 120 p.

5. Industrial work environment and physical conditions of work

ABARBANEL, J.
Redefining the environment; behavior and the physical setting. Ithaca, 1972. 37 p. (Cornell University. New York State School of Industrial and Labor Relations. Key issues series, No. 9.)
Paper intended as a background for discussions of the relationship between job behaviour and the physical work environment.

ARBEIDSFORSKNINGSINSTITUTTENE. ARBEIDSPSYKOLOGISK INSTITUTT, Oslo.
Arbeidsmiljø og vernearbeid. Kartleggning av problemer og forslag til endringer. /The working environment and its protection. A statement of the problems and proposals for change./ Oslo, 1974. 224 p.

Bättre arbetsmiljö. /Better working environment./ Stockholm, Allmänna förlaget AB, 1972.

BERG, M.M.
Information om arbetsmiljön. /Information on working environment./ /N.p./, 1976.

BOLINDER, Erik.
Arbetsmiljö. Svenska erfarenheter och framtida problem. /Working environment. Swedish experiences and future problems./ Stockholm, Bonniers, 1972. 118 p.

BOLINDER, Erik.
Individen och den industriella miljön. /The individual and the industrial environment./ Stockholm, Prisma, 1971.

BRUNET, R.; DEROD, J.M.
Méthode d'analyse et d'évaluation de la sécurité et des conditions d'environnement du travail. /Methods of analysing and evaluating safety and conditions in the working environment./ Limoges, Caisse Régionale d'Assurance du Centre Ouest. /n.d./

CENTRAL LABOUR INSTITUTE, Bombay. - SOCIETY FOR CLEAN ENVIRONMENT, Bombay.
National seminar on industry, environment and man, Bombay, 1975, proceedings. Bombay, 1975, x, 164 p.
Conference report on the work environment in India. Includes discussion of occupational health and safety and the humanisation of work.

CHAIGNEAU, Y.
Contributions à une prospective du travail; présentation et conclusions essentielles du rapport rédigé pour le Commisariat Général du Plan. /Contributions to forecasts of labour trends; presentation and main conclusions of a report for the General Planning Commission./
Report of a working group on present and future trends in working conditions and the environment in France. Covers such aspects as factory organisation, occupational structure and job enrichment.

CLARKE, Thomas E.
"The work environment and mental health." Studies in personnel psychology, Oct. 1971, pp.83-94.

COTTIN, J.
"O.S., esclaves de notre temps." /Slaves of our time./ Etudes Paris, Dec. 1973, pp.695-708.
Examines working conditions and the working environment of semi-skilled workers in France.

COUNCIL OF TRADE UNION CONFEDERATION OF YUGOSLAVIA.
Protection and improvement of the working environment and the activities of the Yugoslav trade unions in this sphere. Belgrade, 1974.

THE DANISH WORK ENVIRONMENT GROUP.
Arbejdsmiljø. Graensvaerdier, arbejdstiden, meningsfyldt job, udstødningen. /The work environment. Threshold values, hours of work, meaningful jobs, ejection from the labour market./ Copenhagen, 1975. 201 p. (Its: Report No. 3.)

THE DANISH WORK ENVIRONMENT GROUP.
Arbejdsmiljø. Skader, omkostninger, målsaetning, naerdemokrati, planlaegning. /The work environment. Injuries, costs, objectives, participant democracy, planning./ Copenhagen, 1973. 158 p. (Its: Report 1.)

THE DANISH WORK ENVIRONMENT GROUP.
Arbejdsmiljøundersøgelsen. Dårlige rygge, stress, høreskader. /The work environment investigation. Bad back, stress, loss of hearing./ Copenhagen, 1974. 207 p. (Its: Report 2.)

ELDERING, H.B.
"Het internationale zoeklicht gericht op het arbeidsmilieu." /The working environment in the international limelight./ Sociaal maandblad arbeid, 30(11), Nov. 1975, pp.663-675.

EMMELIN, Lars.
"La planification de l'environnement en Suède: un projet de nouvelle législation s'appliquant à l'environnement du travail." /Environmental planning in Sweden: a new bill on the working environment./ Actualité suédoise, (72), Apr. 1976.

ERIKSEN, Hanne; KEIDING, J.T.
Arbejdsmiljøforskningen i Danmark. /Work environment research in Denmark./ Copenhagen, 1976. 43 p. (Review No. 5 - A supplement, containing a directory of ongoing research, will be published September/October 1976.)

"Formation massive aux problèmes d'environnement du travail." /Training in matters relating to the working environment./ Intersocial, (14), Mar. 1976, p. 13.

GAVIN, James F.
"Employee perceptions of the work environment and mental health; a suggestive study." Journal of vocational behaviour, 6, Apr. 1975, pp. 217-234.

GILWANN, M.
Pracovné prostredie v priemysle. Priemyselný interiér. /The industrial working environment. Industrial surroundings./ Bratislava, Práca, 1972. 160 figures.

GOYDER, G.
Responsible worker. London, Hutchinson, 1975. 144 p.
Covers employee attitudes towards work organisation and the environment in the UK.

HANKER, J. ROVDEROVÁ, M.
Optimalizácia pracovného prostredia pri komplexnej socialistickej racionalizácii. /Securing an optimum working environment in comprehensive rationalisation along socialist lines./ Bratislava, Práca, 1975. 202 p.

HERZBERG, Frederick.
The mental health effects of the work environment. Ann Arbor, Mich., University of Michigan, Foundation for Research on Human Behavior, 1962.

KATRIAK, Martin; KARÁSEK, Josef; HORA, Štefan; POLJAK, I.
Sociologický výskum pracovného prostredia a podmienok práce v priemyselných závodoch na Slovensku. /Sociological research on the working environment and working conditions in industrial works of Slovakia./ /Záverečná správa/ Bratislava, Ministerstvo Práce a Sociálnych Vecí, 1970. 246 p.

KOHOUT, J.; RŮŽIČKA, J.; MALANIUK, R.
Člověk v pracovném prostředí. /Man in the working environment./ Praha, Práca, 1971. 158 p.

*LANDSORGANISATIONEN I SVERIGE.
Arbetsmiljön. Rapport till LO-kongressen 1976. /Working environment. Report submitted to the LO Congress 1976./ Stockholm, Prisma i samarbete med LO, 1976. 156 p.

LANDSORGANISATIONEN I SVERIGE.
Rapport om arbetsmiljön. /Report on working environment/ Gemensamt av LO och TCO, Stockholm, 1975. /n.p./ (Available in English.)

LANGMEIEROVÁ, D.
"Několik poznámek k společenským a zdravotním aspectům pracovního prostredí." /Some notes on the social and health aspects of the working environment./ Bezpečnost' a hygiena práce, 18(6), 1968, pp. 118-181.

MAGNUSSON, Egon.
Kontroll av arbetsmiljön. /Control of the working environment./ Stockholm, Prisma i samarbete med LO, 1972. 54 p. (LO informerar, No. 11.)

MARRI, G. "Lotte sull'ambiente e riforma sanitaria." /Health reform and the struggle to improve the environment./ I Consigli, (15-16), June-Sept. 1975, pp. 43-45.
Considers the significance of the workers' struggle to improve the environment. Studies the contents of agreements relating to the environment and the organisation of work.

Metodologija za utvrdjivanje uslova radne sredine i zaštite na radu. /Methodology for establishing working environment and safety at work conditions./ Niš, 1972.

Naše tehničko-tehnološke i ekonomske mogućnosti zaštite i unapredjenja čovekove radne i životne okoline. /Our technical, technological and economic possibilities in the protection and enhancement of working and general environment./ Mostar, 1975.

NEDOROST, J.
"Některé poznatky z komplexního průzkumu pracovního prostředí." /The findings of a comprehensive survey on the working environment./ Odbury a společnost, (5), 1969, pp. 26-40.

REGIE NATIONAL DES USINES RENAULT.
Réception des postes de travail. /Approval of work places./ Paris, 1974, 80 p.
Manual which seeks to improve existing work places rather than to create new ones through a method which would compare the present state of work places with a set of rules or ergonomic reference values and raise questions regarding safety, environment work load and comfort of posture at each work place.

RENKER, U.
Gesundheit und Arbeitswelt. /Health and world of work./ Berlin, Verlag Volk und Gesundheit, 1976.

ROHMERT, W.; RUTENFRANZ, J.
Arbeitswissenschaftliche Beurteilung der Belastung und Beanspruchung an unterschiedlichen industriellen Arbeitsplätzen. /The scientific assessment of mental stress and demands on a worker's capacity at different industrial workplaces./ Bonn, Bundesministerium für Arbeit und Sozialordnung, 1975. 293 p.
Report on mental stress and physical capacity in different industrial work environments as seen from an industrial engineering view point.

ROSIVAL, P.; MACHÁČ, D.
"Výsledky prieskumu pracovného prostredia v priomysle strojárenskom a v priemysle textilnom a konfekčnom." /The results of an investigation of the work environment in the machinery industry and the textile and clothing industries./ Bezpečná práca, (5), 1971, pp. 24-27.

STANKOVIĆ, Života.
Ekonomika zaštite na radu. /Economy and safety at work./ Niš, 1974.

"Sweden: final report of the Work Environment Commission." Social and labour bulletin, (3), Sept. 1976, p. 263.

TJÄNSTEMÄNNENS CENTRALORGANISATION.
Tjänstemännens arbetsmiljöer - arbete - hälsa - välbefinnande, en kartläggning av arbetsförhållandena inom tjänstemannaområdet. /Working environment of white-collar workers - work- health - wellbeing, a survey of behaviour patterns of white-collar workers./ Stockholm, 1976. (Its: Rapport 1.)

UNION DES INDUSTRIES METALLURGIQUES ET MINIERES, Paris.
L'environnement des lieux de travail et l'esthétique industrielle. [The working environment and industrial design.] Paris, 1957. 68 p.
Considers theoretical aspects of factory organisation and the work environment including architecture, ergonomics and psychological aspects.

VEDER, V.
Pracovní prostredí. [The working environment.] Praha, Práce, 1970, 235 p.

YUGOSLAV COUNCIL FOR PROTECTION AND ENHANCEMENT OF HUMAN ENVIRONMENT.
Science, technology and human environment: a collection of papers from the 2nd Session. Belgrade, 1974.

6. Social indicators of the quality of working life

ANDREWS, F.; WHITEY, S.
"Developing measures of perceived life quality; results from several national surveys." Social indicators research, 1, 1974.

BARNOWE, J.T.; MANGIONE, T.W.; QUINN, R.P.
"Quality of employment indicators, occupational classifications, and demographic characteristics as predictors of job satisfaction." In: QUINN, R.P.; MANGIONE,T.W. The 1969-1970 survey of working conditions: chronicles of an unfinished enterprise. Ann Arbor, Survey Research Centre, 1973, pp. 385-392.

BIDERMAN, Albert D.; DRURY, Thomas F., eds.
Work quality measures as social indicators. Washington, Bureau of Social Science Research, Inc., /n.d./

BRADBURN, Norman M.
Is the quality of working life improving? How can you tell? And who wants to know? Doc. prepared for the Symposium on Social Indicators of the Quality of Working Life, Ottawa, 1973. Ottawa, Canada Department of Labour, 1973. 28 l.
Conference paper which discusses the question of changes occuring in the quality of working life as highly industrialised countries move into the post-industrial era. The two main question examined are: (1) The conceptualisation of the variables to be examined if attempts were made to monitor changes in this area; and (2) the proper role of government in monitoring such changes. Concludes that changes in the quality of working life will produce no unitary obvious trends in psychological wellbeing and that they must be investigated separately before one can decide whether QWL is improving or not. Does not consider government monitoring of changes in QWL appropriate, feeling rather that it is a matter for individuals to work out for themselves with their employers.

BRADBURN, Normann M.
"Is the quality of working life improving?" Studies in personnel psychology, 6(1), Spring 1974, pp. 19-35.

CAMMANN, Cortlandt, et al.
Effectiveness in work-roles. Report 1: Validating quality of employment indicators. Ann Arbor, Survey Research Center, 1975. 293 p.

CAMPBELL, Angus.
"Measuring the quality of life." Michigan business review, 26(1), Jan. 1974, pp. 8-11.

CANADA ECONOMIC COUNCIL.
Economic targets and social indicators: eleventh annual review. Ottawa, Information Canada, 1974.

CANADA, STATISTICS CANADA.
Perspective Canada, a compendium of social statistics. Ottawa, Information Canada, Jul. 1974.

CENTRE DE RECHERCHES ECONOMIQUES PURES ET APPLIQUEES.
Essai d'élaboration d'indicateurs micro-sociaux. /Attempt to elaborate micro-social indicators./ Paris, Université de Paris IX Dauphine, /n.d./, 95 p.

CENTRE DE RECHERCHES ECONOMIQUES PURES ET APPLIQUEES.
La mesure sociale: forces et faiblesses des instruments actuels, nouvelles propositions. /Social measurement: strengths and weaknesses of existing instruments and new propositions./ Paris, Université de Paris IX Dauphine, /n.d./, 66 p.

CENTRE DE RECHERCHES ECONOMIQUES PURES ET APPLIQUEES.
Les performances sociales des organisations. /The social performance of organisation./ Paris, Université de Paris IX Dauphine, /n.d./, 106 p.

CHARNES, A.; COOPER, W.W.; KOZMETSKY, G.
"Measuring, monitoring quality of life." Management science, 19(10), June 1973, pp. 1172-1189.

CHERRINGTON, David J.
"The effects of a central incentive-motivational state on measures of job satisfaction." Organizational behaviour and human performance, (10), Oct. 1973, pp. 271-289.

DELORME, François; LAROUCHE, Viateur.
"La mesure des besoins des individus en situation de travail: Elaboration d'un inventaire." /The measurement of individual needs in work situations. The elaboration of an inventory./ Revue de psychologie appliqué, Paris 1974.

FALGOS-VIGNE, J.L.; MARTIN, G.
Matériaux pour une analyse des conditions de travail sous l'angle des indicateurs sociaux. /Materials for an analysis of working conditions by using social indicators./ Grenoble, Institut de recherche économique et de planification, Jul. 1974, 132 p.

FINLAND, ECONOMIC PLANNING CENTER.
Quality of life: social goals and measurement, Helsinki, 1973. Report of the Finnish Economic Council on the question of the possible utility of social indicators as an aid to social planning. The areas examined included working conditions.

GASS, J.R.
"Education, work and the quality of life." The OECD Observer, (67), Dec. 1973, pp. 6-10.
The need for increasing flexibility between education, working life and leisure is weighed against the social concerns agreed upon by the OECD member countries as a first step towards developing a set of social indicators.

HAASE-RIEGLER, Peter.
Grundmethodik zur Klassifizierung von Arbeitserschwernissen. Arbeitswissenschaftliche Beiträge für Wissenschaft und Praxis. /Basic methodology for the classification of labour problems. Labour scientific examples for science and practice./ Dresden, Zentrales Forschungsinstitut für Arbeit, 1972. 104 p.
The basic methodology for the systematic classification of labour problems by order of importance is a tool of scientific management enabling any labour problems that may exist at key points in the undertaking to be attenuated or eliminated in an orderly manner.

HELZEL, M.F.; GOODALE, J.G.; JOYNER, R.C.; BURKE, R.J.
Development of a quality of working life questionnaire; item discrimination study. Doc. prepared for the Symposium on social Indicators of the Quality of Working Life, Ottawa, 1973. Ottawa, Canada Department of Labour, 1973. 1 v.
Conference paper which describes an item discrimination study of a quality of working life questionnaire designed to measure perceived social adjustment, workers' adaptation and job satisfaction. The authors evaluate the research method and social indicators chosen.

HERRICK, N.Q.; QUINN, R.P.
"The working conditions survey as a source of social indicators." Monthly labor review, 94(4), 1971, pp. 15-24.

INSTITUT NATIONAL DE LA STATISTIQUE ET DES ETUDES ECONOMIQUES.
Données sociales. /Social data./ Paris, Imprimerie national, 1973, 1974.

LABORATOIRE D'ECONOMIE ET DE SOCIOLOGIE DU TRAVAIL.
Recherches d'indicateurs sociaux concernant les conditions de travail. /Research on social indicators of the conditions of work./ Aix-en-Provence, 1973.

MACY, Barry A.; MIRVIS, Philip H.
Measuring quality of work and organizational effectiveness in behavioral economic terms. Ann Arbor, Survey Research Center, 1974, 32 p.

NADLER, David A., et al.
"A research design and measurement package for the assessment of quality-of-work interventions." In: NATIONAL ACADEMY OF MANAGEMENT. Proceedings 1975. /n.d./ 3 p.

ORGANISATION FOR ECONOMIC CO-OPERATION AND DEVELOPMENT.
Indicators of the quality of working life. Note prepared for the Working Party on Social Indicators, Paris, 1975. (Roneoed, restricted.)
Lists the aspects of the quality of working life which can only be measured using long and medium term indicators and develops short term indicators for other aspects such as working conditions, earnings and working and work related time.

ORGANISATION FOR ECONOMIC CO-OPERATION AND DEVELOPMENT.
List of social concerns common to most OECD countries. Paris, the OECD Social Indicator Development Programme (1), 1973, 27 p.
A report of the first phase of the OECD's Social Indicator Development Programme containing a list of Social Concerns. Eight major areas of interest are defined and twenty-four fundamental social concerns identified among which are, the availability of gainful employment for those who desire it, the quality of working life and individual satisfaction with the experience or working life. This list of concerns forms the basis for the second phase of the programme - the development of short and medium term indicators for each area of interest.

QUINN, Robert P.
"Strategy issues in the development of quality of employment indicators." In: AMERICAN STATISTICAL ASSOCIATION. Proceedings 1974. /n.d./, pp. 8-12. Also presented at the Conference on Quality of Employment Indicators, Silver Spring, Maryland, April, 1974.

QUINN, Robert P.
The 1972-1973 quality of employment survey. Ann Arbor, University of Michigan Institute for Social Research, 1974, 328 p.
One of the two surveys designed to assess the frequency and severity of work related problems, to develop measures of job satisfaction and to assess the impact of working conditions upon the wellbeing of the worker, the study presents data on topics such as the meaning of work, job satisfaction, physical working conditions, fringe benefits, work related injuries and illness, discrimination and wage loss.

RESEARCH COMMITTEE OF THE NATIONAL LIVING COUNCIL.
Social indicators of Japan. Japanese Economic Planning Agency, Tokyo, 1974, 270 p.
A scheme for a system of social indicators including coverage of such areas as employment and the quality of working life and classes and social mobility. The report also outlines social goal areas and the indicators which are intended to measure progress towards the attainment of these goals.

SEASHORE, Stanley E.
"Defining and measuring the quality of working life." In: DAVIS, Louis E.; CHERNS, Albert B.; eds. The quality of working life. New York, Free Press, 1975.

*SEASHORE, Stanley E.
Indicators of the quality of working life. A paper prepared for the UNESCO Conference on the "Quality of life", Dec. 1976. This paper discusses the various purposes of indicators of the quality of working life and clarifies the way in which these purposes require different indicators. Examples of current practice are included to show a certain consensus between conception and practice.

SEASHORE, Stanley E.
"Job satisfaction as an indicator of the quality of employment." Social Indicators Research, 1(2), Sept. 1974, pp. 135-168. The author explains the importance attached to the measurement of the quality of employment by drawing attention to the fact that as work is prevalent and occupies a large part of the available time of adults its ramifications affect virtually all other aspects of the quality of life. He attempts to clarify conceptual issues that are basic to its effective assessment, comments critically on the currently popular conceptions of the nature of job satisfaction and its role as a social indicator, suggests a broader view of the nature of job satisfaction and recommends priorities for research and action.

STRUMPEL, Burkhard, ed.
Economic means for human works: social indicators of well-being and discontent. Ann Arbor, Survey Research Center, Institute for Social Research, University of Michigan, 1976.

TAYLOR, James C.
Concepts and problems in studies of the quality of working life. Los Angeles, University of California, 1973, 56 p.

UNITED KINGDOM, CENTRAL STATISTICAL OFFICE.
Social trends, (1-5), London, Her Majesty's Stationery Office, 1970-1974.
A compendium published annually containing collections of tables and charts, as well as, some theoretical analyses of current concerns with social indicators.

UNITED NATIONS.
Current national and international activities in the field of social indicators and social reporting. Report of the Secretary-General. (E/CN.5/518, 2 Jan. 1975.)

UNITED NATIONS ECONOMIC, SOCIAL AND CULTURAL ORGANISATION.
"Les indicateurs socio-économiques: théories et applications." /Socio-economic indicators: theories and applications./ 37(1), 1975. Revue internationale des sciences sociales

UNITED NATIONS STATISTICAL COMMISSION.
System of social and demographic statistics (SSDS), potential uses and usefulness. Report of the Secretary-General, (E/CN.3/449, 19 June 1974)
Report of a study designed to develop international guidelines on social indicators of levels of living, covering ten areas including earning activities, employment services and social security and welfare services.

UNITED STATES OF AMERICA, EXECUTIVE OFFICE OF THE PREDIDENT.
Social indicators, 1973. Washington, United States Government Printing Office, 1973.
A government-sponsored study directed towards the conceptualisation of social indicators on a multi-sectoral level. Presents one hundred and sixty indicators of individual and family well-being in eight social areas including employment, income and leisure and recreation.

VAN DER MERWE, R.; MILLER, S.
"The measurement of labour turnover. A critical appraisal and a suggested new approach." Human relations, 24(3), 1971, pp. 233-253.

VAN DUSEN, Roxann A., ed.
Social Indicators, 1973: a review symposium. New York, Social Science Research Council, 1974.

WALTON, Richard E.
Criteria for the quality of working life. Paper prepared for the International Conference on the Quality of Working Life, Arden House, New York, Aug. 1972. (Roneoed.)

WALTON, Richard Eugene.
QWL indicators, prospects and problems. Doc. prepared for the Symposium on Social Indicators of the Quality of Working Life, Ottawa, 1973. Ottawa, Canada Department of Labour, 1973. 21 l.

7. <u>General literature on the humanization of work and the quality of working life</u>.

"Arbeid (de) vermenselijken ... maar hoe?" /Humanise work .. but how?/ ACV-Vakbeweging (28), 1973, pp. 3-11.

BALDUIN, Siegfried.
"Humanisierung der Arbeitswelt" /Humanisation of work./ Die Quelle, Dec 1974, p.489.

BALDUIN, Seigried.
"Menschenwürde im Betrieb - Humanisierung und Demokratisierung der Arbeit. /Human dignity in enterprises. Humanisation and democratisation of work./ Das Mitbestimmungsgespräch (7), 1972.

BARTHOLOMÄI, Reinhard.
"Probleme de Humanisierung am Arbeitsplatz im internationalen Vergleich." /International comparison of humanisation of work problems./ Stimme de Arbeit, (5), 1974, p. 107 et seq.

BEST, F.
Future of work, Englewood Cliffs, Prentice-Hall 1973, x, 179 p.
A compilation of articles speculating on the future meaning and nature of employment and working conditions. Discusses historical aspects, changing human motivations and educational needs, the impact of technological change, leisure options, flexible hours of work, the idea of a guaranteed income and the humanisation of work.

"Better working lives : a symposium." Occupational psychology, 47 (1), 1973, pp 15-31, 47 (2), 1973, pp 33-46.
(Contents : WARR, Peter B. "A university psychologist's view," pp 15-22. CHERNS, A.B. "A social scientist's view." pp. 23-28. JACKSON, Peter."An organisational consultant's view." pp. 29-31. PYM, Denis. "A personal viewpoint," pp. 33-46.

BRODBECK, B. ; HERMANN, G. ; WEISS, K.
"Industrieroboter, ein Mittel zur Humanisi erung de Arbeitswelt." /Industrial robots, a means of humanisation of the world of work./ Forschrittliche Betriebsführung und Industrial Engineering, 24(2), 1975, pp.83-87.

BRUNNER, Otto.
"Selbstverwirklichung der Arbeitnehmer durch Demokratisierung der Wirtschaft." /Self-fulfilment of workers through democratisation of economy./ Die neue Gesellschaft (5), 1971, p.321

BUNDESVEREINIGUNG DER DEUTSCHEN ARBEITGEBERVERBÄNDE.
"Arbeitsberichte des Ausschusses für soziale Betriebsgestaltung bei der BDA: Humanisierung der Arbeitswelt." /Work reports of the committee for social interprise organisation at the BDA: Humanisation of work./ Informationen für die Betriebsleitung, 36, 1975.

BUNDESVEREINIGUNG DER DEUTSCHEN ARBEITGEBERVERBAND. AUSSCHUSS FUR SOZIALE BETRIEBSGESTALTUNG.
Humanisierung der Arbeitswelt. /Humanisation of work./ (Its: Arbeitsbericht, No. 36.) /N.p./, 1974.

BRUNZ A.R.; JANSEN, R. ; SCHACHT. K.
Qualität des Arbeitslebens. /Quality of working life./ Bonn, Bundesministerium für Arbeit und Soziales, 1975.

BUTTERISS, Margaret.
The quality of working life : the expanding international scene. London /n.d./ (Great Britain. Department of Employment. Work Research Unit. Paper No. 5.)
Considers the industrial and social background to the present interest in the quality of working life and details policy, research and activity in the field, several countries including Britain, Australia, Belgium, Canada, Denmark, France, Germany, Italy, Japan, Netherlands, Norway, Sweden, Switzerland, Turkey and the USA. The author also outlines policies of the EEC and OECD in this field.

CAMPBELL, Bonnie.
"How to implement the humanizing process. Extracts from speeches given at 10th Annual Conference on IRRI, Queen's University, Kingston, 1973." Labour Gazette, Aug. 1973, pp. 522-524.

CAMRA, J.J.
"Wegweiser zu menschengerechten Arbeitssystemen." /Pointers to more human work systems./ REFA-Nachrichten, 29(1), 1976, pp. 35-37.

CARPENTIER, J.
"Organisational techniques and the humanisation of work." International labour review (110), Aug. 1974, pp. 93-116.
Having analysed the conceptual basis of work organisation and the historical factors that encouraged the development of mass production, the author examines the present situation and the various means by which work may be humanised, particularly through revised organisational techniques.

* CENTRAL LABOUR INSTITUTE, New Delhi.
Humanisation of industry. Proceedings of the National Seminar 8-9 Feb., 1974, organised by the Central Labour Institute, National Safety Council and National Productivity Council. /New Delhi?/ 1974, 176 p.
The proceedings of the first national Seminar on Humanisation of Industry in India, containing 14 technical papers by eminent experts and social thinkers covering various aspects of productivity, participation and protectivity. The papers illustrate the present thinking of a developing country like India on this emerging area of humanisation of industry. The deliberations covered such topics as man and his environment, how to vitalise safety in industry, productivity bargaining, sharing the gains of productivity, impact of new management strategy in India, ergonomics in industry, unions' role in accident prevention, health care in industry etc.

CENTRALE CHRETIENNE DES METALLURGISTES.
Qualité de la vie dans l'entreprise. Congrès des 15-16-17 octobre 1976. /Quality of life in the undertaking./ Bruxelles, 1976. 55 p.

* CHRENS, Albert B.
Perspectives on the quality of working life. A paper to the British Sociological Association, 1975.
A discussion of the basic assumptions and values of the QWL movement which considers also the various criticisms levelled at QWL experiments. Comments on one theory of the differential growth of industrial democracy in different European countries and discusses the process of diffusion in different cultural contexts.

CHICHESTER-CLARK, Robin.
"On the quality of working life." Personnel management, No.v 1973, pp. 26-29.

CONFERENCE ON NEW CONCEPTS OF WORK, Ottawa, Mar. 1973. Proceedings, Ottawa 1974. (Sponsored by the Canadian Council on Social Development.)

CONFERENCE ON QUALITY OF WORK CONTROVERSY. 2nd, Chicago, Dec. 9-11, 1973. Proceedings (preprints). Chicago 1973.

COUILLAULT, Serge.
L'humanisation du travail dans l'entreprise industrielle. /Humanisation of work in the industrial undertaking./ Paris, Epi. 1973, 157p.

COUNCIL OF EUROPE
Report on the humanisation of working conditions in industrial society. Strasbourg, 1974, 26 p.
Considers the humanisation of working conditions in the E.C. countries. Includes both a draft resolution on the subject and an explanatory memorandum dealing with such issues as job satisfaction, alienation and boredom, workers' participation flexible hours of work, and job enrichment.

DELAMOTTE, Yves,; WALKER, Kenneth F.
"Humanisation of work and the quality of working life in trends and issues." International Institute for Labour Studies. Bulletin, (11), 1975, pp. 3-4.
Reviews the present position and future prospects of the interest and activity in the field of the humanisation of work, discussing its various dimensions, the issues involved, the problems encountered and the roles, attitudes and reactions of the three industrial relations actors, the social scientists and the international organisations. Predicts that the interest in the humanisation of work and the quality of working life will grow, but stresses the need for dialogue between unions and management with regard to innovations and experiments in work organisation.

DAVIS, Louis E. CHERNS, Albert B.
The quality of working life. T 1-2. New York, Free Press, 1976. 2 vols.

DICKSON P.
Future of the workplace; the coming revolution in jobs. New York, Weybright and Tally, 1975. vi, 378 p.
Monograph on the future work environment and the prospects for humanisation of work in the USA, which covers job enrichment, workers participation and changes in hours of work.

DOERKEN, Wilhelm.
Menschengerechte Arbeit - Schlagwort oder Realität? /Human work - slogan or reality?/ Refa-Nachrichten, (5), 1976, pp. 145 - 150.

DONNADIEU, J.L.
Amélioration des conditions de vie au travail. /Improvement of the quality of working life./ Management France, (8-9), Aug. - Sept. 1975, pp. 30-36.
Article on the improvement of human relations in the work environment through the creation of conditons favourable to change.

DRAGER, Werner.
"Humanisierung der Arbeit." /Humanisation of work./ In: PLESSER; DRAGER, Werner, Das Unternehmen im Dienste des Menschen und der Gesellschaft. Köln, 1973, p. 25 et. seq. Bund Katholischer Unternehmer.

DRUCKER, Peter.
Management: Tasks, responsibilities, Practices. New York Harper and Row, 1974, (Chapter 19 :"Worker and Working: theories and reality" also chapter 21: "The responsible worker.") Analyses the philosophies of such behavioral scientists as, Douglas McGregor, Abraham H. Maslow, F. Herzberg Warren Bennis and others in terms of the virtues and shortcomings of their propositions.

DUBIN, Robert, ed.
Handbook of work, organisation and society. New York, Rand McNally College Publishing Company, 1976. 1068 p.
This handbook contains 37 chapters on future of work, work organisations, the social system of work. Topics included are : sociotechnical reorganisation of work; work and social power; work and political power; the postindustrial culture; relationships between technology, organisation and job structure; incentives for work; organisation development; the decision-making process in work organisations.

DYSON, William A.
Social policy in Canada: a quest for humanisation. Paper co-sponsored by the Maritime School of Social Work and the Nova Scotia Department of Public Welfare, Dalhousie University, Halifax, 1973.

EHMKE.
"Forschung und Entwicklung zur Humanisierung des Arbeitslebens. /Research and development work on humanisation of work./ Bulletin (35), Mar. 14, 1974. pp. 331-336.

EMPLOYERS' FEDERATION OF INDIA.
Humanisation of industry ; seminar proceedings. New Delhi, 1974.

EMPLOYERS' FEDERATION OF INDIA.
Quality of working life; seminar proceedings. New Delhi, 1976.

ENGELEN-KEFER, Ursula.
"Humanisation of work in the Federal Republic of Germany: a labour-oriented approach." International labour review 113 (2), Mar. - Apr. 1976.
The author contends that work is no longer only a means of satisfying material needs and suggests that security of employment and humane working conditions now rival wage levels as subjects of worker concern. In this context humanisation of work is seen as referring not only to ergonomic factors but also to the need for self-development and participation in decision making. The author feels however, that the latter aspects are still largely neglected and suggests the need for a new comprehensive policy that would entail broader responsibilities for workers' representatives.

EUROPEAN COMMUNITIES.
Conference sur l'organisation du travail, évolution technique ~~et~~ motivation de l'homme, Bruxelles, 5-7 Nov. 1974. /Conference on the organisation of work : technological progress and human motivation. Brussels, 5-7, Nov. 1974./ Luxembourg, 1974, 250 p.
A conference report on problems of work environment, workers participation and the humanisation of work in EC countries which discusses automation, motivation, continuing education and training, job enrichment, polyvalence, productivity and job satisfaction.

"European Communities : programme for the humanisation of work." Social and labour bulletin, (3), Sept. 1976 p. 257.

EVANGELISCHEN AKADEMIE BAD BOLL; ARBEITSGEMEINSCHAFT ZUR FORDERUNG DER PARTNERSCHAFT IN DER WIRTSCHAFT e.V.
"Humanisierung der Arbeitswelt - Herausforderung der Industrie"; /Humanisation of work - its challenge to industry./ eine Arbeitstagung mit Erfahrungsaustausch für Unternehmer, Manager, Betreibsrät und Techniker in der Evangelischen Akademie Bad Boll, /A symposium for entrepreneurs, managers, members of works councils, and technicians at the Bad Boll Evangelical Academy./ 14-16 Nov., 1976. Junkersdorf, 1974.

FISCHER, Guido.
Humanisierung der Arbeit. /Humanisation of work./ Personal, (8), 1974, pp. 340-342.

GERMANY (FEDERAL REPUBLIK). BUNDESMINISTERIUM FUR FORSCHUNG UND TECHNOLOGIE; BUNDESMINISTERIUM FUR ARBEIT UND SOZAILORDNUNG.
"Aktionsprogramm Forschung sur Humanisierung des Arbeitslebens." /An action programme of research into ways of humanising working life./ Bundesminister für Arbeit und Sozialordnung. Sozialpolitishe. Information, 8, 1974.

GLASER, E.M.
Improving the quality of working life. Los Angeles, Human Interaction Research Institute, 1974.

GLASER, E.M.
State-of-the-art questions about quality of worklife. Personnel, May-June 1976, pp. 39-47.

GULAS, S; FUSKO, Z,; HOLAS, E.
Tvoriva cinnost v organizacii a riadeni. /Creative thinking in organisation and the entreprise./ Bratislava, 1973. 153p. (Ceskoslovensky Vyskumny Ustav Prace, Bratislava. Studie a materialy, 22).
A monograph on creative thinking in the entreprise, with particular reference to factors in the work environment which may influence creativity, covers its theoretical and psychological aspects and includes survey data compiled in Czechoslovakia. Contains an English abstract.

GULDEN, Klaus; KRUTZ, W.; KRUTZ-AHLRING.
Humanisierung der Arbeit?- Ansätze zur Veränderung von Form und Inhalt industrieller Arbeit. /Humanisation of work? Proposals for changing the form and content of industrial work./ Berlin (West), 1973.

GYLLENHAMMER, Pehr G.
"Für eine Vermenschlichung des Arbeitsplatzes." /Humanisation of the workplace./ GDI topics, (6), 1973, p. 57.

HARMAN, S.
"The transforming influence of a work quality program." SAM advanced management journal, 41 (1), 1976, pp. 4-12.

HELFEART, M.
"Gesellschaftliche Bedingungen der Arbeit und Humanisierung der Arbeit setzt Demokratisierung voraus." /Social conditions of work. Humanisation of work presupposed democratisation./(4), 1974, p.299 et seq. i (5), 1974, p.391 et seq. Die neue Gesellschaft.

HERBST, P.G.
Socio-technical design: strategies in multi-disciplinary research. London, Tavistock Publications, 1974, 233 p.
Demonstrates the application of socio-technical theory and methods to design of new organisation forms; which are capable of responding to the demands of a rapidly changing environment and of satisfying the human needs of the individuals and groups involved. The book also explores three different approaches to a fundamental problem of socio-technical theory, which is how to integrate the physical and behavioural sciences.

HERRICK, Neal O,; MACCOBY, Michael.
"Humanizing work : a priority goal of the 1970's." In : UNITED STATES. CONGRESS COMMITTEE ON LABOUR AND PUBLIC WELFARE. Worker alienation, 1972, hearings, 92nd Cong. 2nd sess., S. 3916, July 25 and 26, 1972. Washington, U.S. Govt. Print Off. 1972, pp. 311-353.

HERZBERG, Frederick.
"The wise old Turk." Harvard business review, Sept.-Oct. 1974, 11 p.
A list of eight ingredients of a good job which is useful for the redesigning of jobs. The author also delineates four different approaches to job enrichment.

HETTINGER, Theodor.
Humanisierung der Arbeit. Die Anwendung der Arbeitswissenschaft in der betrieblichen Praxis. /Humanisation of work. The application of labour sciences to industrial practice./ Köln, Arbeitgeberverband der Metallindustrie im Regierungsbezirk Köln, 1975.

"Humanisierung der Arbeit und Wirtschaftlichkeit der Betriebe. Streit zwischen Praktikern und Ideologen; ein Seminar in Königstein." /Humanisation of work and economic efficiency of enterprises. Dispute between practicians and ideologists. A seminar in Königstein./ Frankfurter Allgemeine Zeitung, (84), Apr. 1974, p. 14.

HUND, J.
"Humanisierung der Arbeit - Humanisierung der Ausbeutung? /Humanisation of work - humanisation of exploitation?/ Socialistische Politik, 7(33), 1975, pp 63-70.

INSTITUT DER DEUTSCHEN WIRTSCHAFT.
Die Humanisierung - Industriearbeit im Wandel. /Humanisation - changes in industrial work./ 1976.

INTERNATIONAL LABOUR CONFERENCE. 60th SESSION, Geneva, 1975.
Making work more human : working conditions and environment. Geneva, International Labour Office, 1975, iv, 122 p. (Its : Report 1(1).)
Plans the first stages of a vigorous and long-term ILO campaign to help all member states to take urgent measures to improve working conditions and environment. The three main points are: the problem of safety and health in the work place, the problem of more flexibility in hours of work and leisure and the problem of the content and organisation of work. Having analysed these problems and sketched out a programme of action for the ILO, the report concludes that this organisation can contribute to the humanisation of work organisation through research, practical cooperation with member states and international standard setting.

IVALDI, J.P.
"La qualité de la vie dans l'entreprise." /The quality of life in the undertaking./ Hommes et techniques, (366), Apr. 1975, pp. 236-245.
More than an increase of their remuneration workers demand better working conditions and greater responsibility. The author analyses the motivations of workers, studies the problems of management and considers possible solutions such as job enrichment, socio-technical systems and rearrangement of working hours.

JAPAN PRODUCTIVITY CENTRE.
Methods of adapting to medium level economic growth. Tokyo, 1975. (In Japanese.)
An overall view of the labour situation in Japan, given the present reduced rate of economic growth, which stresses the importance of achieving a balance between the economic cycle and employment. The two part report includes suggestions for the promotion of worker participation in an era of economic stagnation and describes the situation of industrial relations, employment programmes, wage determination etc, in 1974.

JARDILLIER, P.
Organisation humaine du travail. /Human organisation of work./ Paris , P.U.F., 1973, 122 p.
Monograph of contemporary industrial sociology in developed countries, which refers especially to working conditions and problems related to the humanisation of work. Describes the principles of Taylorism in assembly-line work and the current trend to promote job satisfaction through job enrichment and group work.

JUNGK, Robert.
"Krise der Arbeitsmoral, Krise der Epoche, Humanisierung der Arbeitswelt ist gesellschaftliche Notwendigkeit. /Crisis of the work ethic, crises of the era. Humanisation of work is a social necessity./ Manager-Magasin, 9, 1974, p. 98.

KASTELLEINER, R.
Humane Arbeitswelt - Schlagwort oder Realität? /A human world of work : slogan or reality?/ Düsseldorf, 1974.

KIRCHNER, J.H.
"Praktishe Elemente für die Humanisierung der Arbeitswelt - Beitrag der Arbeitswissenschaft." /Practical proposals for humanisation of work : contribution of a labour expert./ Zeitschrift Arbeitswissenschaft, 29 (4), 1974, pp. 193-197.

KLINKENBERG, Peter.
"Auf dem Weg in eine menschlichere Arbeitswelt. Abschied vom Fliessband?" /On the way to a more human world of work. Goodbye to the assembly-line./ Sozialdemokrat Magazin, (7), Jul. 1974, p. 14.

KOWALEWSKA, S.
Humanizacja pracy, /Humanisation of work./ Warszawa, Wydawnictwo Zwiazkowe, 1971. 185 p.

KULPIŃSKA, J., SARAPATA, A.
System społeczny przedsiebiorstwa. /The social system of an enterprise./ Warszswa, 1966.

KUTTA, F., SOUKUP, M.
Řízení v období vědeckotechnické revoluce. Principy socioekonomickéhe řízení. /Management in the scientific and technological revolution. Principles of socio-economic management./ Praha, Svoboda, 1973. 326 p.

LANDESVEREINIGUNG BADEN-WURTTEMBERGISCHE ARBEITGEBERVERBANDE e.V.
Humanisierung der Arbeitswelt - eine internationale studie aus fünf Ländern. /Humanisation of work. An international study of 5 countries./ Stuttgart, 1976.

LAWLER, Edward E. III.
"For a more effective organisation; match the job to the man." Organisational dynamics, summer 1974, pp. 19-29.

LAWLER, Edward E. III.
"Quality of working life and social accounts." In: Corporate - social - accounting. /N.P./, 1973.

LEMINSKY, Gerhard.
Qualität des Lebens - Herausforderung an die Wert - und Zielvorstellungen in der Arbeitswelt /Quality of life - a challenge to values and goals in the world of work./ Referat im Sozialamt der Evangelischen Kirche von Westfalen im Haus Villigst, 27. April 1972.

LIFE, E.A.
Behaviour in the working environment; an introduction to some recent thinking and research. Henley-on-Thames, 1970. 28p. (Administrative Staff College, Henley-on-Thames. Occasional paper, No. 10.) (Reprint of 1968 ed.)
Literature survey of research into theories about human behaviour in the work environment.

MADERA, J.
"Plán i pro humanizaci práce." /The plan for the humanisation of work./ Bezpečnost a hygiena práce, 20(2), 1970, pp. 28-29.

MILLS, Ted.
"A taste of social equity." Training and development journal (29), May 1975, pp. 12-23.
Discusses improvement in the quality of working life.

MILES, Ted.
Quality of work; an emerging art and science. London, Working Together Campaign, 1973. 18 p.
The author defines the quality of work movement as one which views workers as entire persons, capable of reasoning, rather than as mere cogs in a machine. He postulates that the inclusion of workers in shop-floor decision-making will increase both their productivity and their identification with the organisation. He outlines the American Government sponsored Quality of Work Programme and considers the potential and the limitations of such efforts, listing thirteen possible problems including management and union resistance, the diversity of available altenatives and the difficulties of diffusion.

NATIONAL QUALITY OF WORK CENTER.
The quality of work program: the first eighteen months /N.P./, 1976. 56 p.

O'TOOLE, J.
Work and the quality of life; resource papers for work in America. Cambridge, Mass. M.I.T. Press, 1974 xv, 414 p. Anthology of working papers on work environment in the USA which covers such subjects as job satisfaction, alienation, occupational health, the humanisation of work and job enrichment, vocational training, labour mobility and the labour market, and social policy considerations.

"Personnel management : from work to quality of worklife." Industry week, 186 (8), Aug. 1975, pp. 30-33.

PLANOWANIE.
Społeczne w zakładzie pracy; aspekty humanizacyjne. /Social planning in the undertaking : humanisation aspects/ Warszawa, Instytut Wydawniczy CRZZ, 1974. 271 p.

POHLER, W.
"Soziale Voraussetzungen und soziale Konsequenzen veränderter Kooperation bei Aufhebung der Fleissarbeit." /Social conditions and social consequences of changed cooperation through the abolition of the assembly line./ In: Humanisierung des Arbeitslebens, Symposion des RKW zu Möglichkeiten neuer Formen der Arbeitsorganisation am 6. Nov. 1972.

PORTIGAL, Alain H.
"Current research on the quality of working life." Relations industrielles - Industrial relations, Oct. 1973, pp. 736-762, (French summary, pp. 763-767). Reviews some viewpoints on QWL and comments on some of the studies purporting to document the apparent dissatisfaction of workers with the prevailing working conditions. Contends that QWL must be viewed not only from the perspective of the workers but also those of government and employers if findings are to be comprehensive and relevant.

POSTH, M.
"Humanisierung der Arbeitswelt. /Humanisation of work/ Der Arbeitgeber- 14, 1974. p. 536 et seq.

PROKOP, K.
"L'humanisation du travail - utopie ou nécessité sociale? /Humanisation of work - a Utopia or a social necessity?/ Monde du travail libre. (297) Mar. 1975, pp. 5-7. Humanisation of work as the basis for the activities of the new study centre of the Austrian Confederation of Trade Unions.

The quality of life concept: a potential new tool for decision-makers. Washington, Environmental Studies Division, Environmental Protection Agency, 1973.

RAO, V. Rukmini
"Quality of life in an industrial township. An initial survey." National Labour Institute bulletin. 1(10), Oct. 1975, pp. 8-12.
A paper arising out of the research project, "Attitude towards Quality of Work Life, Family Planning and Change - a study among Industrial Workers in Bharat Heavy Electricals Ltd. (BHEL) Factory at Hardwar. Based on visits to the homes of 120 workers' families, the author has highlighted aspects of communication in the family planning and family life of a worker's wife.

RAO, V., Rukmini; SRIVASTAVA, B.K.
"Attitude towards quality of work life,family planning and change. A study among industrial workers at BHEL Factory in Hardwar". To be published in National Labour Institute bulletin.
A study designed to explore the linkage between work life and family life. Data was collected from 120 workers and their families. The data included factors such as quality of work life, job satisfaction, attitude towards family planning, caste, religion, determinants of family life satisfaction, etc.

"Rapport du groupe de réflexion recherche scientifique - amélioration des conditions de travail." /Report of the Study Group on Scientific Research into the Improvement of Working Conditions./ Progrès scientifique, May - June 1975, pp 73-84.
Recent technological progress the basic objectives of which have been economic advancement and immediate profitability, has had a profound impact on conditions of work at all levels of responsibility or performance. In particular it has helped to reduce physical work loads. However it has obviously not solved the over-all problem of working conditions but has continually changed its nature. Faced with this problem, the General Delegation for Scientific and Technological Research convened a meeting of the Study Group on Scientific Research into the Improvement of Working Conditions, which has drawn up an inventory of research in priority sectors.

"REFA zur Humanisierund der Arbeit. /REFA on humanisation of work./ REFA-Nachrechten, (3), 1976, pp. 151-152.

ROSOW, J.M. ed.
The worker and the job: coping with change. Englewood Cliffs, Prentice-Hall, 1974, i-x, 208 p.
This book stems from a conference organised by the American Assembly in 1973. It contains two 'overview' papers by Daniel Yankelovich on "The Meaning of Work", and by Eli Ginzberg on "The Changing American Economy and Labour Force". In Part Two, on "Contemporary Issues", there are papers on "Worker Attitudes and Adjustments"; "Unions: a New Role?" "Economic Effects of Industrial Change", and on "Worker Adjustments". Part Three: "New Horizons" opens with a paper by Richard Walton: "Innovative Restructuring of Work",

which gives an extended discussion, of a very inclusive kind of the situations which lead to work restructuring and to the difficulties which have appeared in a variety of projects of this kind.

SALOVAARA, J.
Role of professional contribution by industrial design for humanising work environment. Helsinki, 1975. 18p. Pamphlet on the role of engineering design in the humanisation of work and the work environment. With special reference to Scandinavia.

SANDER, H.
Humanisierung der Arbeitswelt /Humanisation of work./ /N.p./ Institut der Deutschen Wirtschaft. Vortragsreihe, 35. 1974.

SAXBERG, Borje O,; SUTERMEISTER, Robert A.
"Today's imperative : humanising the organisation." Personnel administrator, 19, Jan. - Feb. 1974, pp. 53-58.

SCHEIPS, Charles D.
"The humanisation of work." Personnel, Sept. - Oct. 1972, pp. 38 - 44.

SCHMIDT, H.
"Menschengerechte Gestaltung der Arbeit und der Beschäftigung, Aktivitäten der Bundesregierung." /Human organisation of work and employment, activities of the Federal Government./ Gewerkschaftliche Monatshefte, 24(1), 1973, pp. 52-59.

SEASHORE, Stanley E.
"Assessing the quality of working life: the US experience." Labour and society, 1(2), Apr. 1976, pp. 69-79. Article on the use of social indicators in evaluation of the quality of working life (comprising working conditions and job satisfaction, etc.) in the USA - covers the use of social indicators in enterprise level surveys and includes methodological issues, etc. References.

SERVAN-SCHREIBER, J.L.
L'entreprise à visage humain. /The undertaking with a human face/ Paris, Robert Laffont, 1973, 266 p. Deals with problems of job satisfaction and humanisation of work, including alienation and fatigue of workers and supervisors. Devotes particular attention to the situation in France and the United States. Other subjects dealt with are hours of work, work on the assembly line, workers participation and the social role of the undertaking.

SHAPIRO, Irving S.
"The job ahead : enriching the quality of life in America." Nation's business, June 1976, pp. 64-68.

SHEPPARD, Harold L.

"Some selected issues surrounding the subject of the quality of working life." In: INDUSTRIAL RELATIONS RESEARCH ASSOCIATION. Proceedings of the 25th Anniversary Meeting, Dec. 1972. Madison, Wis., 1973.

SPINK, Peter.

"Some comments on the quality of working life." Journal of occupational psychology, 48, (3), 1975, pp. 179-184.

STEWART, Gail.; STARRS, Cathy.

Re-working the world; a report on changing concepts of work. Ottawa, 1973 (Roneogr.).

STIRN, H.

"Möglichkeiten und Grenzen der Humanisierung der Arbeit." /Possibilities and limits of humanisation of work./ Arbeit und Leistung, 28 (2), 1974, pp. 52-54. Report on a debate held in Darmstadt on 24 November, 1973.

SWEDEN. ROYAL MINISTRY FOR FOREIGN AFFAIRS.

The human work environment; Swedish experiences, trends and future problems. A contribution to the United Nations conference on the human environment. By the Royal Ministry for Foreign Affairs and the Royal Ministry of Agriculture. Stockholm, 1971.

TAKEZAWA, Shin-Ichi.

"The quality of working life: trends in Japan." Labour and society, (1) 1976, pp. 29-48. The present position of the quality of working life in Japan is explored within the context of its historical background and nature, the signs of a movement towards a new definition of the term and the exploration of new solutions to the problem of alienation. Contending that the quality of working life could become a major labour issue, the author sees lessons for the future in current experiences in this field.

TAYLOR, James. C.

Concepts and problems in studies of the quality of working life. Los Angeles, Graduate School of Management, 1973. 56 p. (Roneogr.).

THOMASON, G. F.

Improving the quality of organisation, London, Institute of Personnel Management, 1973. 109 p. A monograph on management techniques for improving the quality of business organisation in the UK. It covers organisation development, job enrichment and work design and the administrative aspects of management.

TIETZE, B.
"Humanisierung der Arbeitswelt : theoretisches Programm und politische Praxis," /Humanisation of work : theoretical programme and political practice./ Arbeit und Geistung 28, Dec. 1974, pp. 309-315.

UNITED STATES. DEPARTMENT OF LABOR. MANPOWER ADMINISTRATION.
Jobs analysis for human resource management: a review of selected research and development. Washington, G.P.O., 1974. 83 p. (Its : Manpower research monograph, No. 36.)

"United States; National Productivity and Quality of Working Life Act of 1974." Social and labour bulletin, June 1976, pp. 157-158

VARADAN, M.S.S.
"Organisational development; the HMT way." Lok udyog, 9 (5), Aug. 1975, p. 19.
A case study in the application of modern management techniques to a giant public enterprise which after six years of growth, found itself in the grip of a recession. The steps taken to define corporate goals and weld the management and workers into an effective, dynamic team are traced.

VETTER, H.O.
"Für eine Humanisierung der Arbeitswelt." /Humanisation of work./ Metall, 20 Feb. 1973, p. 2.

VILMAR, Fritz.
"Humanisierung der Arbeitswelt." /Humanisation of work./ Radius, (2), 1974, p. 29.

VILMAR, Fritz.
"Unsere Arbeitswelt muss menschlicher werden." /Our world of work must become more human./ Der Angestellte, Zeitschrift der Deutschen Angestellten-Gewerkschaft, (11), 1974.

VILMAR, Fritz.
"Was heisst Humanisierung am Arbeitsplatz? Effizienz und Humanisierung als gleichwertige Ziele für die Zunkenft. /What does humanisation of work mean? Efficiency and humanisation as goals of equal value for the future./ Mitbestimmungs-Information; Zeitschrift für demokratisierung der Arbeitswelt, (1), 1974, p. 2.

VILMAR, Fritz. ed.
Menschenwürde im Betrieb. Modelle der Humanisierung und Demokratisierung der industriellen Arbeitswelt. /Human dignity in the enterprises. Models for humanisation and democratisation in the industrial world of work./ Reinbek. 1975.

VOLPERT, W.
"Die 'Humanisierung der Arbeit' und die Arbeitswissenschaft." /Humanisation of work and labour sciences./ Blätter für deutsche und international politik June - Jul. 1974, pp. 602-612, 709-719.

WAHNER, Hartmut.
"Humanisierung der Arbeit." /Humanisation of work./ Links, Sozialistische Zeitung, (58), Sept, 1974. p 11.

Vermenschlichung d. Arbeitswelt; /Humanisation of work./ Bundeskongress d. OeGB Wien, 15. - 19. Sept. 1975 Arbeitskreis 2. Wein Verlag d. OeGB, 1975.

WACŁAWEK, J.
Problèmes de l'humanisation du travail et des fonctions éducatives des entreprises industrielles de la République populaire de Pologne. /Problems of humanisation of work and the educational functions of industrial undertakings in the Polish Peoples' Republic./ Warsovie, WSNS, 1972. 59 p.

WALKER, Kenneth F.
"From Hawthorne to Tapeka and Kalmar." In: CASE, Eugene L. ZIMMER, Fredrick G., eds. Man and work in society. New York, Van Nostrand-Reinhold, 1975, pp. 116-134.

WALKER, Kenneth F.
"Using social psychology to create a new plant culture." In: DEUTSCH, Morton; HORNSTEIN, Harvey A. eds. Applying social psychology : implications for research, practice, and training. Hillsdale, Lawrence Erlbaum Associates, 1973.

WALTON, Richard E.
"How to counter alienation in the plant." Harvard business review, 50 (6), 1972, pp. 70-81.
The author uses the example of a comprehensive organisational redesign effort in a large pet-food manufacturing enterprise to support the contention that the total restructuring of the workplace and the organisation of work is necessary to encounter alienation, to meet the changing expectations of employees and to increase productivity.

WALTON, Richard E.
Improving the quality of work life. Harvard business review, May-June 1974, pp. 11, 16, 155.

WALTON, Richard E.
"Quality of working life: what is it?" Sloan management review, Fall 1973, pp. 11-21.

WEAVER, Charles N.
"What workers want from their jobs." Personnel, May-June 1976, pp. 48-54.

WEIL, Reinhold.
"Gedanken über die Bedeutung des Begriffes menschengerechte Gestaltung de Arbeit." /Reflections on the significance of the concept of human organisation of work./ Mitteilungen des IfaA, (38).

WEIL, Reinhold.
Humanisierung der Arbeit - Antwort auf Engfremdung? /Humanisation of work - a response to alienation?/ Köln, 1975. (Institute für Angewandte Arbeitswissenschaft, Köln Schriftenreihe. Heft 4).

WEISER, Günter
Menschengerechte Arbeitsplatzgestaltung im Betrieb /Organisation of industrial work along human lines./ München, C. Haeuser-Verlag, 1974.

WHITSETT. D.A.
"Where are your unenriched jobs?" Harvard business review 53, 1975,
A discussion of eleven structural clues for recognizing opportunities to improve jobs and also the productivity and satisfaction of those filling them. The author warns, however, that job enrichment is not an overall problem-solving technique that can be used indiscriminately and should, therefore, be undertaken only when organisational conditions call for, and favour its implementation.

"When workers help call the tune in management." U.S. news and world report, 11 May, 1976, pp. 83, 85.

WILKEN, Folkert.
Die Befreiung der Arbeit. Die Uberwindung der Arbeitskämpfe durch assoziative Betriebsverfassung.
/Liberation of work. Overcoming labour disputes by participative works constitutions./ Freiburg i.B., Verlag Die Kommenden, 1965.

WILSON, N.A.B.
On the quality of working life; a report... London, H.M.S.O. 1973, 52 p. (Great Britain. Department of Employment Manpower papers, No. 7.)
The quality of working life depends on both the output and the satisfaction of workers. The present report describes the effects that some of the characteristics of modern industrial systems have, first on the work experience of employees and then on their feelings of responsiblilty and their enthusiasm for their work. Noting that one must take into consideration the fact that conditions of the future will be very different from those of today, the report makes several recommendations for future government action in this area.

WINTERHAGER, Wolfgang Dietrich.
Humanisierung der Arbeitswelt. Gesetzliche Vorschriften, Pläne, Modelle und Kontroversen. /Humanisation of work. Legal prescriptions, plans models and controversies./ Berlin, 1975

Work in America; report on a special task force to the Secretary of Health, Education and Welfare. Cambridge, Mass. MIT Press, 1973, 262 p.
Alternately criticized for its research methods and hailed as a breakthrough in the acceptance of public responsibility for the quality of working life, the report presents an analysis of the problems of work in America and recommends some solutions. It defines work, analyses its functions in American society and indicates that there is a growing sense of alienation among both white and blue collar workers and suggests possible reasons for this. Special attention is paid to the problems of minority workers, young workers and women workers. The relationship between work and retirement and work and health are explored. Suggested solutions to perceived problems include redesigning jobs, increasing workers participation and opportunities for self-fulfilment, massive worker retraining programmes and seven-yearly sabbaticals for all workers. Concludes that the government has an important role to play in planning future strategies for the improvement of the working environment.

"World of work." Dialogue, 7(4), 1974, pp. 3-52.
A compilation of articles on employees attitudes and society's expectations with regard to job satisfaction, humanisation of work, and other aspects of the work environment in the USA.

8. Bibliographies relevant to the subjects covered.

ALABAMA. UNIVERSITY OF ALABAMA IN BIRMINGHAM. CENTER FOR LABOUR EDUCATION AND RESEARCH.
Bibliography on worker participation in management decision-making. Birmingham, 1973.

"Attitudes to work; a selected bibliography." Part I: "Job satisfaction." Part II: "Motivation." Personnel practice bulletin, Mar. 1972, pp. 78-89; June 1972, pp. 177-184.

"Bibliographie sélective sur les conditions de travail. Les principaux centres de recherche sur les conditions de travail." /Selected bibliography on working conditions. The main centres engaged in research into working conditions./ CFDT aujourd'hui, (16), Nov.-Dec. 1975, pp. 85-92.
Bibliographical listing of the most recent studies on working conditions carried out in France, with details of some of the centres active in this field.

CARROLL, Bonnie.
Job satisfaction; a review of the literature. Rev. and updated by Mary W. Blumen. Ithaca, New York State School of Industrial and Labor Ralations, Cornell University, 1973. 57 p. (Key issues, No. 3.)

CLARKE, R.O., et al.
Workers' participation and industrial democracy; a bibliography. London, London School of Economics, 1969.

DWORACZEK, M.; MATTHEWS, C.J.
Recent innovations in work scheduling; a bibliography. Toronto, Ministry of Labour, 1974. 66 p.
Bibliography on various innovations in hours of work - including the compressed work week, flexible working hours, effects on leisure etc.

FRANKLIN, Jerome L.
Organization development; an annotated bibliography. Ann Arbor, University of Michigan, 1973. 108 p.
Bibliography focusing on the improvement of organisational performance with emphasis on the social aspects of organisation functioning.

GAUDIER, Maryse.
Workers' participation in management, 1974-1976. Geneva, International Institute for Labour Studies, 1977. (To be published.)

GREVE, R.
Selected and partially annotated bibliography on certain aspects of the quality of working life, with special reference to work organization, 1970-1975. Geneva, International Institute for Labour Studies, 1976.

KINGSTON, ONT. QUEEN'S UNIVERSITY. INDUSTRIAL RELATIONS CENTRE.
Absenteeism: a bibliography. Kingston, 1975. 60 p. (Its: Bibliography series, No. 6.)

LAMPKIN, Paul.
"Bibliography; appendix 2." In its: Job enrichment - Revalorisation du travail. Ottawa, Department of Labour, Union-Management Services Branch, 1975. 1 v.

MAILO, John R.
Research on job satisfaction. /Monticello, Ill./, 1975. 14 p. (Council of Planning Librarians. Exchange bibliography, No. 762.)

MARCLAY, Annette.
Workers' participation in management; selected bibliography, 1950-1970. Geneva, International Institute for Labour Studies, 1971. 108 p.

ONTARIO DEPARTMENT OF ECONOMICS AND DEVELOPMENT.
Labour mobility: an annotated bibliography. Ottawa, Department of Labour, 1966.

RUNYON, J.
Quality of work life; a bibliography. Hull, Canada, Supply and Services Canada, 1975.

TAGGART, David.
Bibliography on job satisfaction. Princeton, /1973/ 3 p. (Princeton University. Industrial Relations Section. Selected references, No. 168.)

TAYLOR, James C., et al.
Quality of working life: an annotated bibliography. Los Angeles, Center of Organizational Studies, Graduate School of Management, 1972.

TEGA, V.
Flexible working hours and the compressed work week: technical and practical aspects, implications; an international selected and annotated bibliography. Montreal, Ecole des Hautes Etudes Commerciales, Bibliothèque, 1973. ix, 217 p.
Annotated bibliography on flexible working hours and the compression of working hours. Also contains critical evaluations of the theoretical and practical aspects of such innovations, with special emphasis given to the growing trend in this area in Canada.

VAN HOLLE, Roland; GAUDIER, Maryse.
Workers' participation in management; selected bibliography, 1970-1974. Geneva, International Institute for Labour Studies, 1975. 58 p.

AUTHOR INDEX

A

B

C

D

E

F

G

I

J

K

L

M

N

O

P

Q

R

T

U

V

W

Y

Z

ADDITIONAL REFERENCES

I. Relations between working conditions and job satisfaction

DIVERREZ, J.
Améliorer les conditions de travail. Paris, Entreprise Moderne d'Edition, 1976, 151 p.
Monograph on the improvement of working conditions of both managers and workers in France. Presents new concepts and methods of work organisation, and discusses ergonomics, occupational safety, job satisfaction, wages, job evaluation, the work environment, hours of work, etc. Includes a bibliography.

ROUSTANG, G.
"Why study working conditions via job satisfaction? A plea for direct analysis." International Labour Review (Geneva), 115(3), May-June 1977, pp. 277-291. This article on improving the work environment and working conditions points up the reliability of job satisfaction measurements and advocates a methodology, developed in France, for the evaluation of working conditions. Contains bibliographical references.

II. Other literature on job satisfaction

FLUDE, R.A.
"Development of an occupational self-concept and commitment to an occupation in a group of skilled manual workers." Sociological Review (Keele), 25(1), Feb. 1977, pp. 41-49.
Article based on thesis material concerning the mechanisms of occupational choice, commitment and job satisfaction amongst skilled workers in the United Kingdom - contributes to a general theory of socialisation. Includes references.

SARASON, S.B.; KRANTZ, D.
Work, aging, and social change; professionals and the one life-one career imperative. New York, Free Press, 1977, XIII, 298 p.
Monograph on the psychological aspects of job satisfaction and occupational change among professional workers in the USA - discusses the relationships between social change and the individual's sense of ageing and of the quality of life, and includes case studies. Contains bibliographical references.

THURMAN, J.E.
"Job satisfaction: an international overview."
International Labour Review (Geneva), Nov.-Dec. 1977, pp. 249-269.
Aricle presenting an international comparison of job satisfaction levels and trends - shows that much still needs to be done to improve career development prospects and job content if workers' rising expectations are not to be frustrated.

TIEFENTHALER, J.
"Berufliches Selbstverständnis und Berufswirklichkeit des öffentlich Bediensteten (eine empirische Unterschung im Magistrat Linz)."
Arbeitsmarktpolitik (Linz), (21), 1977, pp. 1-239.
Article on a sample survey of employees' attitudes and job satisfaction of public servants in the urban area of Linz in Austria - describes the applied survey methodology and contains research results on social status, sex and behaviour comparisons with other employees and office workers.

WNUK-LIPINSKI, E.
"Job satisfaction and the quality of working life: the Polish experience." International Labour Review (Geneva), 115(1), Jan-Feb. 1977, 53-64.
Article on job satisfaction and job enrichment experiences in Poland - reviews the principal findings of a number of surveys and of various practical experiments to improve the quality of working life, and assesses trends in the most frequent sources of job satisfaction or dissatisfaction. Includes references.

YOSHIDA, K.; TORIHARA, M.
"Redesigning jobs for a better quality of working life; the case of the Tokyo Gas Company." International Labour Review (Geneva), 116(2), Sep.-Oct. 1977, pp. 139-151.
Article on a large-scale job design project for the humanisation of work and improvement of job satisfaction among the 12,000 employees of the Tokyo Gas Company in Japan. Shows how the project was launched with active workers' participation and how it sought to achieve comparable working conditions for both manual workers and non-manual workers, and includes a brief evaluation of the success of the project based on trade union and management attitudes.

III. New forms of work organisation

BARTOLI, J.A.
Organisation du travail par équipes successives. Aix-en-Provence, Université de droit, d'économie et des sciences d'Aix-Marseille, Institut d'administration des entreprises, 1977, 315 p.
Thesis on the scientific management of continuous shift work - discusses work environment, work organisation and arrangement of working time (includes flexible hours of work), and presents a systems analysis approach with mathematical models.
Bibliography pp. 301-315.

BOERI, D.
Nouveau travail manuel: enrichissement des tâches et groupes autonomes. Paris, Editions d'organisation, 1977, 222 p.
Monograph on innovations in work organisation related to activities of manual workers in workshops - discusses features of group work and describes methodologies of promoting occupational change and job enrichment, and includes two case studies concerning transformations in industrial enterprises as well as an analysis of trade unions' attitudes. Contains bibliographical references.

CENTRE D'ETUDES ET DE RECHERCHES SUR LES QUALIFICATIONS
Organisation du travail et ses formes nouvelles.
Documentation française, Paris, 1977, 292 p.
Monograph on work organisation - contains nine contributions dealing with the planning and introduction of improved working conditions, industrial sociology, job enrichment, workers' participation, workers' self management and ergonomics. Includes a bibliography pp. 281-292.

CUMMINGS, T.G.; MOLLOY, E.S.
Improving productivity and the quality of work life. New York, Praeger, 1977. XVI, 305 p.
Compilation of research papers on the humanisation of work and improved labour productivity - discusses the effectiveness of autonomous group work, job satisfaction and job enrichment, workers' participation in decision making, flexible hours of work, countering alienation at the workplace, experiments in work organisation, etc. Includes a bibliography pp. 292-305.

GLASER, E.M.
Productivity gains through worklife improvements. New York, Harcourt Brace Jovanovich, 1976. X. 342 p.
Monograph on the effects of humanisation of work on productivity in the USA, Europe and Japan - examines changes in employees attitudes and motivations, considers the problems, successes and failures of various experiments in job enrichment and the improvement of working conditions, job satisfaction, workers' participation, etc., and presents guidelines for the introduction and evaluation of job-redesign programmes. Bibliography, pp. 327-335.

HACKMAN, J.R.; SUTTLE, J.L.
Improving life at work; behavioral science approaches to organizational change. Santa Monica, Goodyear Publishing Co., 1977, 494 p.
Monograph on management approaches to humanisation of work in industrial enterprises in the USA - contains definitions of job satisfaction and covers industrial psychology and industrial sociology in career development, motivation and job enrichment through the redesign of business organisation, the impact thereof on absenteeism, the choice of wage payment systems, intergroup relations, personnel management and supervisory roles, government policy on interest group activities, etc. Includes bibliographical references.

HAMMER, T.H.; BACHARACH, S.B.
Reward systems and power distribution in organizations; searching for solutions. Cornell University, New York State School of Industrial and Labor Relations, Ithaca, 1977, 119 p. (ITS: Frank W. Peirce memorial lectureship and conference series, No. 5.)
Monograph and essays and research in the social psychology of behaviour control, with particular reference to the factors bearing on work organisation and job design as they influence motivation and job satisfaction. Includes references.

INTERNATIONAL INSTITUTE FOR LABOUR STUDIES
Implications for trade unions of the trend towards new forms of work organisation (new forms of work organisation and quality of the workplace); research paper, Netherlands. Geneva, 1977, 32 p.
Research paper presenting trade union attitudes on work organisation and humanisation of work trends in the Netherlands - discusses labour relations, government policy, working conditions, job content, job design, the introduction of autonomous group work (including case studies from industrial enterprise), etc., and presents evaluations.

INTERNATIONAL LABOUR OFFICE
Selección de tecnologias y condiciones de trabajo: esquema para un estudio comparativo.
Seminario regional sobre promoción y coordinación de estudios e investigaciones en materia de condiciones y de medio ambiente de trabajo en América Latina, Lima, 1977. Geneva, 1977, 9 p.
Working paper prepared for an ILO meeting on the promotion and coordination of research with regard to working conditions and the work environment in Latin America (PIACT). Discusses the effects of technology transfer on the welfare of manual workers and defines the role of ILO in investigating occupational health, work organisation within the enterprise, living conditions, etc.

INTERNATIONAL LABOUR OFFICE
Textiles Committee, 10th Session, Geneva, 1978.
Conditions of work in the textile industry including problems related to organisation of work, Geneva, 1977, IV, 87 p.

MEADOWS, I.S.G.
"Innovative work arrangements; a case study in job enrichment, Philips Electronics Limited, Leaside, Ontario." Ministry of Labour, Toronto, 1976, 20 p. Employment Information Series, No. 17.
Research paper based on a case study of changes in work organisation and job design at the Philips Electronics Industry factory in Leaside, Ontario - evaluates each of the changes in terms of effects on job enrichment. References.

WILD, Ray.
Work organization: a study of manual work and mass production. Wiley - Interscience publication. London, 1975, 226 p.

YORKS, L.
Radical approach to job enrichment. New York, Amacom, 1976, XII, 209 p.
Monograph presenting a radical approach to job enrichment - explores the relationship between business organisation, organisation control and employee behaviour and motivation, presents a model for effectively implementing job enrichment, and examines support systems (includes wage incentives, management development, etc.)

IV. Economic costs and benefits of new forms of work organisation

SIBSON, R.E.
Increasing employee productivity. New York, Amacom, 1976, IX, 210 p.
Monograph on how to increase labour productivity in industrial enterprises - discusses management of human resources, personnel management, business organisation, motivation and financial and non-financial incentives (such as wage incentives, job satisfaction, etc.).

V. Humanisation of work and the quality of working life

3. Shop-floor participation

LAWLER, E.E.; JENKINS, G.D.; CAROOZE, S.D.
Employees participation in pay plan development. Ann Arbor, 1976, XV, 237 p.
Report on research into the impact of workers participation in the design of a wage payment system, particularly a wage incentive plan, on employees attitudes in a small manufacturing firm - examines resulting changes in absenteeism, labour turnover, labour productivity, job satisfaction, etc. through replies to questionnaires.

RENAUD, Y.
200 000 emplois pour la qualité de la vie. Paris, Stock, 1977, 391 p.
Monograph on the role of the supervisor (foreman) in industrial enterprise in France - discusses responsibilities with regard to working conditions, job satisfaction, good labour relations, and as link between workers and management, etc.

SZANIAWSKI, Ignacy
Die Intellektualisierung der Arbeit: Beruf und Arbeit zwischen Diagnose und Prognose. Braunschweig, Georg Westermann Verlag, 1975.

4. Flexible working hours and other time arrangements

CAULKIN, S.
"Strange scandal of overtime". *Management today* (London), Apr. 1976, pp. 53-55, 110.
Article asserting that enterprises in the United Kingdom are overly dependent upon overtime - finds that high levels of overtime are associated with low wages, low investment, and low productivity.

COTE, L.H.; LEWIS, N.; BOULARD, R.; TURGEON, B.
Horaire variable au Québec : rapport d'enquête. Québec, ministère du Travail et de la Main-d'oeuvre, Direction générale de la recherche, 1976. X, 207 p.
Report on a questionnaire survey on flexible hours of work in Quebec, Canada - concerns workers' adaptation to this system and the impact on the enterprises in several industries, etc.

GROSSIN, W.
"Evolution des durées de travail dans 14 branches d'activité industrielle de 1965 à 1974". *Revue française des affaires sociales* (Paris), 30(1), janv.-mars 1976, pp. 81-125.

INTERNATIONAL LABOUR CONFERENCE
62nd Session, Geneva, 1976.
Holidays with pay for seafarers. Geneva, 1976, 45 p.
Conference paper on holidays with pay for seafarers - includes extracts from a conference paper to the Preparatory Technical Maritime Conference, and the text of a proposed ILO convention revising Convention No. 91.

INTERNATIONAL LABOUR CONFERENCE
64th Session, Geneva, 1978.
Hours of work and rest periods in road transport. Geneva, 1977. Report VII(1), 77 p.
Conference paper comprising a preliminary law and practice report on existing national, international and regional regulations, etc. Governing hours of work and rest periods in the road transport sector and a questionnaire concerning the adoption of new related international labour standards. Includes references.

INTERNATIONAL LABOUR OFFICE
Economics of hours and hourly working patterns. Symposium on arrangement of working time and social problems connected with shift work in industrialised countries. Geneva, 1977. Participant paper No. 13, 33 p.
Conference paper on recent trends in the arrangement of working time in relation to existing economic theory concerning hours of work, and with particular reference to the impact of collective bargaining - considers various permutations of standard hours, viz. overtime, shift work, part time employment, dual job holding, flexible hours of work and the compressed working week, etc., and possible trends in the form of leisure, e.g. increased length of annual holidays.

Arrangement of working time. Geneva, 1977, working paper No. 1, 14 p.
Working paper in the form of a conference paper on the arrangement of working time (new trends in arrangement of hours of work) - covers the continuous working day, the compressed working week, staggered hours of work, flexible hours of work, part time employment, staggered holidays, etc. References.

MARIC, D.
Adapting working hours to modern needs; the time factor in the new approach to working conditions. International Labour Office, Geneva, 1977, VIII, 50 p.
Monograph outlining new trends and approaches in developed countries with regard to hours of work and the arrangement of working time - includes the compressed working week, staggered hours of work, flexible hours of work, part time schemes, etc., and discusses annual and lifetime distribution of working time. Bibliography pp. 47-50.

TESSIER, B.M.; TURGEON, B.
Horaire variable : rapport de la mission d'étude en Allemagne et en Suisse. Québec, ministère du Travail et de la Main-d'oeuvre, Direction générale de la recherche, 1976. XIII, 224 p.
Report of a study tour examining the economic implications and social implications of flexible hours of work in Germany (R.F.) and Switzerland - covers legal aspects, labour relations aspects, employees attitudes, management attitude, etc., and includes summaries of interviews with trade unions, employers' organisations, etc.

UNITED STATES CONGRESS. SENATE. COMMITTEE ON LABOR AND PUBLIC WELFARE.
Changing patterns of work in America. Washington, Government Printing Office, 1976. V, 497 p.
Record of hearings on alternative hours of work and work arrangements in the United States - covers part time employment, flexible hours of work, job sharing, etc., considers the implications for job satisfaction, and suggests national employment policy measures, etc.

ZBARSKII, M.I.
Sotsial'no-ekonomicheskie problemy rabochego dnia pri sotsializme Moskva, Mysl', 1976, 222 p.
Monograph examining some social and economic problems linked to hours of work in socialist society. Covers theoretical aspects of working full time, time budgeting, leisure, labour productivity, etc.

7. General literature on the humanisation of work and the quality of working life

BELLONE, L.
Amélioration de la condition de l'homme au travail; manuel d'ergonomie. Paris, Editions d'organisation, 1976, 192 p.
Reference book on applied ergonomics in the work environment, with particular reference to contributions from industrial sociology and the behavioural sciences - discusses psychological aspects of group work, job enrichment, motivation, etc. and the effects of fatique, mental stress and hours of work. Includes a biliography.

FORM, W.H.
Blue-collar stratification: autoworkers in four countries. Princeton, Princeton University Press, 1976. XX, 335 p.
Comparative study of social stratification amongst industrial workers in the automobile industry in Italy, Argentina, India and the USA - discusses the effects of industrialisation on the working class, and covers aspects of workers adaptation and job satisfaction, trade unionisation and degree of social integration. Includes a bibliography.

GOHL, J.
Arbeit im Konflikt; Probleme der Humanisierungsdebatte. München, Wilhelm Goldmann Verlag, 1977, 310 p.
Monograph of readings on the humanisation of work, with particular reference to Germany (R.F.) - discusses the controversies concerning prerequisites for and economic and technical aspects, sociological aspects, psychological aspects of and problems raised by the improvement of working conditions and the quality of working life. Includes a bibliography.

GLASER, E.M.; IZARD, C.E.; CHENERY, M.F.
Improvement in the quality of worklife and productivity; a joint venture between management and employees. Los Angeles, 1976. VI, 161 p.
Final report on a humanisation of work research project carried out in a pharmaceutical industry enterprise in a rural area in the United States - outlines project activities and results in respect of determining whether increased workers' participation, etc. improves labour productivity and job satisfaction, and includes a summary of conclusions and recommendations. Includes a bibliography.

8. Bibliographies relevant to the subjects covered

SHONYO, C.
Job satisfaction; a bibliography with abstracts, search period covered: 1975 - October 1976. Springfield, Va, US National Technical Information Service, 1976, IV, 153 p.
Updated annotated bibliography including 153 abstracts of Government-sponsored research on job satisfaction, both civilian and military. Covers personnel management techniques, motivation, etc., and includes surveys of employees attitudes.

YOUNG, M.E.
Work attitudes in the civilian sector: a bibliography with abstracts, 1964 - March 1976. Springfield, Va, US National Technical Information Service, 1976, IV.

ONAL AUTHOR INDEX